D1602633

Buffalo, Elephant, & Bongo

Buffalo, Elephant, & Bongo

Alone in the Savannas and Rain Forests of the Cameroon

by

Reinald von Meurers

Safari Press Inc.
P. O. Box 3095, Long Beach, CA 90803

BUFFALO, ELEPHANT, & BONGO copyright © 1999 by Reinald von Meurers. All rights reserved. No part of this publication may be used or reproduced in any form or by any means, electronic or mechanical reproduction, including photocopy, recording, or any information storage and retrieval system, without permission from the publisher.

The trademark Safari Press ® is registered with the U.S. Patent and Trademark Office and in other countries.

Meurers, Reinald von

Second edition

Safari Press Inc.

1999, Long Beach, California

ISBN 1-57157-160-4

Library of Congress Catalog Card Number: 98-60867

10 9 8 7 6 5 4 3 2

Readers wishing to receive the Safari Press catalog, featuring many fine books on big-game hunting, wingshooting, and sporting firearms, should write to Safari Press Inc., P.O. Box 3095, Long Beach, CA 90803, USA. Tel: (714) 894-9080 or visit our Web site at www.safaripress.com.

TABLE OF CONTENTS

Foreword

The late Professor Ernst A. Zwilling, a longtime professional hunter and world-renowned expert on Cameroon, wrote in 1989:

"For several years now I've known of Dr. Reinald von Meurers and his expeditions in Cameroon. I admire his ability to arrange traditional foot safaris and explore undisturbed game paradises far off the beaten path, while still managing to keep the old-style traditions of yesterday's hunter intact. He is always eager to walk for his passion, and it's not only the 'extra mile,' but usually some twenty extra miles! Anyone seeking to follow in his footsteps must know the French language fluently, have a feeling for the mentality of the locals, have experience in African wilderness, and have plenty of tolerance for a definitively slow governmental administration system.

"Many people shudder at the thought of a stay for weeks without the modern amenities of daily life—much less having to share unknown food from horrible sources at a campfire with a crew of natives. Von Meurers's knowledge was acquired during many solo safaris, executed entirely on his own, and the experiences related in the following chapters will no doubt be of great use to any outdoorsperson. Especially useful are the many practical hints and ethnological references he offers, as well as advice about various local diseases (he is also an M.D.), and recommendations for disease prevention.

"How I would have loved to join von Meurers on his exciting canoe expedition as the first white man to ever travel over 130 miles on the unexplored rapids of the Sanaga River."

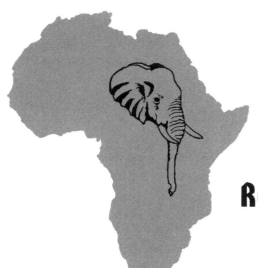

Chapter I

Remote Access

Our small canoe careens downstream at breakneck speed. Full of enthusiasm, I paddle furiously along the narrow, forested river, a mere nine to eighteen feet wide. Behind me sits Hassan, a local fisherman, who tries desperately to steer the canoe with his paddle. My frantic action accelerates us, but makes it difficult for him to keep us clear of obstacles such as numerous submerged trees and other forest debris. An accident here is not akin to springing a leak on the local pond at home!

Our journey began early yesterday morning in a remote village that was a long and difficult trek from Cameroon's capital. When we arrived in the village, my old porters and trackers greeted us cheerfully. I quickly outfitted three other white hunters with their own crew and organized local food supplies for the porters to carry. Then we all marched our separate ways through uninhabited savanna and gallery forests. No footpaths, no huts, just game. This is truly a paradise—*my* paradise!

Some local men carried my gear, which consisted of two duffel bags and the folded canoe. In about three hours we had reached the relatively small mouth of this lonesome river. Half the village accompanied us to see this crazy white man's inflatable *pirogue* (dugout)!

I still had to inflate the canoe—a very time-consuming job—and the sun burned hot. Noisy villagers found my actions fascinating and cheered me on. Finally we had the canoe loaded and afloat, and set out to a chorus of wild cries from the locals.

For an entire generation, no black man had floated down this river to the next village some fifty miles away because of three major rapids—all capable of upsetting a dugout. Reportedly no white man had ever done it either—at least no white man who survived to tell the tale!

The only link between the next village and the modern world is a small, seventy-five-mile-long footpath that originates at the railroad. Only thirty people live in the decaying huts of the little village, and they subsist mainly by fishing and some snare trapping. After several expeditions, I realized this was an ideal place for big-game hunting. Only one other dyed-in-the-wool white hunter—an extremely experienced Frenchman—hunted there, and he regularly took huge forest elephant.

At the evening campfires on my safaris I used to listen to the porters' tales about the Frenchman, Colonel Pierre Ruffinoni, and he did the same when his people related their adventures with "the Doctor"—me! For years, due to differing time schedules, we had both ventured into the same remote areas of the rain forest without ever meeting. During my third safari into that game paradise, I hired a tracker from the next village. He was the son of the local chief and had served Colonel Ruffinoni earlier that season. He just happened to have the Colonel's business card. I was quick to note his phone number and called him in France after I returned to Europe. This was the beginning of a profound friendship.

When we finally met, I was very impressed by the depth of his knowledge of Africa and related activities: The old

soldier was a flyer and had participated in almost all the-
aters of war since 1939. In World War II he escaped with
General de Gaulle to the United Kingdom; flew in the Battle
of Britain in a B-26 aircraft with the Free French; and
accompanied General Leclerq, who had twice attempted to
attack Rommel in the flank by crossing the Sahara from the
south after entering via Chad. The North African theater
over, he went on a long leave to Alexandria, Egypt, with two
years' pay in his pocket to celebrate the victory. From the
fire that flickered in his eyes as he told me the tale, I figured
he must have had a wild time.

Later he took part in the invasion of Sicily, and after
WWII, the Berlin Air Lift, Indochina, and finally the Algerian war. Afterward he was appointed director of the French
air force survival school based in Gabon. During most of
the campaigns he had found time for the occasional hunt,
and had a plethora of fascinating hunting stories that one
could listen to tirelessly. He was an endless source of knowledge, and it is a pity that he never conducted seminars on
hunting in the wilderness under difficult circumstances. As
you will note, however, his safari preparations always kept
roughing it to a minimum!

Pierre invited me to join him for his last hunt into the
remote areas—a traditional walking safari intended to last
nearly three months with a long file of porters to carry all
kinds of amenities. Being a Frenchman, he set great store
in the proper food. His crew carried big boxes filled with
canned food, jars of red and white wine, liquor, and many
delicacies for almost seventy-five miles. His base camp was
maintained in the fishing village mentioned earlier, and from
there he ventured out for five-day excursions into the primary rain forest, always searching, for huge tuskers.

By then he had downed 106 elephant—all trophy
animals with huge tusks. He praised the use of "enough

gun" under the difficult conditions of the rain forest. Eighteen elephant had been brought down with his .378 Weatherby Magnum, a caliber he highly praised, but only if utilizing full-metal-jacket bullets. In his opinion, their penetration was unrivaled—a useful characteristic considering the bad shooting angles sometimes imposed by the thick undergrowth. It usually took him only one or two shots to down an elephant. Later he switched to the more powerful .460 Weatherby and never ceased to compliment its use in the heavy cover of the rain forest.

I was delighted when Pierre invited me, but I could not walk in with him since I had already agreed to organize hunts for three friends in a northern area. I had to get all four of us with guns and gear to the last village. From there I planned to float down the river to the Colonel for three weeks of pure hunting. I had promised him I would be there by December 22 *insha' Allah*—if God wills in Arabic—quite an ambitious project since no one knew the river, but I was young, optimistic, and eager.

My fisherman friend Hassan had warned me that it would be impossible to use a dugout due to three major "killer" rapids, so I brought an inflatable expedition canoe capable of carrying a 700-pound payload. My luggage allowance had been used up by other gear, so I carried the folded but still-bulky boat as hand luggage onto Sabena's aircraft. The flight attendants gave me disapproving looks, but my reddened face, broad smile, and uneasy shoulder shrugging disarmed them. I managed to get the bulky 50-pound canoe onto the plane and behind a seat unmolested. I think God looks after hunters, even slightly demented ones!

The time schedule for reaching the Colonel was quite unrealistic; it had been conceived in my scientific ivory tower far from the wilds. I had to cram the trip to both places into a four-week holiday. No one had ever paddled up or down that stretch of the river, but I had full confidence

4

in the qualities of the Kevlar-reinforced rubber canoe and in courageous Hassan. During the planning period, I was unaware that his knowledge extended only to the upper twenty-five miles of river, prior to the first major rapids. Ignorance is such bliss!

My reasoning had been that if the rapids were too rough, we could unload and portage, even though it would be very tough in the oppressive heat. But I expected to collect some fine trophies as well.

Advance planning has become reality. We are sitting in our rubber boat and doing fine. Slowly and quietly we float along the countless bends. The brown water is rich with sediment and doesn't allow us to see the bottom. The banks are covered with a tangle of dense bushes growing rampant and unchecked. They crowd into the creek, sometimes leaving just a small tunnel for our passage.

The splashing noise of falling objects intrigues me, but Hassan waves patiently: "Just water snakes, escaping from their sunbath in the twigs." Most reassuring! However, I am not sure whether all sunbathing snakes are nonvenomous, so I silently vow to repel all boarders savagely. Harmless? Too bad for them!

Strange yellow flowers are embedded in the dense green bushes; and sometimes the vegetation gives way to open savannas, where whole banks are covered with huge, white, deliciously scented lilies. Typical for these waterways are enormous trees with wide, stocky branches that bend toward the water. Thick liana vines creep up around the trees, sometimes so woven into the structure that both appear to be one plant. When these weakened   giants fall victim to violent tropical storms, they crash across the stream and half-submerged collect all kinds of driftwood—nature's own dams.

Our fast start comes to a quick halt at the next turn, where the first in a seemingly endless series of fallen trees blocks our way. Hassan readies his machete and purpose-

5

fully hacks a path through the tangle while I pull the boat through the slowly opening channel. Meanwhile, a haze of musty dust mixed with small spiders drifts down from overhead—not exactly my idea of a pleasant journey!

Finally we are through and gather speed again until the next barricade. This exercise repeats itself too often. Sweating profusely, we labor all day until finally the creek becomes a river and logs can no longer bar the entire width of the waterway.

Hurrah! Now we literally race downriver. With this speed, we should be able to keep to my less-than-flexible timetable. Typical white man: In the blink of an eye he travels by plane into the heart of remotest Africa, then spends hours pushing man and nature to reach his goals!

Suddenly, an unpleasant ripping noise warns that we have rammed a log and the bow instantly elevates. We concentrate on the pointed remains of a root base that has pierced the hull! *Tshshshshshhsh.* A sudden stream of bubbles indicates our predicament—Nature: 1, Kevlar: 0! This is a disaster, and I'm not sure we'll be able to repair it. Slowly we float to the next bank, the boat's bottom and my spirits deflated. Fortunately, the rubber canoe consists of separate compartments, so we aren't at risk of sinking.

Relieved to reach terra firma, we jump onto the sand. Imagine the shock we experience after unloading and turning the boat over for inspection: A four-foot-long gash has ripped the bottom wide open, and my repair kit contains only a couple of small patches and a large tube of glue. You've heard the expression "up the creek without a paddle and with a hole in the boat"? Well, the only good news right now is that we still have the paddle!

It's too late to attempt any repairs today, and we are both too exhausted anyhow. Fortunately, the designated campsite for the other hunters is nearby. We decide to carefully float there to find help. Instead of a triumphant arrival at full speed in a proud warship, we limp in slowly like a battered tramp steamer in our low-riding craft, muddy water lapping at our freeboard.

The others are just arriving after a long stalk and greet us happily. One hunter has shot a cob, so soon there will be delicious antelope meat on the fire for everyone. Combining our forces, we haul the canoe onto a log "drydock" and clean and grind the material around the rip with a file that our porters use to sharpen their machetes.

After dinner, my spirits renewed, I decide to try out an idea for the repair. For greater comfort on my cot I carry an inflatable lightweight rubber mattress consisting of individual inflatable compartments. I can sacrifice one row on its outside edge and cut out a piece long enough to patch the rip. Fortunately, the repair kit contains that oversized tube of glue, an ample amount for the task. Fascinated by the white man's experiment, our porters gather around and gladly help by pounding the two parts together.

The night is uneasy. Visions of a sinking boat—a miniature Titanic—followed by a desperate march with heavy gear through hostile forests keep me tossing and turning. Early the next morning we anxiously await the outcome of our repair job as air is cautiously pumped into the boat.

For safety reasons I don't inflate it to full pressure, and the repair seems to be holding. We are relieved that we cannot find any treacherous air pockets that would indicate a leaking seal. Perhaps the pendulum of fortune has swung back over to our side. *"Al-hamdu llilahi"*—Thank God in Arabic. Hassan is always happy to hear me using these apt expressions. He is Muslim, the predominant religion in northern Cameroon—his birthplace.

Still uneasy, we load bags, containers, machetes, and guns and continue our journey. We are completely on our own for the next forty-five miles; no friendly camp awaits around the bend. If we have to abandon the boat,

7

it will be very difficult, if not impossible for the two of us to reach civilization again. The only alternative would be to cut our way out alongside the river. Cross-country travel would mean a week's march and innumerable obstacles in the extremely dense and wholly uninhabited rain forest.

Surrounding this remote river is eighty by one hundred miles of jungle, rolling hills, and muddy swamps rich with game. It is an El Dorado for red forest buffalo (*Syncerus caffer nanus*), *kob de buffon* (*Kobus kob kob loderi*) in the small savannas, bongo (*Tragelaphus euryceros euryceros*) around tiny forest creeks, and sitatunga (*Tragelaphus spekei gratus*) along the bigger streams. Not a single footprint mars this vast and lonely area—a hunter's dreamland!

Since the accident, I am doubly cautious and leave all the paddling to Hassan. He steers us safely around each log and rock, and the journey is much more enjoyable for me as I watch and doze.

At noon we hear some distant noise that increases to a thundering roar as we come closer: Rapids—our first encounter! The thought of the thin repair on the boat's underside makes me more than a little uneasy, but Hassan happily signals me to stay put. At this point I am all "watch" and no "doze"! More and more rocks protrude above the surface while racing white foam forms in small channels. Passing through these, the boat picks up a significant amount of speed. Now we are racing along!

Hassan navigates cold-bloodedly through whirling waterways. Suddenly, we become airborne as the boat flies up and over the edge of a big flat rock shelf and drops three feet into a big pool where an eddy keeps us swirling around for some time until Hassan paddles us clear. This last part makes me shudder, and my knees turn to rubber. It is fortunate that I am sitting down because they wouldn't support me right now. After that unexpected trip, I won't require any laxative for a while.

I envision us swimming in swirling whitewater while enthralled crocodiles lick their chops. Once we're in the clear, it suddenly seems like fun, and we have more faith in our repair. We haul the boat out and inspect the previously damaged area: It looks OK; so we increase the air pressure for better speed.

I recall my five-year-old son Philip at home when I first inflated the canoe. He inspected it, and I sat inside to show him how it's rowed. He liked the idea, but asked what I'd do about the crocodiles—Nile crocodile or *Crocodylus niloticus*—called *ngato* by the Pygmies.

I just laughed and showed him how I would hit them on their toothy snouts with the steel rim of the paddle. At first he smiled, but his smile soon turned into bitter weeping and he pleaded with me: "Papa, don't go to Africa. Stay home!"

This was the first rapid that Hassan had ever navigated. He'd only heard about them from downriver fishermen who told him that the upcoming second set of rapids was impassable for dugouts. Nice time for me to find this out!

Late in the afternoon we slip ashore at a game path leading from the water and try to hunt the next savanna. But stalking here is quite impossible since the thick, nine-foot-high elephant grass (*Pennisetum purpureum*) bars all vision. Only the whistling of alerted cob indicates game is nearby.

Here lies a typical hunter's dilemma: Near occupied lands this tall grass would be reduced as the savannas are burned off for crops, but here in no man's land it gets reduced only occasionally by lightning-set fires late in the season. Now it is at its thickest and most savage.

Discouraged but not defeated, we try our luck from the water, but this also proves very difficult. During the planning stage of this journey I had counted on hunting these remote areas from the boat, but now I am disillusioned. Floating on the open water is not advantageous. On the contrary, the game stays well hidden in the shady vegetation of the river banks, and easily spots us first. By the time we catch sight of anything, it's already escaping into deeper cover.

We slowly drift close to the shore in order to remain hidden for as long as possible in the shade of the tangled mass of liana, branches, twigs, and thick leaves of the huge trees, many of which hold large figlike fruit. I believe they are a type of ficus.

It's our second day alone and we have to find fresh venison. Our lengthy safari depends upon supplementing our supplies with meat. Suddenly, a reddish spot appears between the bushes—a grazing red-flanked duiker (*Cephalophus rufilatus*). My .22 Hornet kills the 35-pound animal instantly. Now meat will be abundant for the next few days at least.

My "second" gun, the popular German Drilling (two shotgun barrels over a rifle barrel), is well designed for hunting various game. Inside the upper right shotgun barrel is an inset barrel for the popular and efficient small-bore caliber, the .22 Hornet. So it's now a four-barrel!

We quickly learn that rafting is not exactly a pleasure in Africa, even if the view is splendid. Unfortunately, many small critters want to profit from us hapless humans, nipping and sucking everywhere. Number one on my hit list are the big black horseflies that slip under any bit of clothing and bite viciously. Buttoned-up long-sleeved shirts are the uniform of the day on *our* yacht, even in the oppressive jungle heat. More dangerous are the infamous tsetse flies that spread sleeping sickness. In spite of the intense heat, I button my coat to prevent these attacks, and sweat pours out from under my armor.

We have covered enough distance today, and after "hauling out," we camp on the sand protected by wide, thick, outspread branches. Hassan is quite pleased with my rubber canoe and tells me that his dugout would have taken twice as long to reach this point. Yeah, but no repairs would have been needed either. I can just imagine trying to get his canoe behind seat 23-B on Sabena!

I am always mindful of the prospect of sharing our campout with crocs! While I unload the duffel bags and two light watertight metal barrels containing essential gear, Hassan makes camp by cutting sticks, hanging the mosquito net, and covering it with my light Tyvek cover. This provides a great shelter with its sides up in the daytime, and keeps in the warmth while keeping out the dampness at night.

The flames of our fire are flickering high, and Hassan is now busy cooking. This task is too much for him, and the food is terrible! The next morning I try my luck, but with a lot of laughter we agree that it's not any better. Perhaps we should have made room in our boat for the chief's daughter. What I'd give for a Big Mac right now! Hassan is a gifted fisherman, and it is amazing how many fish he flips out of the water in no time, equipped with only a simple stick, some hooks, and twelve feet of fishing line. He is more than worth his pay.

Tonight our talk at the campfire is brief since we are both completely worn out by our strenuous day on the water. Even the beautiful night, with its noisy concert of large and small crickets, shrill monkey cries, flying squirrels, and numerous unidentified creatures, fails to keep me awake.

Enjoying my narrow air mattress on the cot under the reassuring protection of the mosquito net, I sleep soundly and dreamlessly. Nary a thought of crocs that night. Hassan keeps a fire going during the night to ward off the cold, moist air rising from the river. At dawn he passes me a cup of acidic coffee made from the local Arabica bushes. This stuff would wake the dead.

Half an hour later we paddle into the beautiful coolness of an African morning. Without warning, two nice waterbuck bulls splash in startled flight through the low water. Again, no chance for a shot. In this region waterbuck—sing-sing waterbuck, *Kobus ellipsiprymnus unctuosus*, also known as West African defassa waterbuck—are rare, so I try to follow them. As I stalk slowly across the vast floodplain, the wind changes, carrying the terrible odor of a rotting animal toward me.

Our small-game path is blocked by a dead buffalo with a grossly bloated belly. Around his heavily infected left forefoot protrudes the loop of a wire snare. Snared nearby or a distance away? And was his injury the reason he was gored by other buffalo, as evidenced by numerous puncture wounds all over his body? The poor beast was looking for water and died close to it, probably due to internal injuries. Just one of many tragedies caused by the diabolic snares— once set, they are like a commercial fisherman's forgotten gill net and can kill long into the future.

Our stalk of the waterbuck comes to a quick halt as soon as the path turns into a tunnel leading into a patch of tall elephant grass. This stuff is impassable for humans and impossible to hunt in during the beginning of the dry season. There are still many green shoots between the dry yellow stems of elephant grass, so burning isn't possible. It's virtually fireproof this time of year.

Once the grass is dry, normally mid-January in this region, it can be burned. A "burn-off" is quite interesting. First, the fire sets off into a terrible blaze. The small savannas sound like hell itself when the air trapped within the cavities of the *Pennisetum* stems explodes in the heat. The great variety of short and corkscrewlike twisted trees, which effectively block the sight after sixty to eighty yards, suffer carbonized bark and burned branches but survive.

Two weeks later, when the small green shoots of fresh grass flood the land, the burned black savanna becomes enormously attractive to all manner of game.

It is now December, and game is spread out in the forest along the small creeks. Hunting there is much more difficult, but not impossible. New hunters believe it would be fruitless to hunt the forest, and walk on the ground cover of big dry leaves and twigs, making sounds like walking on cornflakes. However, elephant, buffalo, and antelope also make a lot of noise, and since there is no hunting pressure, game is not easily alerted. Walking like Indians and stopping at intervals—instead of the stomp, stomp of human cadence—is the secret to success.

We continue by boat through increasingly beautiful scenery as the river widens. Here and there we are accompanied by bands of colobus monkeys—Guereza or Abyssinian black and white, *Colobus abyssinicus*—with beautiful silky fur. Their long, white back hair hangs down like a coat, contrasting with their jet-black body color. The old males display a prominent cheek beard, making their French name *magistrat* (judge) more than appropriate. Some decades ago these monkeys were close to extinction because clothes makers used their magnificent hair for fashion. Now they are protected and actually quite numerous in remote areas. The locals hunt them for their meat and use their pelts for bags.

We hear big splashes now and then. Spooked crocodiles lunge from their dry resting places among branches or rocks into the safety of the water when they see our boats approach. The size of the wakes indicate the size of the reptiles that make them.

Hassan points out some crocodile holes in the banks. They are the openings of caves, now exposed by the falling water level. It's there that the crocs deposit newly caught prey to rot for a while. Because of a deficiency in stomach acid, they swallow the prey whole when the meat is sufficiently digestible.

The crocodile population in this river is low because the Muslim Hausa tribes from the north overhunt them at night using spotlights, rifles, and even spears. The Hausa want to make as much money as possible by selling the soft belly leather, which is in high demand in Nigeria.

Hassan accompanied a Hausa hunter last year. It took them three weeks to spear one seven-foot croc—frozen by the spotlight—on a sandbank. Fortunately, the poachers' expeditions are kept in check by the local fishermen from the upper river; they do not want the crocodiles killed because they believe that the reptiles living in the wide downstream pools push the big fish upstream.

Ahead, a deep roar gets louder and louder, and the water flows more swiftly as we approach the second set of rapids. Hassan is anxious. He's heard bad stories from fishermen who occasionally venture to this remote spot. We beach the boat and proceed on foot for a closer look before risking boat, gear, and especially our lives!

The view is exciting: For a hundred yards or so the stream narrows by half, and the foamy water races through narrow channels, sometimes dropping over benches. Fortunately, all the rocks have been smoothed and rounded by the water, so there is no particular risk to the boat but dangerous roots or branches might easily be wedged in the fissures. A haze from the rising spray obscures visibility and is accompanied by a deafening roar.

It looks serious and I envision tough work ahead—painstakingly hacking out a pathway, then portaging gear and boat around—but Hassan is confident. As he returns to the boat, he motions me to climb across the rocks to where the river widens. Minutes later he comes into sight, steering the canoe while it goes faster and faster! I hold my breath and pray for him, the gear, and myself. I don't care to be marooned in the middle of nowhere with only my rifle after losing Hassan, the boat, and all the equipment.

Hassan concentrates intently as he speeds along as if in a race, steering his course and choosing the right channel at the last second. Abruptly, he flies across the last bench and splashes into a big pool. It's done! Proudly, he pulls out of the whirling eddies. Good guy! He is a gifted helmsman in a new Olympic event, the "Kevlar Canoe Rapids Shoot." It's a one-man division; I want nothing to do with it! I heave a huge sigh of relief. One must never show any outward sign of fear or concern in front of one's crew. To do so would mean a loss of face, along with their trust and confidence.

Many black-and-white fish eagles (*Pandion haliaetus*) watch us from a safe distance. They know humans signify danger because the natives always long for any kind of fat, and these birds provide a fishy, rancid fat. Hassan tries to motivate me into shooting one now and then, but I always refuse. They are definitely not my idea of a tender stew!

We notice snares on the sandbanks, another sign that we are reaching areas hunted by fishermen. They try to catch the fish eagles by putting fish guts on the sand. Hidden around this bait is a wire loop attached to a bent stick, its end buried in the ground. If the fish eagle picks up the bait, the snare is triggered and the loop is tightened by the upward straightening of the stick.

The river is now forty-five to seventy-five feet wide, and game is everywhere. Sometimes it's a surprised buffalo, quickly escaping from its bath. Sometimes it's a group of kob antelope resting on a sandbank, then splashing wildly through the water. A large water turtle almost three feet long slowly slides into the murky protection of the brown river.

Here and there the heads of big Congo finger otters—cape clawless otters, *Aonyx capensis*—pop up. I count fifteen altogether. They are highly desired by the natives. Strips of the skin of these sleek beauties are highly valued among many of the tribes as powerful talismans, and the medicine men will pay a considerable amount for pelts.

As we continue our journey, the smaller rapids become less menacing as the river widens. Now we enjoy the race through the thundering rocks and jumps across benches, but there is always the same nagging doubt: Will the repair hold until we reach our destination?

I am somewhat ill today. A spider bite on my neck our first day on the water is causing muscular pain and an increasingly severe headache, so I avoid moving around too much. Suddenly huge hippo (*Hippopotamus amphibius*) heads pop out of the dirty brown water all around us. Headache and pain are instantly forgotten, and I am paddling like a madman. These beasts are un-predictable and I've heard numerous horror stories about their aggressiveness. They readily charge all intruders.

Once, a good friend insisted upon collecting a certain old hippo bull. He set out on the Sanaga River with three local fishermen in their swaying dugout to pursue the rogue bull. Finally they located him, and my friend took a shot at sixty yards from the lightly dancing boat in which he stood. An alerted hippo doesn't present much of a target, only its eyes and prominent brows surface to watch the enemy.

Initially, my friend was quite happy when the colossus disappeared in a huge torrent of foaming water, apparently well hit. Shooting a hippo in the water isn't much fun. One has to wait for hours until the stomach has built up enough gas from rotting grass to float the animal to the surface. My friend settled back, prepared to wait and enjoy the sights, but his enjoyment was short-lived. Suddenly the heavy dugout was lifted two feet out of the water with a loud bang. The big bull had not been hit, and had attacked the boat from below!

They were extremely lucky that the unstable boat didn't capsize, because the riverbank was over thirty yards away and had a seven-foot-high vertical bank. If the boat had capsized, the bull would have killed them all, hunting each down in turn. The natives paddled wildly with terror-stricken, ashen faces, and my friend never tried to shoot a hippopotamus from the water again.

Alhough not a member of the Big Five, hippo cause many more fatalities than any of that glamour set. Seeing the horrible scars on an attack survivor's body lends credence to the African natives' tales of the hippo's resilience to damage and its survival skills.

Suddenly I am jolted out of my daydream by strange game standing in a depression on the riverbank. It's the dark shape of a duiker in the foliage. *Camp meat!* I say to myself as I shoot it down. The sudden muzzle blast almost causes Hassan to jump off the boat for a swim. He has been standing and is thrown off balance by the rifle's loud report.

I later determine that the animal had been standing in a natural salt lick. I discover to my deep regret that it is the very rare and almost strictly nocturnal water chevrotain (*Hyemoschus aquaticus*), which is protected in Cameroon. I feel just terrible! The presence of these tiny animals is most often documented by their dainty footprints as they are almost never actually seen. They represent a zoological curiosity—a link between antelope and swine—hornless with long upper canine fangs, dark reddish markings with horizontal white stripes, and weighing between six and twelve pounds.

The *baseng,* as the water chevrotain is called by the Baya, has an almost white meat, which sometimes causes diarrhea, probably due to its diet of certain plants that are toxic to humans. Some claim the tropical plant mimulopsis (*Mimulopsis solmsii*) could be responsible. It flowers irregularly and reportedly causes death among bongo and giant forest hogs (*Hylochoerus meinertzhageni*) during its

17

second year of growth. Mimulopsis also causes a virulent hay fever allergy in humans. Similarly, the crested rat (*Lophiomys imhausi*) causes death among dogs that catch and eat it due to its ingestion of toxins. The mysteries of Cameroon are not confined to wildlife but extend to its huge variety of flora.

When threatened, water chevrotain dive into the water and swim well beneath the surface for cover as I witnessed elsewhere some years later. The experts say that they occasionally prey on fish. None of my friends, not even the experienced Colonel, had collected this very desirable trophy. Professor Zwilling's chevrotain took him ten long years: After spending many months on expeditions between World Wars I and II, he finally collected one for the Natural History Museum of Vienna. It doesn't take me long to skin this small but valuable quarry. It will make a very beautiful full mount and will be one of my fondest memories for many years.

As we continue our journey, I use a rope to drag the skin and the skull in the water behind the boat for several hours. This will leach all blood from the tissues. A skin so treated will be protected from decay because the absence of blood precludes nourishing bacteria. A beneficial side effect is that the skull becomes pure white without any bleaching. Cleaning with something like concentrated peroxide can break up the solid outer layer of bone cells and eventually result in a brown stain caused by dust attaching itself to the uneven surface.

Late in the afternoon we heave a big sigh of relief as we arrive at the harbor of our destination, back to human settlement. "Harbor" is a proud word for a big sandbank with a handful of decaying dugouts of all sizes.

We've done it. We floated down the river, the very first boat to have done so in this generation, and we have even arrived as planned. I send Hassan to the nearby village, and he soon returns with a horde of cheering porters and villagers. Everyone is amazed that we succeeded in navigating this lonely waterway. Even the Colonel was unsure whether we would ever show up. He was so certain we would never arrive on time that he didn't wait until the scheduled meeting date and set out three days earlier for his hunt.

In minutes all the gear and the boat itself are loaded onto the porters' heads and brought triumphantly into the village. Hassan is definitely the hero of the hour and, as captain, walks proudly in front, garnering many admiring glances from the village beauties.

The Colonel has rented a hut here for the past several years and runs his headquarters in style. Solid planks form stable wooden doors, and there is even a central dining saloon well equipped with chairs and a table sporting a real tablecloth, all unknown in African villages.

Other amenities include a real shower—a perforated bucket protected by a palisade ring around the wooden floor. Another luxury is the toilet located fifty yards away. No squatting for us!

The Colonel and I have a decidedly different approach to do-it-yourself safaris: He makes camp in the villages and sets out for short hunts, while I prefer to leave the villages for the entire safari and return only when time and food run out. Otherwise I find there are too many problems with drunken porters, arguments over women, and theft. I think the latter is Cameroon's national sport.

Pierre goes on five- and six-day expeditions with minimal provisions and relaxes between by fishing. But he comes to Cameroon for several months while I have only four weeks.

The porter shows me to a clean room, and after my gear is arranged, dinner is served by the Colonel's cook. I do not believe my eyes. He is dressed in a white jacket and wears white gloves! This is the last thing I expect in the middle of nowhere. "Nowhere" means separated from the nearest track road by sixty miles of a small winding footpath.

The cook apologizes for being unable to serve me an apéritif and wine—compulsory in French cuisine. It seems the knowing Colonel has the "firewater" locked safely away, but the stylish chef proceeds to cheer me up with three hard-boiled eggs on an avocado as appetizer, followed by a superb duiker fillet on rice with a delicious sauce. This fare is a welcome surprise after my sojourn in pristine wilderness with abominably bad cooking.

The spotlessly clean kitchen is very well organized. The walls even boast shelves, an amenity completely unknown to the locals and probably seeming like the eighth wonder of the world to them. For me, wonders one through seven are the goods on these shelves: rows of canned delicacies such as beans and peas; jars of jam and mustard; and all civilized necessities are piled high.

The cook uses a gas cooker even though there are piles of wood everywhere, because the wood might impart an unpleasant taste to the food. This is definitely a Frenchman's camp!

I leave early the next day with a local tracker to hunt some plains game. First we float downriver for an hour in a dugout; then we stalk across some half-burned savannas. As we leave the boat we almost step on a young cob caught in a wire snare. The poor animal is hanging awkwardly with its front leg pulled up by a rope attached to a spring device rigged from a bent tree. The bare soil around the wire's anchor attests to the animal's atrocious suffering. Africa shows little mercy to its inhabitants. Something in the food chain is always after something else.

Our stalk leads us to some swampy areas where the elephant grass is less than two feet tall—great for stalking. A red-flanked duiker escapes just ahead of us into heavy cover with its typical hopping leaps. Then a red buffalo appears in its typical alert posture with upthrust head at the edge of the slightly burned tall grass. Before I can steady my rifle, he disappears into the grass.

20

The loud cracking sounds of bursting grass stems indicate his escape route. We try to follow the bull into the next forest gallery since hunting on this savanna is too difficult. We are able to track the buffalo's spoor for an hour; then we lose the trail in some dry rocks. A mark in wet clay catches my eye: a fresh bongo track! It crosses our trail in a stretch of dense vegetation beside a small river.

My pulse beats faster as we concentrate on tracking this huge spiral-horned antelope for two hours. A very desirable trophy! Although we are unable to catch up with him and finally give up the stalk, our efforts are not totally fruitless: Constant bending under branches and liana is the best exercise for the spine. Later we stop to call in duiker, but are not successful. It has not been one of my better days.

We are exhausted, empty-handed, and it's getting late, so we reverse course and arrive back in the village just after sunset. I am thankful that the always cheerful Hassan is awaiting us. The good man saved the day again with his fishing skill, enabling the cook to serve up a delectable dinner of catfish on rice.

Tonight I have company, a tall, proud, solid man named Lamda, owner of the hut. As brother to the chief, he is a highly respected local dignitary with certain traditional hunting privileges. He arrived today by dugout from down river and complains of feeling weak. Being a physician, it is my obligation to care for the ill, so I examine him.

My examination reveals an arrhythmic heartbeat. He is fortunate that I am in this remote spot and have brought along an ample supply of medication, including the appropriate remedies for his problem.

The next day he feels much better; his pulse is stable and regular. By now everyone in the village has heard the news, and half the population is patiently sitting in front of our hut, enthusiastically waiting for treatment by the white medicine man.

Health problems in rural areas are rampant. Nearly everyone suffers from some form of tropical disease ranging from malaria and unknown viral fevers to many kinds of worms. Microfilaria—small worms concentrated in blood vessels and muscles—are very common. The disease is called *Loa Loa*. It causes the skin and joints to swell and triggers allergic reactions including an irresistible need to scratch. It weakens the lymphatic vessels and years later causes monstrous swelling of the legs referred to as *elephantiasis*.

Malaria afflicts everyone here. In most victims, a series of attacks produces a kind of immunity that lasts for some months. When the immunity vanishes, there is a relapse into *falciparum* malaria (*Plasmodium falciparum* is the worst form of the malaria parasitic microbe). Chronic infection causes many locals to sport big bellies from swollen livers and spleens, as well as yellowish eyeballs.

I can cure most of these diseases temporarily. My medication is given free to my crew and their families, but other patients have to bring food, the amount based on what they have and can spare. Their payments are much less than the value of the drugs, but I want to make them understand that the medication is valuable. If I handed it out for nothing, the well would come to cadge, and the unwell would not value it. Even the missions sell medicine because the African mentality necessitates such logic. But then, items given away free in our own society do not receive the consideration attached to that which is paid for, and so it goes.

Many villagers reek of the palm wine and corn booze they consume, and nearly all money obtained by fishing and hunting is immediately converted into alcohol. This Babute tribe has quite a reputation for hard drinking, reminding me of some fellows I knew in my youth.

During the German colonial era, each village was allowed to cut off the head of only one palm tree each year. This hypothetical law was difficult to enforce because the country is spread out, and illicit palm wine fueled many happy days and nights.

Later in the morning, Lamda takes me to his private brewery. A simple ladder made of two large vertical bamboo stalks with horizontal branches secured by strips of bark allows access to the top of a palm tree. The tree's top is cut off, and a hole is drilled three feet to the center of the trunk. Soon, a milky fluid begins to drip into a pot made from a dried pumpkin.

During the first few days Lamda collects about five gallons of the precious drink each morning and three more gallons each evening. Gradually the flow of sap decreases, and after about four weeks the tree dies.

The cool juice is incredibly delicious and has only small amounts of alcohol in it. If left standing for some time, however, the sugar ferments, resulting in a higher concentration of alcohol and a bitter taste. It is easy to tell when someone has stepped out for a quick one owing to the pungent breath and skin odor caused by drinking palm wine.

While driving through Cameroon, you will see big glass jars in front of huts. This means that the occupants sell palm wine for about twenty cents a quart. These are good places for a break and a pint, but not for the driver or anyone meeting him on the road. The truck drivers in Cameroon are usually half-drunk, so the jungle is not the only place one meets dangerous denizens!

Lamda digs out some dried pumpkin-shell cups and offers me a freshly poured drink, which I readily accept. We chat about hunting around the village. Lamda is a privileged man and has exclusive traditional hunting rights to several game-rich forests. This helps me plan for hunting plains game in case my French friend does not show up soon.

At noon the cook serves another delicious meal. I savor the food, knowing that without him I would suffer from my porter's cooking. All locals use liberal amounts of a hot pepper they call *pili-pili*. It is hotter than cayenne pepper and is poured generously over all their food. It is probably effective as a germ killer and possibly even a delicate tourist or two. I have become accustomed to it over my twenty years of hunting in Cameroon, and even carry some powdered *pili-pili* or an oil extract with me.

Once, after I had disembarked a flight from Cameroon, a female customs agent found a vial of *pili-pili* while examining my luggage. She unscrewed the top and was beginning to sniff it when I shouted "Stop!" My waving arms brought armed officers to her side, weapons trained on me. After a brief explanation, I saved my precious vial and the woman's even more precious nasal passage!

It is easy to make this extract. First, the red pepper shells are crushed and mixed in vegetable oil, then allowed to sit for several days. When it turns a reddish color, the oil will have absorbed the fiery capsicum, and the new solution can be used to season food cautiously.

Both tribes in this area, Baya and Baboute, abuse the substance. Once a user gets accustomed to the substance, he has to increase the dosage to feel the same burning sensation previously experienced with smaller amounts of capsicum. I have wondered whether carried "pepper spray" (supposedly effective against a charging grizzly) would work on those natives who are "immunized." Well, not to worry—I know a spray of .458 Winchester Magnum will!

I am awakened from a peaceful siesta by an imperious voice in the dining room. My French friend, Pierre, has returned from his first elephant hunt and is giving orders to porters and trackers regarding camp routine. Everyone jumps eagerly to his task; the old colonial officer has his crew tightly under control. Seemingly relieved and with a broad grin, he shakes my hand. It's not just that he wants my company; I also bring badly needed cash to help with expenses.

Today there is no shortage of apéritif and wine since the Colonel has unlocked his supplies. Engaged in animated discussion, we stay up until late in the evening sharing our adventures. Then he retires to his well-equipped private room to sleep. His gas lantern gives out an extraordinarily bright light (I do not even carry a puny petroleum lamp with me on my safaris) and attracts every night-flying insect known to man plus a few unknown varieties, many of which seem to place *Homo sapiens* high on their culinary charts.

The next morning we depart in different directions. Pierre, who is a very good fisherman, acknowledges Hassan's skill and takes him out to fish with him. This proves advantageous for Hassan. By evening a happy and smiling Hassan will have caught three times more than the slightly dour-looking Colonel. I do not ask about the one that got away for fear that the contents of the kitchen shelves might be denied me!

My destination is one of Lamda's personal reserves, a northeastern forest named Krisa, renowned for its giant, bright-red bongo. Pierre and his friends have shot one of the spiral-horned antelope on almost every trip there.

We track a huge bull's spoor for hours as it gets fresher and fresher. Confidence rises, and our anticipation of a rare and valuable trophy is almost palpable. Suddenly we hear a crashing sound and a red whirlwind vanishes behind a wall of leaves and interwoven twigs. Too bad we spooked the old bull, but the wind had shifted in his favor. Today we must be traveling under a bad spell; from the lost bongo until near dusk only duiker come into view. Today was his day, but tomorrow will be ours.

Back home I find an angry Pierre. His luck was no better. He had ventured out in a dugout rowed by his backup porters from the next city. The amateurs capsized the unstable canoe in the largest and deepest loop of the river, sending Pierre for an unscheduled swim. He struggled in his armor-like clothing in the muddy water, and the blacks still chuckle silently as he gives an agitated account of his mishap. Fortunately, no crocodiles were around (or they were not interested in white meat), but the incident proves that not even full colonels are waterproof!

Tonight we feast on the rewards of my medical practice: chicken, sweet potatoes, fish, and for dessert, rich, sweet dates, the Algerian *Deglet Nour* (Finger of the Light) from my provisions. At the end of this culinary orgy, I struggle to my cot with my full belly. This is my final indulgence, because tomorrow we leave at dawn for big-game hunting far away.

It is tough to be up by 5 A.M., but adventure calls and soon our small crew is ready. Six porters carry our five-day supply of tackle and food. We proceed quickly on the villagers' path, but soon it peters out and we continue on narrow game trails and large elephant paths. Sometimes we cut across the abundant vegetation to find the fresh track of a worthy bull. Our guides are the compass and a detailed map. Pierre shows me remnants of the German colonial era; although abandoned for some sixty years, a six-foot-wide path is still visible.

Thousands of heavily loaded porters stomping along year after year have compressed the path almost two feet deeper than the surrounding soil. The bark of rubber trees—*Kikxia* or *Ficus lutea*—shows spiral cuts from collecting the white sap over seventy years ago. The natives from the colony of *Kamerun* (Cameroon, see appendix) used to pay the German government a head tax, part of which consisted of rubber sap. Rubber exports peaked in 1914 with 47,345 tons worth 11.5 million reichsmarks (now around 100 million dollars U.S.). The rubber required 50,000 porters. No wonder the paths are sunken!

Ivory was also a major export article from *Kamerun*. In 1914 the value of ivory exports was 530,000 reichsmarks (5 million dollars U.S.), while the ivory exported from German East Africa, nowadays Tanzania, totaled just 360,000 reichsmarks, with another 40,000 reichsmarks from the German colony of Togo. *Kamerun's* ivory exports peaked in 1905 with 1.27 million reichsmarks (10 million dollars U.S.), up from its average of around 900,000 reichsmarks. Unfortunately those game-rich days are gone, and now big tuskers are rare.

Against all odds, a few years ago the Colonel brought down a giant bull with magnificent tusks of $84^1/_4$ and 86 inches. Forest ivory is smooth without any cracks or fissures, and it is much harder than ivory from the savanna. It is yellowish, with large brown and black blotches from the daily influence of abundant plant juice. Some call the forest variety "rose" ivory because a lamp held in the hollow at the base of a tusk will cast a reddish tint. Others attribute this tint to a special variety of elephant in Gabon. Its surface displays a clear texture with a fine network of lines, and I think it's the prettiest of all ivory.

We continue our search for a bigfoot day after day, walking for hours in creeks because they are sometimes the easiest way. The tracker whacks with his machete for hours on end while we twist through the small openings. At the end of another tough day we have covered just three miles "as the crow flies" on these winding trails. The detailed map is helpful, but often we just guess which of the many small creeks we are in.

Ten years later, a Global Positioning System (GPS) unit makes it a piece of cake to pinpoint positions, but then it was tough. Another reason to wonder "How did I ever manage without . . . ?"

Imagine our disappointment twice during the second day when we meet eager young black men armed with modern big-bore rifles who "hunt" for influential Cameroonians. Fortunately they do not venture as far as we do. Still, elephant are taking a heavy beating from these men who bang away at every bull regardless of tusk size. Several times we come across decaying bones. The big leg bones and the skull last the longest, and we can tell by the skulls how big the tusks were.

One day we're stalking buffalo and reach a small savanna near a swamp in the big rain forest. The buffalo track leads us through high grass toward a sun-bleached elephant skull. This animal died around two months ago. The skull looks untouched, with no signs of having been cut into. Usually tusks are chopped out with an ax or a machete, leaving obvious marks. Was he wounded far away and did he die here without his poachers at his heel? This means there is a good chance of finding the tusks. Everyone fans out, eagerly searching the thick grass and dense bushes for ivory. Finally one porter shouts from the swamp. He has found one half-immersed tusk twenty yards from the skull.

Small rodents such as porcupine carried it away and gnawed on it for its mineral content; then it was protected by the flooded swamp during the rainy season. The thick, solid frontal portion is still three feet long and weighs eleven pounds; only the hollow root of the tooth has been eaten away. The furrows from the rodents' teeth give the stump an elaborate, almost artistic design. Originally it must have been a beautiful tusk about five and one-half feet long, weighing around thirty-five pounds. Except for this pick-up trophy, our first excursion results only in small game.

I bag several duiker and bushpig (*Potamochoerus porcus*, red pig or red river hog), so our daily provisions are guaranteed, but once our rice is gone, we have to head back to base camp in the village. We rest for a day, then set out again. This is my last chance for big game. Although the journey down the river was very interesting, it reduced my time to hunt big game to only two weeks. I must still float fifty miles down a huge river with several rapids to reach a railway station and board a train to Cameroon's capital, Yaoundé.

Many small insects, ants, and thorns await us in these virgin forests. Our clothing must be well chosen to protect us. The Colonel is especially well-clad in armor similar to a medieval knight's: light woolen sweater on bare skin, long cotton jacket completely buttoned to the jaw, high leather boots, leather gloves, and a small hat. Too hot for me. I just wear long-sleeved light clothing, canvas boots, and gaiters.

We try very hard to penetrate deep into the forest, but Diana resists. We are unable to locate fresh big bull tracks for the first two days. On the third day, we hear the sounds of a herd of elephant feeding. Trees are pushed and crack with a dull sound, and limbs and liana burst with a high-pitched noise. For elephant hunters in the forest, a scattered herd is just about the worst-case scenario. In such conditions it is impossible to locate a big bull. Each source of sound must be stalked to see whether it is a shootable bull, until sooner or later the animals catch our wind, at which point all hell breaks loose—hell being a behemoth bent on harm!

I am shocked when Pierre orders me to stay with the porters while he sneaks up on the animals, accompanied only by his tracker. Even the tracker looks at me in disbelief, but this is not the time to argue. I have too much respect for the old hunter to disobey, so I stay and wait. Ten minutes later shrill trumpeting sounds through the peaceful forest as elephant scatter, uprooting and crushing trees underfoot. They got wind of Pierre early. The porters leap like cats up the closest trees, but I rely on my rifle and wait confidently.

Suddenly three cows break through the bush and pass only ten yards away from me. Soon the show is over, and the peaceful chirps of birds and crickets fill the air. The

Colonel shows up unhappy. He is angry that his stalk failed and feels uneasy about having left me behind like a child. I propose we hunt separately for the remaining two days, so we split up the next morning.

I am relieved to be on my own and able to make my own decisions. I push my crew, and we soon come across relatively fresh bull spoor. After thorough examination at the next muddy spot, my tracker confirms that the bull passed by here last night.

It is now or never. We pursue the spoor as quickly as possible. By noon we are getting close. The bull's droppings are fresh, and no dung beetles have invaded it. Now it is necessary to move as silently as possible since elephant rest from about noon until 3 P.M. During this period they doze, standing almost motionless. It is easy to blunder into them and scare them away, so we move painstakingly slowly, turning big leaves and small leafy bushes to avoid any treacherous noise.

Hour after hour passes, and our attention lessens. Before we know it, we are suddenly in front of the bull. He realizes his imminent danger and turns to run off with shrill trumpeting. I glimpse the tusks. He carries more than enough to be legal, and this is my very last chance this hunting season. Wanting to fill my permit, I aim carefully for a spinal shot one hand above the root of the tail.

My .458 Winchester Magnum belches tremendously, and the bull's hindquarters collapse. He levers himself around, savagely smashing branches and leaves with his trunk, trying to get close to me. In one swift motion I chamber another cartridge and finish him with a shot to his forehead, directly on the third wrinkle above the eyes. The effect is dramatic as he crashes into the bush and all movement ceases. The angle was poor, so I am not sure whether I hit his brain or just stunned him. The elephant's brain is relatively small—around the size of a football—and is well protected by the bones of the massive head.

Safety first. I move quickly to his neck and place a sure shot into the brain. A final quiver marks the end of these dramatic seconds. Certainty is a must because many a "dead" jumbo has risen to smite its tormentor.

Now I have time to look at the short but thick tusks. They are bright yellow, with beautiful black and brown stains from plant juices—very typical for a forest elephant.

The crew is even happier than I. The village is close, and one porter is dispatched immediately to summon the villagers for a feast. With no load he will reach a path in the evening and move through the night unprotected! He must love a good feast, but had better watch out or he could become the feast. A Pygmy would not make such a trip at night; these Baya and Babouté tribesmen are definitely more courageous.

By 10 the next morning our lonely forest is filled with excited locals carrying knives, machetes, and axes. After a few hours of fierce whacking and cutting, only bones remain in a lake of blood and excrement. Blazing bonfires all around us smoke meat and entrails. These tasty treats are piled high on tables of freshly cut saplings and covered with huge leaves to keep off the flies.

I can't hang around until the tusks are removed; I have to start back to the village today. In four days the skin around the skull bones will have rotted sufficiently to extract the ivory. No chopping for these trophies. The Colonel will carry them with him when he returns to civilization in another month. I have confidence in this crew. They have been well trained by the Colonel and will not dare to steal the valuable ivory. Normally, it is wise to keep them under strict control at all times.

A friend of mine killed a magnificent bull elephant last year. He continued his quest for buffalo and other game, and had his porters carry the heavy tusks weighing 93 pounds in and out of some seventy miles of uninhabited forest for fourteen days. He didn't let those beauties out of his sight!

31

At the village I meet up with Pierre. He congratulates me on my medium bull and is quite optimistic that he will find a big one in the four weeks he has left to hunt. But the rainy season has been over for three weeks, and it gets drier each day. It will be difficult to keep following a bull's trail for days on end.

I realize that the golden era of elephant hunting in this part of central Cameroon is long gone. "Too many hunters are the fox's death," and there are far too many poachers here, even one being too many. At the end of his first safari into this remote area five years ago, the Colonel caused a terrible uproar when he arrived at the railway station in the bush with a heavy load of ivory.

Four years ago Pierre and two friends exported three pairs of the most beautiful rose ivory tusks weighing a total of 350 pounds. Just two years ago he killed a huge tusker with ivories weighing seventy-two pounds each only a day away from the village.

I wonder whether the success of sport hunters draws poachers to an area. Does our "meat feast" push hungry villagers to illegally take more elephant? The latter is doubtful since they do not have the necessary firepower, unlike native "hired guns" from the city.

Pierre now regrets having to stay behind alone. He will have no one to listen to his endless and interesting stories at the campfire. I am restocking his larder with the proceeds of my final consultations. He has never had so many eggs or such a variety of vegetables!

Hassan has rested well during the past two weeks and is eager to travel. He loves the river and we have only a short fifteen-mile stretch left. Then it flows into a much larger river, and we will paddle fifty more miles to the railway station.

The porters think it is fun to inflate the boat, so I leave them that task. The heat gets their sweat flowing freely, but the river is close and they enjoy a quick dip after each turn, wildly splashing each other—big children with zero regard for man-eating crocs!

The boat's repair looks fine, so we inflate it fully to allow it to float high on the water. After all the gear is stowed away, we depart at full speed, both of us paddling furiously. The villagers and Pierre's crew yell wildly until we disappear around the first bend.

Now we relax and enjoy a peaceful journey on the 40- to 60-yard-wide river. At dusk we make camp close to the big river and listen to upriver rapids create a distant thunder. After feasting on smoked elephant trunk and fresh roasted peanuts, we sleep very soundly.

Daybreak brings a white mist. We embark and soon reach the beautiful Sanaga River, which is several hundred yards wide at this point. We float quickly with the current. The water is relatively clear during the dry season, and we can see several feet down. The banks are entirely covered with dense rain forest, but the occasional small savanna helps keep kob antelope alive by sending warning whistles into the air upon our approach.

We frequently encounter fish otter, both the big Congo clawless otter—*Aonyx (Paraonyx) congica* Lönnberg—with its shiny white breast and long fingers, and the smaller, entirely brown Cape clawless otter—*Aonyx capensis* (Schinz). They move in small groups and dive away elegantly when we get too close. Their spoor is everywhere on the muddy banks where they dig for worms. The river sometimes forms an inner delta and divides into many channels that meander around several large and small isles, all covered by a thick green mass of trees and bushes.

Small rapids are no problem for the flexible rubber boat and make a full-speed passing great fun. In the afternoon we reach the first village and hear a surreal thundering: A distant train is rumbling through Africa's outland.

The villagers tell us that we can board only at noon some twenty miles farther, so we rush to catch the train. After night falls we continue for two hours in bright moonlight to reach the big rapids close to our goal. Suddenly the distinctive rumbling of a slow freight train and the light from its headlights close to the river create a ghostly impression. It is so out of place in this beautiful scenery—a ghost train from a movie.

We have trouble finding an open bank for our camp, but finally come across an abandoned fishing camp. Hassan is tired, so I cook some rice with smoked meat and onions—not fancy, but enough to stave off hunger.

We are afloat again before dawn. The morning is beautiful: Birds sing, and a thin white mist gives the contours of the forest a dreamlike appearance. But soon we must concentrate on the dangerous rapids that the villagers warned us about. They stretch for two miles along the river that is now a mile wide. The water foams across and between many rocks in small channels. We feel uneasy because the river is so wide and Hassan has never been here before, but he stays on the right side as advised by the villagers. Once committed to a channel, we must stay there until it ends, because there is no way to stop and we are very far from the riverbank.

The boat gains more and more speed, and suddenly visible rocks scrape dangerously at its bottom and sides. Hassan is steering fine, but a white wall of foam suddenly rises before us. We have no time to react as the boat plunges through it, flying over a rock ledge into the air to land with a bang five feet deeper into the wild eddies.

Fortunately there are no other obstacles farther on. We have passed the worst part of the rapids and are very relieved as the thundering roar softens, and the river flows quietly again. The tension and fear of the past few minutes expel themselves in loud laughing and shaking hands—but my knees turn to rubber again. Some hippo lift their heads to watch us, and we speed up again to put a safe distance between them and us.

Huge fish—Nile perch, catfish, and some species unknown
to me—are visible as they coast along beneath the surface.
"Perch" brings to mind a small fish, but these babies can reach
weights in excess of three hundred pounds!

By now we don't care much for our environment, and
paddle like galley slaves to reach our destination on time. I
am reminded of a "good news/bad news" joke: Drum beater
to galley rowers—good news: It's Sunday, Captain declares
a day off./bad news: He wants to go waterskiing!

It's crucial to catch the train at noon because the next
one doesn't come until tomorrow, which would leave us
little time in Yaoundé to obtain the export permits for our
trophies. In addition to my own, I am responsible for the
paperwork for the three German friends I left in the bush
at the beginning of this expedition. By now they should
also have an impressive array of souvenirs.

At 10 A.M. we pull into a small village. The locals are bewildered by the sight of a white man in a strange craft arriving
from nowhere! We deflate the canoe and pack everything in
duffel bags while a large crowd watches our every move.

There is still time to make a fire and heat some water
to shave my four-week-old beard. Even with the soft water
from the river, it hurts! Then I recruit some porters and
walk an hour until we reach the train station. We pass the
game department's hut where several impressive gorilla
skulls are spread out on the bench in the window.

The villagers complain that these primates create havoc
on their small plantations and suggest I shoot some! That is
absolutely out of the question; apart from the ethical problem,
they are protected. Fortunately lowland gorilla are still very
numerous in Cameroon. The "lowland" or "western" gorilla
(*Gorilla gorilla gorilla*) is highly endangered. The "mountain"
or "eastern" gorilla (*Gorilla gorilla berengei*) is extremely endangered. As of this writing, the lowland/western gorilla can be
legally taken on a hunting license in Cameroon.

Surprisingly the train arrives on schedule. Hassan boards the luggage coach to guard our equipment—four bags totaling 200 pounds including the deflated and rolled canoe. I climb into the first-class car: This rusty, dirty, and badly damaged coach would not be suitable for animal transport in Germany. Even if I had preferred coach, "face" dictates that I occupy this car. By now it seems almost luxurious to me, and I relax on a torn plastic-covered bench as the train rattles along at twenty miles an hour for the remaining two hundred miles.

The only advantage to riding in first class is space. The second class is wall-to-wall locals, chickens, goats, and anything else they can cram in. It would be tough to turn around in there, much less try to snooze.

There are very few stations along our way but at each stop picturesque vendors rush to the windows to sell bananas, papayas, and avocados, as well as many hard-to-identify foods. All are displayed in plastic bowls balanced elegantly on their heads. "Batons" are frequently offered—manioc sticks wrapped in banana leaves and boiled. Hygienically they are safer than the other foods. Some are very hot, but the pepper does kill microbes.

That night we arrive in Yaoundé's noisy train station, a world of difference from this morning's peaceful camp on the lonesome riverbank. Now it really gets dangerous because we are back in civilization and must take great care to prevent theft of our luggage. Young men rush toward us from all sides and press me to hire them to carry the luggage from train to taxi. They charge a tremendous amount of money, so it is important to agree on payment before assigning the job and to sort out the serious workers from the thieves.

It is a nightmare; these fellows try to create confusion to maximize their profit. I remain calm, pick out some more or less reliable-looking men, and chase the others away, which is not an easy task. They try to threaten those who were hired, but take off when they hear me negotiate with the taxi driver for *le department de police*—the police station! With my olive duffel bags and military haircut they probably think that I could be a foreign adviser. I am glad to have Hassan with me and relieved when everything is safely loaded into a cab. We are on our way to see my old friend, Al-Hajj Yacoub.

We arrive and I can finally relax. His wives bring food and drinks, and take care of my luggage—a safe haven at last! Yacoub is a Fulani (also Fulbe or Peul) merchant from the grasslands of west Cameroon, a Bamoun tribesman. He is Muslim and has traveled to the holy city of Mecca three times, thus the title "Al-Hajj" (the pilgrim). In his youth he was a very poor villager and is still illiterate. However, he is clever and worked hard to save enough money to buy a beaten, rusty Land Rover. Now he travels to remote areas in central Cameroon, where he sells goods and buys dried fish, smoked venison, and all kinds of vegetables. Two of his three wives are at the market every day selling the food he has purchased.

The profit margin is high. Yacoub owns several houses and has even built his own small mosque. He is a wealthy man by Cameroonian standards. Now he is in the bush collecting my three hunters. Late that evening they arrive completely worn out but fairly content. One brings a huge set of 95-pound tusks from the bush!

Two of the hunters were novices. One carried a busload of unnecessary gear—an incredible 180 pounds! He boasted before leaving that his wish had always been to hunt where there were no roads or fences. Now his wish had come true in the extreme; he walked forty miles into desolate bush. He eventually got buffalo, a medium elephant, and several antelope, but during the first week he couldn't bag anything and was very depressed.

The third hunter is less downbeat. He has been on many safaris in southern Africa and knows the value of a red   forest buffalo. He is happy with his big bull, which ended up in the renowned Rowland Ward Record Book.

The next day my boat is inflated, thoroughly waxed, and hung from the ceiling of Yacoub's uncle's room for use on later safaris. The small old man looks rather grimly at the huge boat hanging low over his bed, so I feel uneasy. Yacoub just laughs and tells me that his uncle doesn't pay any rent anyhow.

Reassured, I relax and enjoy Yacoub's hospitality. At dusk, two of his wives return from the market and join the third one, who has been taking care of the household. Then there is no TV in Cameroon, so his three wives sit at the table to read and sing verses from the Koran in Arabic. I listen, and later we talk about daily life in Cameroon and Germany; they are curious and want to know all about my family. It's hard for them to comprehend that I have just one wife and, even worse, only one child. As a respected and, in their eyes, rich doctor, I should do better. More than one wife under one roof with western female attitudes? A minefield!

After a while they gather enough courage to ask me what kind of magic I use to survive in the bush, hunt successfully, and return safely without disease. Africans fear the bush and prefer to crowd together in big cities—a human trend or the herd instinct? I tell them that I rely on my powerful rifle, but they giggle and reply: "You live in a civilized country, have a job requiring no labor, drive a car, yet do not suffer from insects and tropical diseases. How could you possibly avoid all our plagues without very strong magic? You just don't want to tell us your secret."

Many native Africans believe in magic. They are sure that nearly all events in life are influenced by magic. This belief is deeply rooted even in educated Christians and Moslems of higher social status. Being a Westerner, I don't try to argue. I just go with the flow and smile. Even in Western civilizations, the effectiveness of medication depends upon the power of suggestion around 30 percent of the time; in Africa it's more than 80 percent. Few Westerners can begin to comprehend African thought processes, and the reverse is also true. Many failed development projects have proven this time and again.

One white hunter I heard of used to order Carter's Little Liver Pills from the U.S. and give them to his crew. The pills are completely harmless and are supposed to improve liver function. They also turn urine green, so the magic is visible! That hunter's porters worked better than they would have if they had been paid double wages.

Once I set out on a safari for elephant and recruited a crew of porters and two trackers in a village. I turned down an old hunter who wanted to be engaged as a highly paid tracker. He reeked of palm wine, and his physical condition was very poor. I decided he would not be too useful and would probably just slow down the safari.

We had to cover around thirty miles on a difficult footpath in two days in order to reach the hunting areas. The plan was to camp and take long side trips with minimal luggage, pursuing elephant through pristine forests with intense undergrowth. This is very hard work for the tracker, the point man who has to constantly cut the way with his machete. It requires excellent physical condition. The drunkard would not take a polite no for an answer and dogged me to hire him. Fed up, I finally told him to leave me alone. He walked on, grumbling out loud about the stubborn white man, but I paid him no further attention.

During our first day, one extremely strong and reliable porter joined me at a break in the march to tell me that in case the hunt went poorly or any accidents occurred, I should report to the police that the old drunkard was responsible for the bad luck. I was completely surprised, and since I respected this porter who had worked for me before, I refrained from making fun of him.

I inquired politely why I should blame the old drunkard. I had completely forgotten that hiring incident, but apparently the old man had not. My porter said he had seen the old man follow me to the river during our departure and cast a bad spell by burning some herbs over my footprint in the mud. By now I could not help laughing and told him that the police would send me away thinking white man got too much sun.

"No, no, they will put the sorcerer in jail and accuse him," answered my porter seriously, and it was true. Even high-ranking government officials thought the same way. One widespread popular belief is that bad witch doctors change into dangerous animals during the day. When shot, such an animal changes back into human form. The locals believe that hunting accidents are caused by black magic, so safari porters and trackers need to have a lot of confidence in their boss.

The boss is called *patron* in French and is addressed as such. He is responsible for solving almost all problems encountered during traditional foot safaris, and on a safari of several weeks' duration, many problems arise. Newcomers invariably suffer difficulties. It is best to stay calm and allow the locals to sort out problem with minimal guidance. But after the omnipotent *patron* has been the boss for several weeks, deeper relations form and he must face all kinds of demands. He must distinguish between the good and the bad workers. Some just want more money, and some really need help.

Once I responded to a desperate letter written on behalf of my porter and skipper Hassan. Besides having rendered valorous services, Hassan was always a cheerful porter of heavy loads and represented to me the very best elements of adventure and the hunt. He told me that he had been imprisoned for failure to pay taxes on an inherited shotgun for many years. He was a fisherman and did not hunt, so the gun had just lain at home. Now he needed $700 U.S. to get free. I did not want to just pay the money or post it to the prison as requested, fearing that it would never reach him and end up in some official's pocket. I asked my old friend and clever businessman, Al-Hajj Yacoub, to take care of the matter and put $800 U.S. at his disposal.

The information gathered by Yacoub told a completely different story: Hassan was accused of dealing hashish, which in Cameroon means up to five years in prison. Cameroon's prisons are meant to deter people from a life of further crime through harsh conditions such as heavy labor, miserable food, and rough treatment. They are not hotels like some Western prisons. In Cameroon five years' imprisonment is tantamount to a death sentence.

Hassan told Yacoub that he was accidentally in the house of a hashish dealer when police raided it. That could be true as Hassan was not smart enough to be a dealer. He could be a buyer, but not a dealer. Anyhow, he was in big trouble, and I told Yacoub to do whatever was necessary with the $800 to get Hassan out of jail, knowing that a major part of the sum would land in Yacoub's own pocket. Two months later, after several interventions by lawyers, some gift-giving, and lots of talk, I was $800 poorer and Hassan was out of jail—one expensive porter!

This is an example of the filthy lucre circulating in most parts of Africa, one of a safari's many hidden expenses. I got a long thank-you letter from Hassan, who said that he included me in at least one of his five daily prayers to Allah. This little story should alert a novice to the indirect costs that must be calculated into the expense of a safari, unless one plans to follow a scorched-earth policy and never return. Upon returning, such a person would encounter a surprising number of small obstacles created by unhappy and uncooperative personnel.

Diplomacy is paramount, whether in or out of Africa. Sometimes authorities or acquaintances from safaris show up for visits in Europe and must be housed and entertained.

Letters containing orders for goods can add significantly to indirect safari costs, so I always travel like a heavily loaded mule. Even if one has perfect contacts with important people in Cameroon, unexpected problems often arise and must usually be resolved with expensive presents.

Even if all paperwork and equipment is perfectly correct and legal, one can still spend days at one of many checkpoints if the local potentate wants something, as he often will upon seeing a white man. It does no good to get angry. The key to success is staying friendly and making small talk. If nothing else helps, the inevitable dash for beer or *cadeaux* (presents) will open doors. It's no different from a trip to India, Mexico, or any other country where graft is common.

After ten years, I still have vivid memories of this adventurous expedition. I doubt whether I would now go on a similar journey without gathering and thoroughly examining all available information. I was young and eager then, and very confident in my ability to handle all problems. Still, I was the first and only white man to travel down this wild river through hostile forests and savannas. Even if the hunting was not what I had anticipated, it was good fun and I have many spectacular memories. Numerous photos, trophies, and other mementos remind me of insignificant but meaningful things.

This hunt took place ten years ago, and now heavy poaching has diminished game populations, leaving no big tuskers. This is a terrible shame, not just for the animals but also for the locals, whose economy benefits greatly from the influx of sport hunters, especially the do-it-yourselfers who spend a lot of money directly in the area. Nonetheless, I derive immense satisfaction from having been the pathfinder—the very first!

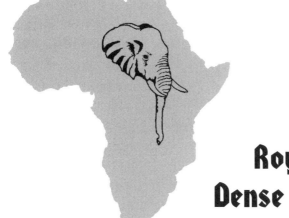

Chapter 2

Elephant— Royal Game in Dense Rain Forest

I hurry along a narrow forest trail with long strides. My bearers half-run to keep up. Since yesterday, I have been pushing my crew northeast in the general direction of the porters' home village, our starting point three weeks ago. We have seen no vehicles, road tracks, or huts the entire time—just twenty-plus days of a tremendously exciting safari.

I have stalked forest buffalo, large antelope, and many kinds of small game, but still yearn for the one game animal that has eluded me. I badly want a trophy elephant bull— "Royal Game." I am hoping for a last stalk so I hurry the porters along. My gait is powerful, and I am filled with anticipation. We follow a swiftly flowing 35-foot-wide river to reach the mouth of a small creek before nightfall hoping for a last try at jumbo in our few remaining days.

We could take a two-day excursion into a remote, swampy forest where I have located elephant several times before. They prefer the swamps, and there is also a good chance for sitatunga there. If necessary we could extend the hunt another day since the porters' village is just a hard day's walk from our camp.

These days very few countries have elephant populations stable enough to permit the harvesting of surplus trophies. In the few that do, it is extremely rare to bag the classic "100-pounder." A weight of 100 pounds per tusk is the minimum for entry in the Rowland Ward's *Records of African Trophies*, which has been in existence for more than a century. The tusks of the No. 1 record bull are displayed in London's British Museum, and viewing them is a memorable experience. Each tusk is taller and heavier than the average person. Imagine the stately beast that carried them. Formidable!

A black slave named Senussi, poaching for the famous and feared slave merchant and ivory hunter Shundi, killed that heavily laden bull on the steep slopes of Mount Kilimanjaro. In 1898 the tusks were sold at the traditional ivory market in Zanzibar. The British Museum was later able to purchase the pair, each of which had a separate owner. In 1962 they still weighed 214 and 226 English pounds respectively. Their lengths of 10 feet 2$^{1/2}$ inches and 10 feet 5$^{1/2}$ inches are exceeded by other tusks—the longest known measuring 11 feet and 11 feet 5$^{1/2}$ inches—but their weights remain the highest recorded.

Since forest ivory has always been much smaller than savanna ivory, a hunt for forest elephant in Cameroon will never bag a 100-pounder. Both types of elephant live up to sixty years. They grow three sets of molars in the daily quest for fodder; and when the last one wears down, the animal starves to death. It can be rewarding to examine the jaws. Several times I have located two- to four-inch long, dark brown, and shiny worn plates, which were all that remained of those last molars—wonderful souvenirs!

Estimates of Cameroon's elephant population are difficult to come by, but it is probably around eight thousand. The CITES (Convention on International Trade in Endangered Species of Wild Fauna and Flora) quota for permits to export hunting trophies to Europe was sixty for the 1995 season. Various organizations, including Safari Club International, have battled with the U.S. Fish and Wildlife Service to establish a quota for the United States.

Banning the ivory trade slowed down elephant poaching in Cameroon by causing the black market price for ivory to drop significantly. Before the ban, the price per pound had risen to $25 U.S.; now it is down to $7 U.S. However, since the black market price of a single .375 H&H Magnum or .458 Winchester Magnum cartridge is only $20–$30 U.S., and since elephant meat is still in high demand, poaching on a smaller scale continues regardless of the amount of ivory the elephant carries.

Early the next morning my best tracker, two porters, and I cross the river to enter a small game trail somewhat farther up the creek. Two hours later we come to the first of a series of swamps. We close in on them covertly but are disappointed time and again. Only old elephant tracks are visible, and no sitatunga seem to have visited these swamps for quite some time. By 10 A.M. I change our plan. We will not continue along the series of swamps. Instead we will go west and circle the dense forest in an attempt to pick up tracks.

An hour later my tracker—Sumano—excitedly shows me fresh elephant tracks. Elephant pull out small trees and lianas and strike the roots against other trees, so the amount of moisture in broken roots indicates the amount of time that has passed since they were pulled out. These elephant passed through barely an hour ago. Perhaps we will get lucky! We follow these slight signs (it always amazes me how few tracks these giants leave, considering their enormous feet are like flexible rubber soles on a huge tennis shoe) until the animals cross some mud. Only then can we accurately judge our chances for a good bull.

Some time later we step into a small creek, and with a sudden charge of adrenaline akin to a lightning bolt, my heart starts racing. This must be a truly worthy bull! Huge, round, deep tracks promise superb ivory.

Hunting the rain forest is very different from stalking elephant in open savannas. Normally, the hunter tries to find a single spoor; then he follows it until the track crosses some wet soil or mud that will indicate the size of the round front foot. The bigger and clearer the front nail marks, the older the animal and the better the chance of big tusks. But the tracker must carefully examine several tracks, since animals often step over a log or prominent root, causing their footfall to be heavier and the spoor to be deceptively larger.

If the foot measures about sixteen to eighteen inches, it is probably an older bull. But forest elephant can be good tuskers and still have small footprints, so it is very important to evaluate the nail marks. Several times I have unwillingly followed small spoor, suspecting that my Pygmy tracker wanted me to shoot the elephant in self-defense to provide his tribe with eagerly desired meat, and actually ended up finding bulls with rather good tusks. A good tusk in Cameroon these days is anything from around five feet and thirty pounds on up.

Once the tusks are cut out of the jaw, it is easier to judge age; up to around twenty-five years the cavity gets larger; then it starts to shrink. The older the animal, the smaller the cavity and the heavier the tusk. Tusks continue to grow throughout an elephant's life, around $3^1/_2$ to $4^1/_2$ inches a year, but wear down when used to excavate roots or minerals in the soil, break trees, and strip bark. Similar to humans who generally have either a dominant right or left hand, elephant tend to favor one tusk, resulting in one being shorter. While approximately 20 percent of *Homo sapiens* are "lefties," it is not known what percentage of elephant are southpaws.

The odds of finding this particular bull are high, even though its tracks have joined those of a small herd that is moving slowly and spreading out to feed along the way. We isolate the big bull's tracks and follow them as quickly as possible. Sumano is an experienced tracker who knows his job. He is a member of the Baya tribe of middle Cameroon, traditionally very clever hunters. As he carefully picks out the sparse signs, he is nearly running after the elephant.

It is important to catch up as quickly as possible, so we can close in before he stops for his noonday rest. The bull will stand motionless until about 3 P.M., and the dry ground will make it almost impossible for us to get close. The elephant has poor eyesight, but compensates with excellent senses of smell and hearing. This year's rainy season was not very wet. The most recent drops fell over four days ago, and now everything is bone-dry.

I barely manage to keep up with Sumano. He bends like a cat under the liana and low-growing branches. Heaven forbid we should encounter a green mamba (*Dendroasdis viridis*). One strike from this angel of death—seven feet long, slim, and terribly quick—and the victim is history. Antivenin is effective, but it requires refrigeration and cannot be carried on these journeys into *Dendroasdis's* domain.

Normally Sumano cuts a wide path for me with his machete, working with the elegance and enthusiasm of a Japanese samurai wielding a *katana*. But now he just cuts through a small liana here and there with his knife. The heavy blade of the machete would make too much noise and give us away to the ever-vigilant quarry.

I am glad this marathon is taking place after the fourteen days of grueling intensive "training" I have just been through; a rugged solo safari in Cameroon's dense rain forest is the best exercise for the back and stomach muscles. It is much easier to bend and twist, but I still sweat profusely.

Before noon we hear the sounds of cracking branches and liana that elephant produce as they move slowly through the forest. It sounds promising, and I pray silently that we will come across the big bull and not a cow. The odds increase as the track of the big one moves to the left into a dense thicket—his noon nap site? We hear the other elephant on a small ridge to our right.

Its solo journey improves the odds that this elephant is a bull. The porters hang back, put their loads safely between some large roots, and look for easy-to-climb trees out of harm's way while Sumano and I begin the final stalk.

My Mauser .458 Winchester Magnum (this hunt took place before I developed the trusty Bullpup .460 Weatherby Magnum design) is loaded with three full-metal-jacket cartridges in the magazine and one cartridge in the chamber. I carry the rifle high on my left with the safety lever still engaged on the right side, ready for instant release. The danger of a charge in this dense foliage is very real.

We move with extreme caution through dense thickets of raffia-palm. Our progress is slow. My heart is racing, and sweat trickles from every pore. Knowing that I must face the world's most dangerous and powerful land animal at a visibility of fifteen feet at most, relying on my wits and big-bore rifle, adds to the suspense and makes us move even more cautiously. Fortunately the slight breeze is in our favor.

I take some dust from a termite mound and let it fall from my palm. It drifts slowly to our rear, but at noon wind direction in the forest changes quickly. On several previous hunts I had harrowing moments when once-promising stalks quickly turned into near disaster.

The bull is barely 150 feet away when we hear the awful sound of breaking twigs and branches moving away from us. What a disappointment—the tusker of my dreams was so close!

With a smaller bull, this would not necessarily mean that the hunt was over. We would follow and most likely get another chance after he eventually slowed down to find out what had scared him off. But this is an old rogue. He knows the signs of danger and will keep moving without stopping until nightfall. I can't understand what gave us away. Did the slight wind circle and drift down toward him? Very unlikely in the forest, but I have no time to wonder.

The other elephant hear their leader move away and decide to join him. Noisy and impressive, they run through the jungle with us in their way. Four bulls, trumpeting loudly, pass with long strides through a relatively open spot just 45 feet away. The first one is small, the second a medium (legal) bull, and the last are two pygmy bulls. This is really my last chance to fill the license, and I do not hesitate.

For a better sight picture I am forced to shoot from a crouched position. I shoulder the weapon and begin swinging with the fast-moving elephant. Thirty feet farther along is another clear spot, and as soon as the second elephant moves through it I aim at the shoulder and fire the big-bore. Five-hundred grains of solid-jacketed bullet throw the bull down, but he continues to trumpet shrilly while trying to regain his feet.

I am now lying on my back (too much recoil in that unstable posture!) with my prescription glasses somewhere in the dry leaves. The enraged elephant is less than a stone's throw away, and a charge seems imminent. Without my glasses I can barely see the bull, so a killing shot is impossible.

Sumano is so excited that he does not realize my problem and decides to shoot the elephant himself. But a full-jacketed 7x57R out of my three-barrel Drilling has no effect on an elephant's chest! A 7x57R or "rimmed" equals a .257 Roberts—puny medicine for such a huge adversary. Finally I locate my glasses and manage a clean shot in the right spot. The bull is finished, and once the tension eases my knees suddenly feel like jelly.

Again I understand the famous big-game hunter Professor Ernst Zwilling when he says that "hunting elephant in the rain forest is a royal hunt." Equally descriptive are the words of the well-known professional hunter T. Sanchez-Arino: "For the real hunter who thrives on the thrills of hunting, stalking an elephant must always be the peak of his ambition as a hunter."

I do not believe this world offers a greater pleasure than hunting elephant in thick forest with a fine heavy rifle. From my point of view there is nothing to add. Not everyone understands the beauty of this type of hunt. My wife often asks: "You told me before your first safari that you wanted to hunt just one elephant in your life. Why do you now leave every year for another?"

My answer comes from Sanchez-Arino, who says that one is four times less likely to take a forest elephant than a savanna elephant, and that was several years ago. Now, especially in Cameroon, the chances of obtaining such a prestigious trophy are much lower than they were when Sanchez-Arino penned his remarks. It is a real challenge and a thrilling one. I have hunted elephant on twenty-two safaris, and the thrill never abates.

My safaris in Cameroon and elsewhere in Africa—all solo safaris except for two, where I went with friends—have resulted in my being fortunate enough to bag a total of twenty elephant and forty-nine buffalo. I have placed around nineteen heads of game in the Rowland Ward's *Records of Big Game* (Vol. XXIV-1995), and given enough time and energy any serious hunter could do the same.

We have only three days left before our truck picks us up in the village and takes us to Yaoundé, so this last stalk is real luck. I enjoy my trophy: The bull's 25-pound tusks are a beautiful black-stained ivory. The big old rogue tusker would have had heavier ivory, but under the circumstances I am content.

As mentioned earlier, forest ivory has a different consistency than savanna ivory. It is harder and yellower with a clearly visible network of fine lines. Some call it rose ivory as explained in the previous chapter, but real rose ivory has a definite rose color even when viewed from its exterior and is found only in certain parts of northern Gabon, equatorial Guinea, and Cameroon. This rose color will not last forever. It vanishes after around ten years, probably due to dehydration.

No fissures mar the surface of ivory on forest bulls, and beautiful black and brown stains on ivory from older animals add to its attraction. Ivory consists of approximately sixty percent phosphoric acid calcium and forty percent cartilage. Today it is easy to analyze the most minute particles of ivory and tell by the mineral content whether it comes from Cameroon or Zaire. The hunter will occasionally find holes in the ground where elephant have eaten mineral-rich soil and left long scrapes from their tusks. These earth licks are usually close to springs or certain rocks, especially slate, or sometimes in the root hole of a freshly fallen tree.

Since an elephant's appetite for salt is voracious, the salty waters of Lake Lobéké in southeast Cameroon are an El Dorado for them and for other game. Elephant tend to frequent the same licks for centuries, so the trampled trails they make during their pilgrimages are often deeply embedded in the earth and easy to follow.

We call for the porters with a bird whistle. Its shrill sound can be heard at a great distance without disturbing elephant and other game since they seem to think it's a real bird. I am terribly thirsty and take a bottle from my porter. Even though he was sitting safely high up in a tree, his hand is shaking like the limbs of a storm-tossed aspen. Now he is enjoying the sight of a mountain of meat that will end up in his village and in his stomach!

I sit by my bull's head and admire its beauty. Suddenly strangers materialize out of the thick bushes. One of the black men carries a modern rifle in his hand, and they all look greedily at the nice tusks. I feel uneasy since my rifle is propped against a tree out of my reach. But apparently there is no reason for concern because my crew converses animatedly with the poachers in their tribal language. They, too, must have been following the rogue bull's track.

Sumano translates their discussion: The gun bearer is the younger brother of Pierre, one of the most renowned poachers in middle Cameroon during the 1980s, and the other men are his relatives. At first they were following us, but somehow ended up ahead! Since Pierre walks unshod and bends under all obstacles without doing any cutting, we did not see signs of anyone ahead of us on the rogue elephant's track. Pierre was in dense Aframomum (*Aframomum melegueta*) thickets just fifteen feet from our quarry when the bull got his wind and escaped. Now we know the reason for the old rogue's unexpected flight!

Half an hour later Pierre himself emerges from the forest. He had followed the huge tusker for a while, but my shooting spurred on the bull who did not slow down at all, so Pierre had to abandon his pursuit. An elephant's normal walking pace is much faster than an average human's all-out run!

When I first began hunting middle Cameroon in 1979, the Djerem plain was a bonanza of huge trophy tuskers. Ivory six to seven feet long and weighing thirty to forty pounds was not unusual. Now only some small elephant have survived the heavy poaching. When I last visited there in the mid-1980s, we set out from various base camps on four- to six-day expeditions into the remotest parts of this vast, uninhabited forest region, and each time we would find three to four cadavers. The meat wasn't touched at all; only the tusks were hewn out. The poachers did not select just big bulls. They killed everything, including the smallest cows with tiny two- to three-pound tusks. Six to eight groups of poachers were operating year-round in the forest between Betaré Oya and Yoko.

The two worst were Dodo and the aforementioned Pierre, both around thirty years old. They would remain in the forest with an entire crew for many weeks. Dodo even took several of his wives, porters, and auxiliary hunters with him. He slaughtered without mercy any buffalo he happened across to avenge his father who was killed during an encounter with a red buffalo. They did not even bother with the meat. When he came upon a herd of elephant, he usually killed at least several within a short period of time.

Pierre, whom I had just met, used to hunt with a small crew of four to six people. Most of the poachers used .375 H&H Magnums, so they were wounding more elephant than they killed. This explains why we sometimes found elephant skeletons with the tusks still intact. Bones and tusks don't last long here; within months they are eaten by porcupine and rodents. The old tale of an elephant graveyard filled with piles of tusks is sheer fantasy, and was probably born out of occasional discoveries of tusks in flood zones.

Pierre was wanted by the Cameroonian *gendarmerie*—police—but he always managed to escape. This sparsely populated country with its large uninhabited areas offers easy concealment for fugitives. On a later safari I hired a tracker who, unbeknownst to me, was Pierre's older brother. I did not discover the man's lineage until the safari was over. He was a valuable tracker in spite of his tainted kin.

My initial uneasiness over Pierre's presence was unjustified, since the poachers in Cameroon do not dare to   attack or molest white people in any fashion. They even regard other hunters as more or less friendly competitors. I was especially safe since I was accompanied by his tribesmen. Tribal affiliation is usually quite important to most black Africans, and tribal ties dictate the outcome of nearly all elections.

Cameroon's big cities and the roads in the northern sector are very dangerous, but not the forests. It differs from other African countries such as Burkina Faso (formerly Upper Volta), where two French doctors disappeared in the 1980s while hunting the Arly savanna. No trace of them or their crew was ever found; they simply vanished, probably cannibalized by the locals. "Our" poachers were now quite happy as they loaded up with as much elephant meat as they could carry and quickly faded into the impenetrable foliage.

Elephant hunting is an old tradition among the locals. Before they had firearms, they hunted with poisoned spears and traps, digging out pits on ridges where ancient elephant trails were located. The pits were about eighteen feet long, seven feet wide, and ten feet deep, tapering at the bottom and camouflaged with branches and leaves.

Hunters forced elephant to walk into these traps by barricading the trails on the ridges. An elephant could not free itself once it fell into a pit because its weight kept it down. I have found such remains in areas east of the Djerem River that preceded colonization at the end of the last century. No elephant roam there now.

Once I came across a very interesting site in an open forest of *bimba* trees: A row of ten pits thirty feet apart had been dug parallel to a major creek. Their origin is not known, but it is likely that the local Bantu (the ethnic name for all black tribes in the Congo area) tribes drove elephant in from the river. The Pygmies did not dig pits, and told me that the pits were dug long ago by the "blacks," as they contemptuously refer to the Bantus whose complexion is distinctly darker than the Pygmies' yellowish hue.

My diary describes another encounter with poachers some years later: "This is a nightmare," it reads. "This safari will

54

end in disaster." It was my first hunt in an area, and I had hired a crew from the last village at the end of the track road. The chief had given me his brother, Albert, as a tracker. Albert was an interesting character and full of good will, but useless as a tracker since he did not know the distant forests where I have since pushed my crew with compass and detailed map. Even worse, he wielded his machete without much sense through the dense foliage and tangled mass of the gallery forests around the creeks.

A tracker needs a sixth sense to find his way on old game trails, and this is doubly true for zigzagging old elephant trails. These paths are usually well hidden under the foliage, but a good tracker will sense them. It helps if he walks barefoot because then he can feel the leveled ground where elephant have passed, and push easily through the dense foliage. Albert did not like to wade in the creeks, which frequently offer the easiest route. The relatively cold water is a horror to Africans accustomed to higher temperatures.

But suddenly Albert speeds up. We have hit a poacher's trail and follow fresh cuttings to a large savanna. It is terribly hot, and the sun glares down from a deep blue sky. The temperature has reached 90 degrees Fahrenheit, so I am relieved when we reach the poacher's camp and can rest beneath two dilapidated straw-covered huts.

A powerfully built man with a completely shaven head is sitting peacefully in front of the bigger hut,   preparing special roots from the forest for intestinal worm (*Ascaris lumbricoides*) medicine. Nigeria carefully grinds the dried root into a red powder. At his side lies a huge pile of mushrooms.   He is obviously a skilled and hard-working outdoorsman.   He arrived yesterday with his brother and son after an arduous five-hour trek from the railroad.   He says he plans to hunt with snares and will not admit to having a gun. Later I learn that he owns a .375 H&H Magnum and poaches elephant!

We combine venison and vegetable oil, and share a delicious dinner before spending the night in his camp. Sitting at his campfire, we talk animatedly, and he impresses me with his personality. During our conversation he tells me that two miles north of here they came across the fresh tracks of a huge elephant herd totaling some two hundred animals. They were the smaller pygmy variety, much feared for their aggressiveness.

Two or three varieties of elephant can be found in Cameroon. *Loxodonta africana* lives in the savannas of northern Cameroon. Its long triangular ears, pointed at the bottom and touching at the back, form a map of the African continent. This huge subspecies reaches a height of nine to ten feet but sports small tusks of white and usually quite deeply fissured ivory. A hunter is lucky to find a bull with a twenty-pound tusk. The hunting of *Loxodonta africana* is permitted in the hunting zones around Waza National Park.

Loxodonta cyclotis, the round-eared elephant, lives in the dense rain forests of southern and middle Cameroon. It is a bit smaller, standing seven to nine feet high. Its distinctive rounded ears do not touch in the back like those of *Loxodonta africana*.

A form of dwarf elephant roams in the rain forest that is reported to be very aggressive. Some scientists have named them *Loxodonta pumilio* while others regard them as a variation of *Loxodonta cyclotis*. These Pygmy elephant are very numerous in southern Cameroon. They reach a height of five to seven feet with extremely small, thin tusks ranging in length from thirty-five to forty-seven inches. Even in old bulls the tusks weigh between four and eight pounds; some carry the beautiful yellow forest ivory with its distinctive rose hue.

Albert appears nervous when I announce that we will follow the large herd tomorrow because he fears an attack.

We will determine whether a big bull is with the herd, perhaps even the legendary *Tour* (tower in French)—a huge bull with unusually large feet and big tusks. The poacher Pierre had twice gotten close to *Tour* and fired his .458 Winchester Magnum but could not make the kill. During the first encounter Pierre wounded him; the second time another elephant came between them and was killed instead. Now the clever *Tour* usually moves only in the middle of a spread-out herd, well protected by the others. Getting to him would be very difficult!

Big elephant are extremely tough in dense forest areas, so it is advisable to carry the powerful .460 Weatherby Magnum because it delivers almost double the foot-pound energy of the .458 Winchester Magnum. In the forest elephant offer very small vital-area targets, usually at difficult angles.

Nigeria is the only hope for my safari's success, so I try to persuade him to work for me as a tracker temporarily. It does not take long to convince him since he is a born hunter and the incentive of a huge pile of valuable elephant meat is quite appealing.

A terrible thunderstorm wakes me at 3 A.M. Lightning bolts flash wildly and heavy thunder rolls almost endlessly, followed by a heavy downpour. My porters build a shelter of Tyvek sheets to protect me from the deluge but the edges stop ten inches above the ground, so the raindrops splash inside for an hour. Fortunately I am wrapped in a water-tight emergency blanket and sleep comfortably until dawn.

The next morning I find that the rain has provided excellent tracking conditions and decide that it was a very welcome intercession. By 6:30 A.M. we are moving north toward the mountain called Goum when we reach a day-old track of a small herd of Pygmy elephant that apparently includes a dominant bull.

Hour after hour we follow, mostly in an easterly direction. Sometimes we pause at a special thick liana with the colorful name *Landolphia florida.* At this time of the year it carries orangelike fruits. Inside a thick shell are embedded four to six nuts, and the shell's inner portion tastes refreshingly sour. Combined with water and salt, it offers a welcome treat.

Later Nigeria stops abruptly at a small scrape in the soil adjacent to the trail that indicates a special type of honeycomb. A giant scaly anteater (*Manis gigantea*) had apparently started digging but was chased away. Did the passing elephant herd spook him? In nine previous safaris my crew has never found honey in the ground, but everyone is always excited about stopping for food—especially if it satisfies their sweet tooth.

Nigeria eagerly digs into the red soil with the large blade of his machete until the hole is about three feet deep. Then he brings out a football-size nest consisting of thick, papery layers and looking like an oversized hornet's hive. Its inner shell contains small honeycombs filled with a thin, slightly bitter honey. The bees are tiny and resemble the small savanna flies that crawl into every opening, especially eyes and nostrils. The Pygmies, or *Baka*, as they call themselves and prefer to be known, call this variety of honey *moko*.

We enjoy the sweet liquid, sucking it out of the broken pieces. We are not concerned about getting the bright red soil in our mouths because at that depth it is free of microbes and therefore safe. A good way to cure diarrhea is to dig a hole about two shovel blades deep in natural, non-polluted soil, then mix some clean soil with water and drink it. It enhances the healing properties in an infected and irritated stomach because the considerable surface area of the diluted earth easily absorbs toxic substances.

It is hot again, but we walk as fast as possible for another hour. I am impressed by Nigeria's abilities as a tracker. He has a remarkable eye for the minutest sign of moving game. At noon we rest an hour by a small, clear forest creek. I am exhausted. The oppressive heat and fast march have taken their toll, but twenty minutes of intensive stress relaxation revives my strength and I continue with renewed energy.

It remains hot, and perspiration pours off me all day long. I drink as much water as possible, adding some minerals—especially magnesium tablets—which help prevent muscle cramps. The constant dampness has weakened the fabric of my clothing, and a small branch suddenly tears my right trouser above the knee. At noon I had been quite proud of these durable army trousers (the only pair I carry) and hoped they would last for the next ten days.

By 4 P.M. we are quite close to the herd, which has moved in a big loop to the north, northeast, and east. Half-eaten leaves and bark and fresh droppings begin to look more and more promising, but we are still far behind as the sun drops below the horizon. Nevertheless, it looks good for tomorrow. These elephant feed almost constantly, stopping here and there, so this might allow us to close the gap.

While crossing a creek we find a huge round footprint in the mud that was definitely not made by several elephant stepping into the same place. There seems to be at least one big bull with the herd and I hope he carries good tusks.

Luckily we find a clear spring in a deep forest hollow just before nightfall. What a nice place to camp! It's even better when Nigeria discovers another hive of honey bees in a hollow tree. My crew sets out in the dark with wooden torches to cut down the tree—a most impressive sight.

Later they return triumphantly with pots full of honeycombs filled with delicious dark honey. Besides being a treat, it's also a great energy booster. The first months of the rainy season are renowned for good honey, but this batch is especially fine. I can't eat as much as the locals without getting an upset stomach, so I save my share in a small plastic bottle to sweeten the rice during future meals.

Now I enjoy a refreshing shower, compliments of a bag hung overhead, and a fine dinner with excellent smoked fish and honey-sweetened rice for dessert. Who says a do-it-yourself safari has to lack comfort? After reading under the mosquito net, I fall asleep, only to be awakened at midnight by another wild thunderstorm. This downpour is no surprise since the day's heat was conducive to building a storm front and I enjoy the fresh, cool air.

Each morning is the same: Dress in damp and increasingly sour-smelling clothing and moist canvas boots in the relatively cold, wet morning air. Not fun, but an avocado with honey cheers me. By 6:30 A.M. we are on the march again. It's time to catch up to the herd and to escape the swarming bees that are angrily looking for yesterday evening's plundered honeycombs!

We follow the elephant tracks as quickly as possible until they enter a dense, swampy forest. Nigeria decides to circle around, first toward the Pangar River through a beautiful open forest, then north, and then south. It is extremely hot, especially when we cross a savanna. The midday break is most welcome, and some honey helps to renew our energy. Later we come across fresh buffalo and bushpig spoor, which indicate that hunting pressure is low on this side of the river. Bushpig meat contains a lot of fat, and is sought-after by the locals since most game meat is quite lean. Bushpig are heavily hunted and populations are low near hunting grounds that are regularly frequented by humans.

We continue until evening but still can't find any trace of our elephant herd. I think we have lost them. I have been in this situation several times before and have never found these "shortcuts" to be successful. It is better to stay on a trail.

As we look for a relatively open space to camp, we come across another beehive that produces another pot full of honeycombs. I pity my friends; they look terrible with their hands and faces swollen from bee stings. Some of them still have bee stingers stuck in their skin. Still, no one complains. They are happy about the honey, a considerable improvement over their usual attitude. Normally they complain about the smallest injury in order to get a Band-Aid, and are even worse when they want medicine.

It takes about twenty minutes to build my hut. Albert and some porters cut a couple of sticks, drive them into the ground in a circle, and connect the inward-bending tops with strips of bark. The hut is covered with a sheet of Tyvek, then a plastic tarp to keep out the wind and water, but it is still airy. Tyvek and plastic sheeting together weigh much less than a stuffy tent.

I use the spare time during camp construction to clean and oil my rifle. For the first time I am carrying a .460 Weatherby Magnum. My old friend Pierre Ruffinoni had urged me to switch from my old .458 to the stronger caliber, which delivers almost twice as much energy, and sold me the used gun in perfect condition at a good price. It was well worth it considering the difficult hunting conditions in these dense forests.

Dinner is delicious again. I liberally pour my share of dark, sweet honey from the most recently looted beehive over my rice and select some slices of freeze-dried banana for dessert—not bad. I am always amazed to see the amount of rice and meat eaten by the locals. One portion would be a week's ration for me. What gluttons! It is important to choose the right provisions to carry into the deep bush, and rice is about the best given the ratio of dry weight to calories.

The night is quiet with no thunderstorms, and I sleep soundly until 5 A.M. when it is time to start the daily routine again. We have honey with rice again, and by 6:45 A.M. we are on our way.

My porters walk fast, even with loads over forty pounds each in old wheat bags, which have been improvised into rucksacks with strips of bark. If the country is open, they balance the load on their heads; otherwise they carry it on their backs. I have brought a ski pole with me for the first time. It looks out of place in the tropics, but I plan to use it as a rest for the heavy big-bore rifle while hunting plains game. Now I find that this stick helps me to bend and twist between and under huge roots and liana. It creates the necessary balance and eases tension on the lumbar spine. No more back pain. What a paradox—snow gear in the steaming tropics!

By 8 A.M. we have returned to the place where we left the spoor to circle around the elephant swamp yesterday. We missed where the elephant left the area, confused by too many trails. Now the herd has gained too much distance for us to catch up. We decide to abandon the trail and follow the river, hoping to cut sign as the game moves to water.

My old tracker Albert is talking a lot and does not look down, so he doesn't realize that he has stepped on some fire ants. He is unaware of the danger until I inform him, and narrowly escapes with just a few burning stings. It could have been much worse.

At 9 A.M. we are abruptly stopped by the sound of breaking branches nearby. Elephant are just fifty yards away. One track looks promising, so we ease closer. Luck is with us again. The forest is relatively open, and I recognize a huge gray shape. I anxiously creep forward until I am only forty-five feet away. My rifle is ready with the safety off.

Majestically, the bull lifts his mighty head and curls his long trunk upward like some giant snake. I see the trunk tip flutter as he maneuvers it, exploring the scents in the wind. Something must intrigue him. Then he moves a bit and exposes his tusks. What a disappointment. They are thin and short, barely nine pounds each. This one is definitely safe from me; even if the law permitted it (Cameroon requires a minimum of 11 pounds or 5 kilograms in each tusk), I would not shoot him.

I quickly retreat to a safer position to ward off a possible charge. My companions can't understand my decision.

To them, this huge bull is a mountain of meat that promises fat between the bowels, around the heart, and near the kidneys. Africans love fat! Now the bull has located us by our scent and takes the initiative, charging with shrill trumpeting! My friends climb with incredible speed up the tall trees. Meanwhile, I find a safe haven between the roots of a large tree and wait with my gun at the ready.

The bull advances with round ears out and trunk curled inward—a truly menacing sight. He's very close. When he is only about thirty feet away, he suddenly turns and retreats. I am very relieved because with bulls you never know until the last few feet whether it is making a mock charge or really set on trouble. Still, a "bluff" charge is quite an attention-getter!

My confidence in my .460 Weatherby is reinforced. It is very calming to know that you are able to stop a charging bull with sheer knockout force from a frontal shot, even if it is not fatal.

The forest explodes uproariously as trumpeting elephant break through to follow their leader. Within seconds, they are gone. The rain forest is peaceful again with only the screeching of monkeys in the trees echoing overhead. That was an exciting but fruitless stalk. Still I have another week to find a better bull.

We now move through a beautiful green savanna. It must have started growing immediately after the first rainfall since it is now knee- to waist-high after only two weeks. The lush grass is a magnet for all types of game. A small ridge provides a tremendous view over adjacent savannas and green, forested hills. Partially eaten grass tops and fresh single-game tracks announce the presence of buffalo and kob antelope. We need fresh meat and stalk closer cautiously.

Suddenly, a big kob steps up onto a termite hill thirty yards ahead. Only its head and the line of its back are visible in the tall grass. I aim carefully where its shoulder should be and fire one of my special .460 Weatherby Magnum "reduction" loads at him. It runs off without any sign of a hit, and the dense grass mixed with bushes hides him immediately. My hungry crew is very disappointed. His quick flight seems to indicate a clean miss, but we follow the faint tracks in the dry clay and find him stone-dead thirty yards away. The .45 caliber, 230-grain lead wadcutter bullet went clear through both shoulders! I admire the elegantly curled horns of the 180-pound antelope, which is very similar to the *puku (Kobus vardoni)* of southern Africa.

I am pleased not only with the stalk and the shot but also with my reduction shells. I have developed these special loads to reduce noise and to eliminate the need to carry a second gun in the forest for small game trophies and camp meat. The design of my new load is simple: An exact outer copy of an original .460 cartridge is made of steel on an NC (numeric code)-machine. Then an inside rim and a cylinder are drilled into the steel cartridge from the rear with the precise measurements of a handgun cartridge.

During this safari I carry a prototype of the steel case that was drilled to accept a .45 cartridge. However, it is not accurate at longer distances because the bullet has too much free flight before entering the rifling. Also, the steel wall is too thin at the extractor claws, creating the risk of a case having its rim torn off and disabling the weapon by sticking in the chamber.

After this safari I changed calibers so an inside cylinder for a .357 Magnum cartridge sits in the back of the steel case. The .357 Magnum cartridge (minus the bullet) is inserted, its base level with the base of the steel cartridge. The .357 cartridge is filled only with powder and sealed with beeswax or a greased felt wad. The bore in the steel cartridge runs the length of the neck until the last half-inch, when it opens to the diameter of the .460

Weatherby Magnum. In the neck of the steel cartridge, a light .45 bullet is loaded from the front; I use either a lead or a half-jacketed hollowpoint bullet.

The .45 is slightly undercalibrated, but will be squeezed by the rifling to achieve the proper rotation and gain the necessary accuracy. A lead bullet must not be accelerated to more than 1,360 feet per second, or it will cut through the rifling and lose accuracy. But with 11 to 14 grains of fast-burning powder—like the kind used for a .22 Hornet—the speed is just under that critical level, and the bullet's impact is about 7 inches lower than the original factory load at 80 yards with a spread of about 5 inches, which is perfect. Since shooting distances in the rain forest are usually around 30 to 40 yards, it is not necessary to aim differently with factory ammunition. The power of the .45 bullet out of the reduction shell is amazingly effective.

I once shot a giant forest hog at 90 yards, which is unusually long. The lead bullet passed through both shoulder blades and made a clean exit. The second bullet, fired at a 30-degree angle, passed through both blades and lodged just under the skin at the far shoulder. This was excellent penetration considering the big boar weighed about 240 pounds.

I believe the Cameroon variety of forest hog is a subspecies or a diminutive variation not described in mammal books. Judging by the two I have taken, plus five other sets of tusks from old animals offered to me by natives, the animals in central and southeast Cameroon are much smaller than the ones described in *A Field Guide to the Larger Mammals of Africa* by Jean Dorst and Pierre Dandelot. Those weigh up to five hundred pounds while mine—both very old animals—did not exceed three hundred pounds and their tusks, measuring around seven inches, were also much shorter than the reported length of eleven inches in the Kenyan type. There are no scientific descriptions of them because the Cameroon forest hog is rarely found and taken.

My main reason for developing these special rounds was to reduce the noise level, and their effectiveness is astounding. A normal .460 Weatherby cartridge generates a 162-decibel (dB) sound level and the reduction shell generates a mere 95 dB. A reduction of only 3 to 5 dB results in half the noise level for humans, so a reduction of about 70 dB is an immense lowering of concussion volume. In other words, given the mathematical relationship, sound doubles in intensity with an increase of slightly more than 3 dB! With a regular cartridge and a reduced load, the noise would still be louder, and the risk of a chamber bursting from a secondary explosion caused by the small amount of powder would be considerable. An underpropelled charge could also cause a bullet to lodge in the bore.

A follow-up shot in such circumstances could have terrible results. Carrying a handful of these steel reduction cartridges on the belt with spare .357 Magnum shells and .45 bullets in a pouch, then loading fired cartridges like a muzzleloader from back and front, is an elegant solution for shooting smaller game without a loud bang that scares away the big game. Now I can even shoot guinea fowl with my .460 Weatherby!

The kob provides much needed meat, and my crew is very content with their *patron*. Even though it's just 10 A.M., we stay in one of Nigeria's camps nearby. This is a day to relax, and I enjoy a refreshing swim in the cool water of the Pangar River. It is brown from sediment, and I feel more than slightly uneasy wondering whether crocodiles might soon be feasting on a white man. Crocs are not very common in this area, and the locals assure me it will be safe if I stay close to the banks. Hmmmm—I still owe them wages, so I assume they speak the truth!

What a pleasure to have a siesta under the mosquito net, followed by a late afternoon stalk through the lush

savanna. We sneak to each vantage point (such as a termite mound) with anticipation, looking for interesting game.
We find only a female kob and two buffalo cows grazing
within reach. Nevertheless, our walk in the wilds is beautiful and enjoyable.

Meanwhile, Albert has prepared a delicious dinner
of fresh heart, ribs, and liver from my kob—all roasted in
the embers. The moon is a perfect crescent in the clear
evening sky far above the large treetops. Cicadas in concert are so loud that we raise our voices to hear each
other, and the flames of the fire flicker high. In the distance, thunder from the next storm rolls and lightning is
mirrored on dark clouds to the south. I enjoy the fantastic scenery with all my heart; this is part of why I love to
hunt in Africa.

Some days later I don't have much hope of getting an
elephant in the remaining time. We head back to the village and decide to explore a small area between the Pangar
and Lom Rivers that is seldom hunted by the locals. I
have abandoned hope of finding the famous old rogue *Tour*,
but hate to give up completely.

We traverse the river and hear the sounds of elephant
feeding in the bush. Will I have a last chance? We slowly
move closer, winding around branches and liana until I get
a quick glimpse: The elephant in front of us is a good bull.
No monster, but he carries decent ivory, so I don't hesitate.
There may be a better bull ahead, but one in the hand is
worth two in the bush.

I peer anxiously over the wall of leaves as I wait for a
better position. For a split second I see his left shoulder,
and as the big bore thunders, he literally just topples over.
It's amazing how much more powerful the .460 Weatherby
is, especially on a feeding, inattentive elephant with no
adrenaline coursing through its system. I quickly step behind him, ready for a second shot.

Nigeria darts in closer and with a swift motion of his razor-sharp machete, cuts off the last ten inches of the bull's trunk before I can stop him. Too bad for the photo, but now he feels safer because the elephant would bleed-out if it got up again. He touches the eye of the fallen giant but gets no reaction. Now that he is sure the bull is dead, he yells triumphantly for his friends who are safe in the treetops.

Wild joy sparkles in their eyes. An abundance of meat close to a path that is just a three-day march from their village! Some villagers have never seen an elephant, so everyone inspects the big animal. After the initial excitement, everyone moves around purposefully to prepare the coming feast. A place for the camp is cleared fifty yards farther on, and arm-thick saplings are cut and transformed into huge tables. Firewood is collected and piled up, then everyone gathers around the elephant. With mighty strokes of their machetes, Nigeria and Albert cut the thick hide at the back and in several lines down the legs. Large, strange, shiny green spotted ticks are living in clusters on the animal. Now they need to find a new host as the skin is loosened with knives, pulled off, and laid on the ground with the ears to protect the meat.

Everyone is busy cutting huge chunks and piling them on the hide. After the outside members are boned, the belly is pierced. This is a delicate operation since the gut is already badly distended from the heat. Nigeria carefully cuts a small opening with a spear to allow the gas to blow out. A thick stream of foamy, putrid-smelling brown liquid squirts out. Then he opens up the belly and the huge white intestines slide out. The frenzy increases because the human-waist-diameter intestines have one-inch-thick muscular skin and large quantities of the highly desired fat. The large liver weighing some fifty pounds and the oversized heart of even greater weight are sliced into pieces and passed out. The lungs are relatively small, and their position in a standing animal is well protected behind the legs. A shot at the chest must be taken just behind the leg and not much farther down. A bullet fired at the middle of the animal will pass right through the large intestines, and the elephant will eventually die of infection some days later far away.

I am only the second white hunter who has ever been here. The first was a friend whom I sent to explore the area because it looked promising on a map. Unlike sport hunters, poachers move in at night with a small band and do not bring out meat. They don't want publicity, and they don't bring money into the local economy. They also wound a tremendous number of animals that wander off to die alone.

W. D. M. "Karamojo" Bell describes very specifically in his classic book, *Wanderings of an Elephant Hunter*, the correct aiming points for lethal shots. A head shot is an immediate kill if the brain is hit. However, this vital organ is only the size of a football, and is deeply embedded about twenty inches inside the mighty head. This protected position, combined with the layers of flesh and hide that surround the skull bone, create a veritable mass of natural armor. When shooting from the side, the hunter must aim at the depression in front of the ear hole or at the ear hole itself, depending on the angle of the shot. In the forest the hunter is much closer to his target than in the savanna, so he must fire at a much steeper angle in order to hit the brain. I only realized this after several misses: I used a side shot with a .458 Winchester Magnum and hit an elephant in the temple, but it just shook its head and moved on because the bullets did not reach its brains. I eventually got them all, but only because I am accustomed to reloading and firing rapidly.

However, the frontal shot is different. A .458 will only stun the beast if the brain is not hit. From the front, aim at the second wrinkle a bit higher than the eyeline, or perhaps the third wrinkle, depending on distance, angle, etc. A lot depends on experience. If the head is tilted even slightly upward, it is quite difficult to shoot from the front without damaging the base of the valuable ivories, which are close to the eyes and quite large with little space between them. If the bases of the tusks are hit, they will splinter and impair the beauty of the ivory. In any event, if the animal falls the hunter must quickly move behind it, ready for a second shot at the head. There's no point in conserving ammunition: An elephant is too strong an animal. I cannot stress this second shot strongly enough. Hit him again! Ammo is cheap compared to your life.

Once I hunted in southeast Cameroon north of the famous Lobéké area. We walked in the forest for three days, and had just made camp in the afternoon when I went out for an evening hunt with my tracker and another Pygmy to shoot a duiker for the kitchen. We stalked carefully through a relatively open forest on large elephant trails for a long while, and I was amazed that we did not stop to call duiker. Then I understood. My Pygmies were looking for elephant, which they could hear very far away. Suddenly a feeding duiker moved slowly in front of us. My rifle was ready and up in a swift move with the hammer cocked. The reduced load in the reduction shell gave a short bellow. The duiker lashed out his back legs and ran off clumsily. We found the Peters duiker (*Cephalophus callipygus*) dead sixty feet ahead. Our evening meal was assured, and it was a nice old male with long horns—an excellent trophy.

My friends pierced a hole in the back legs under the knees, then severed the tendons of the front legs under the knee so the large bone protruded. Then they forced the front legs through the narrow slit in the back legs and squeezed the head in between the front and back legs. A strip of bark around the head and through the legs served as a handle for this handy package, which was pulled over the porter's forehead—a duiker rucksack!

I thought we could head for camp, but my Pygmies continue like excited hunting dogs. This must be a promising forest. I do not ask them about their intentions, because they obviously have a plan. They think I have strong "magic" and would lose confidence if I had to inquire about their intentions. The psychology of the African native; it took me a long time to learn!

We stalk on, and a half-hour later I shoot another duiker. Again I silently praise the reduction shells. Their low noise output does not scare game because the sound is not audible 1,000 yards away. Now both Pygmies carry about fifty pounds each as we head back.

During our stalk we heard my friend the colonel shooting duiker on the other side of our camp, two miles away. Normally I hunt alone and send other hunters with their own crew in a different direction, but this was a new area so my friend and I walked together for the first week. He uses a 6.5x57R caliber in a combination gun for small game, and the noise of his shot definitely carries too far. Suddenly my Pygmies stop, listen intently, and very excitedly tell me that an elephant is heading toward us!

I can't hear or see anything. Fortunately the forest is very open here so we can see about ninety yards, which is rare. First I hear the elephant; then he bursts into sight— a single huge bull moving with great strides straight toward us. He must have been alarmed by the colonel's shots. I squat down to hide in the open forest, trusting my Woodland Tarn camouflage. As the elephant passes just twenty-five feet away, I aim at its ear hole and fire. The .460 bullet knocks him on his side. I immediately step behind his head and chamber another round. The bull still moves his feet and the Pygmies urge me to shoot again, but I stubbornly refuse, trusting the powerful caliber.

The elephant paddles with his feet and is suddenly up and on the move. I felt confident until I saw that he was up and moving away. Now I have to shoot from a bad side angle and aim for the heart, but it's a long way to the target, even for a .460 Weatherby. Two more shots only make him run faster until he disappears into the bush.

I had left camp prepared to hunt duiker, so I carried only four big cartridges in my belt. Now I have only one left, with a Trophy Bonded half-jacketed bullet. We follow the blood trail, and suddenly the bush in front of us explodes with a charging, shrilly trumpeting elephant! I have just enough time to quickly swing the rifle up and aim between the eyes. As the shot breaks, the bull stumbles to his knees a mere fifteen feet in front of me. I don't care to wait around to see what happens; with no ammunition left it's better to vacate the area, so I race to catch my long-gone Pygmies. I throw a quick glance over my shoulder and see that the bull is up again! If he persists, I am a goner! Fortunately, he has had enough of me and turns to disappear in the opposite direction.

What a mess! I acted like a stupid beginner after a good dozen elephant under my belt. Had he followed through, I don't doubt that my original overconfidence would have resulted in an unmarked grave in this lonely wilderness. Back in camp that evening, I tell my friend how angry I am at myself: I am the biggest fool around. The night seems endless, and I don't sleep much. I am awakened again and again by the vision of the magnificent bull moving off, but my confidence in the destructive potential of the powerful .460 Weatherby consoles me a bit. The wounded bull should be resting somewhere nearby.

At daybreak we start to track the wounded bull. This time I carry enough cartridges for a small army. The Pygmies find the trail quickly, and we follow easily for the next half-hour. Then the problems begin: Too many fresh tracks across the old trail confuse us. Again and again the trackers follow a trail only to abandon it and return to the last sure tracks. We are very fortunate that it did not rain last night. Suddenly, the sound of moving elephant comes toward us. My heart beats faster. We stalk slowly, only to be disappointed at the sight of some Pygmy elephant (*pumilio*).

We search for ten minutes until we find the spoor of the wounded bull and are very uneasy for fear of losing it. Twice we come across other herds. We are relieved to see that the track is much more visible now. The bull is dragging one hind leg while walking, as if a bone was hit yesterday. Now we follow easily, and at 11 A.M. we see a huge back moving out of a swamp fifty yards ahead of us. The movement is too quick for a sure shot, so we wade through deep, black mud and ease around sharp, thorny bamboo leaves.

As we reach the far bank, a noise suddenly comes from our right. We stalk over there with the wind steady in our faces. It's another herd with one nice bull feeding in a small opening. Back at the bank, a quick search indicates the right direction, and five minutes later I see my injured bull standing in a small clearing. I do not hesitate and aim quickly at the shoulder. As the shot breaks, he collapses and gets another bullet into the skull for safety. This time it was unnecessary, but better safe than sorry (again)!

My Pygmies are very happy. So much meat! And I am even happier about this superb bull with large, heavy ivories. One of the Pygmies, who is revered by the others as a fetishist and a medicine man, stands before the bull and performs a ceremony. He talks to the bull oblivious of our presence, and the other Pygmies slowly retreat. Pygmies consider the bigger elephant to be gods (they used to hunt only the small variety with their poisoned spears), so perhaps the fetishist is trying to console the elephant god.

Later we have a big feast and everyone enjoys the meat and fat. When my Pygmies cut off the head, we find the half-jacketed bullet twenty inches inside the skull. The lead had disintegrated completely, but the remaining jacket still weighs one-third of the original 500 grains—enough to have stopped the bull with my last cartridge and given us time to run away.

I am so happy that I present my wristwatch to Nigeria and explain how to operate the mechanism. The next morning I see him asking a Bantu the time, so I spend half an hour explaining how to read a watch. After the lesson he laughs and tells me he can count only to ten! Ethnologic studies of the Baka Pygmies of southeast Cameroon have found that they can only count to five. Still, Nigeria is very pleased with his shining golden treasure and wears it proudly.

In the evening we enjoy fresh elephant stew cooked in the traditional Pygmy way. The meat is cut into small pieces and placed in small bags of *Phrynium* leaves, which are hung for hours over a low-burning fire. The outer leaves look like charcoal, but the inner layers are green and moist. It takes a long time, but the stew is delicious and my ever-present *pili-pili* seasons it to my taste. No pot is needed for Pygmy cuisine!

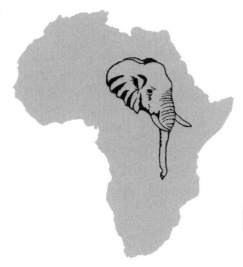

Chapter 3

Powerful and Futile— Forest Buffalo

Buffalo was my major goal when, inspired by various articles in hunting magazines, I first started looking for good hunting grounds in Africa. My starting point was the beautiful, game-rich country of Algeria in North Africa, where I worked for four years. I used that time to equip an 8,000-pound four-wheel-drive truck for my expedition to Black Africa. The Unimog was an incredible vehicle that could go almost anywhere. A camper body, 100-gallon reserve fuel tank, air conditioning, and many other useful features made it extremely tough but also very comfortable to live in while exploring remote areas for expeditions.

Fortunately, I had six months for my initial journey. After crossing the Sahara, I occasionally hunted while traversing Mali, Upper Volta, the Ivory Coast, Ghana, Benin, and Nigeria, until I finally arrived in Cameroon. This was to be a short diversion en route to the magical hunting paradise of the Central African Republic (CAR). However, just before I was to leave Cameroon, free hunting in the CAR came to an abrupt halt. Only guided, extremely expensive hunts were possible for nonresidents, so I scouted intensively for good hunting in Cameroon where do-it-yourself hunts are still legal.

Far away from the large arterial roads I found a very sparsely populated area with a huge and uninhabited, but game-rich hinterland. A German development agent in a lonely outpost, who was vainly trying to teach natives to cultivate expensive potatoes instead of the easier and cheaper manioc, recommended an even more remote village to me. He had recently accompanied a local hunter named Paul into the forest, and came away impressed by his hunting skills.

It was not easy to reach the remote village in my four-ton truck on a terrible track road. Small bridges made of huge logs crossed small creeks and could barely carry my truck. Cold sweat often trickled from my brow as I geared down to crawl like a tortoise on those rotten supports, praying that I wouldn't break through. This is one race that the hare would have won! Finally I arrived, and some thirty miles from the main track road, a dozen or so huts were scattered about the dense green rain forest. It was one of the last outposts before hundred of miles with no permanent human habitation of any kind—true wilderness!

Paul was home and looked bewildered at the sight of my truck, which was beyond the realm of his experience. We talked for a while, and he seemed very interested in guiding me, so we arranged a short excursion for the following morning. I parked my truck behind his hut and set up camp to wait impatiently for tomorrow's hunt. Anticipation of the unknown is a large part of any adventure I embark upon.

It is still dark when we leave the village, our flashlights casting ghostly shadows and illuminating a small path into the forest through cultivated fields and savannas. Heavy dew on the grass intensifies the smell of ash. Thick, half-burned stems of elephant grass hang in our way, smearing wet stripes of black charcoal on our skin and clothing. We soon resemble camouflaged jungle raiders slinking through the bush.

It's February, and we are two months into the dry season. A month ago the grass was burned in several savannas, but now tender, young, green grass sprouts are everywhere. They are quite a delicacy for the game that comes from afar to graze.

Moisture hangs like a dense mist as billions of fine drops form in the early morning air; the dew penetrates and our clothing is sopping wet. With a temperature of 70 degrees Fahrenheit, this is not a concern. Then I carried a 9.3x64, the equivalent of a .375 H&H Magnum. It is completely waterlogged and dewdrops fall from it. I am thankful that I had it coated with matte tape to prevent glare because the tape also protects quite well against humidity.

Now and then the path leads us through dense forest galleries. We bend and squeeze under liana and twigs, jumping over small creeks and muddy spots. We encounter wide creeks, and carefully balance on small logs as we slowly tiptoe across. It wouldn't matter if we fell in; we are already soaking wet from the humidity!

After several exhausting hours we approach our destination, a rocky hill covered with fresh green grass. Several savannas are scattered throughout the forest with grass about ten inches high. Very attractive to game, as the nibbled tops indicate. Stalking is difficult, because thick, half-burned grass stems scrape on our clothing and break when touched. We try to minimize the sounds of our travel by following the crisscrossing patterns of game trails on the savanna, trying to go against the wind. Visibility is only about fifty yards. Warped, fire-charred trees abound on the softly rolling ground.

Three of us walk in single file. Paul, who is only about five feet tall, leads while the porter, Jean Bosco, brings up the rear. With my six-foot-four frame, I can easily see over Paul, who is about the same height as a Pygmy. In fact, he learned his considerable tracking skills from a Pygmy. This stalk intrigues me. This is my first hunt in Cameroon, and I cannot imagine how we could close in on game when visibility is so low and we are making so much noise. It's not just the dry grass; the earth is covered with five-inch-high piles of mud raised by worms and baked hard as stone by the sun. Stepping on one creates a crunching sound, but there is no way to avoid doing so. However, Paul shrugs his shoulders. Apparently a lack of hunting pressure results in game that does not react much, especially since they make similar sounds themselves.

Paul carries his double-barreled shotgun. I could not persuade him to leave it at home, because he is afraid of buffalo. Only one barrel works, and between that barrel and the action is a gap of $^1/_{10}$ of an inch, resulting in a distinctly loose movement of the barrels. Paul is very proud of this treasure—the only firearm for thirty miles. Still, it is good enough for smaller game, so I borrowed it yesterday to hunt guinea fowl in the village's banana plantations. After a few shots, I decided my fingers were worth more than a guinea hen and bought a chicken for the pot.

While musing over Paul's blunderbuss, I neglect to watch the savanna and am surprised by the noisy and successful escape of three big defassa waterbuck (also sing-sing or West African defassa waterbuck). They disappear into a dense gallery forest in an explosion of grass and twigs. Too bad. These very attractive antelope are high on my wish list. Covered with heavy rings, the horns are long and upswept with a distinct forward arc. The three bucks had been standing behind some unburned grass close to a ten-foot-high termite hill, which we had just begun to climb.

With the commotion of the running waterbuck added to all our noise, I cannot imagine there is much hope for hunting this particular savanna, but Paul just laughs and moves on. Two hundred yards farther along we come face to face with a female *kob de buffon* antelope standing only seventy yards away. She sizes us up for several minutes, trying to decide whether we are harmless game or dangerous predators.

We follow another trail into a gallery forest and wade through black, muddy ground—a huge wallow used last night by bushpig, duiker, antelope, and buffalo. The evidence is everywhere, and wet mud still clings to the leaves and tree stems on the game trails. I am very pleased with my canvas boots. The water penetrates easily, but they fit comfortably and lose moisture quickly in the dry air of the savannas.

Around 8 A.M. we come upon another burned savanna with a trail covered by fresh buffalo spoor. The wet clay on the bark of some of the trees, together with large, fresh, flat droppings, indicate that game passed by barely half an hour ago. Paul studies the sky repeatedly but cannot find any oxpecker birds, which usually indicate the presence of buffalo.

The trail turns to the right. We tiptoe as quietly as possible when Jean Bosco suddenly tugs my shirt from behind. On our left a big buffalo bull strides toward us through the grass. He has heard us and is looking for his herd or a rival. He shows the classic alerted bovine posture of a half-lifted head with the nose above the dorsal line—the basis for Robert Ruark's famous line: "He looks at you like you owe him money!"

He stops head-on about sixty yards away. I aim at his chest and fire a 300-grain half-jacketed bullet from my 9.3x64. He reverses course and escapes clumsily. I climb a nearby termite hill for a better view, and the wounded bull is standing just sixty yards away. Another half-jacketed bullet to the shoulder drops him immediately, and we shortly hear the typical "death bellow" of a dying buffalo. The louder the bellow, the higher the hair on my neck stands! I approach cautiously with my rifle and hesitate behind him for a moment. Too many hunters have been killed or seriously wounded by rushing to a downed buffalo.

I am very happy that my first hunt in Cameroon has resulted in a beautiful red forest buffalo with its sharply contrasting black dorsal stripe. I take possession and feel his rough horns with their large, 6-inch bases, 18 inches long, and $16^1/_2$ inches across—definitely above average. Later I learned the true extent of my luck: Not many hunters get a "true" forest buffalo. Bagging this secretive game usually requires a lot of walking and difficult stalking in very remote areas. They are truly a trophy animal!

A photo-and-video session follows; then my companions process the game. They are so thrilled over this mountain of meat that it scares me to watch them! After divvying the spoils, they start a fire and roast a delicious breakfast of kidneys and fillets that we savor in the heat of an African day. This is safari at its best, exactly as I had hoped it would be. Sometimes dreams do come true!

African buffalo (*Syncerus caffer*) are divided into two disparate forms—the better-known Cape or southern buffalo (*Syncerus caffer caffer*) and the dwarf forest buffalo (*Syncerus caffer nanus*). The smaller variety is also called red buffalo because of its color, which ranges from bright chestnut over yellow, to dark brown. This diminutive form has a fringe of long, fine hair on its ears. It also differs in horn shape and in size—1,700 pounds (Cape buffalo) to 500 pounds (dwarf buffalo). Between these two subspecies are intergradations of size, color, and horn form, the most prominent of which is the northern buffalo (*Syncerus caffer aequinoctialis*).

Southern Cameroon is home to the shy and secretive "real" red buffalo. The farther north the animal occurs, the darker the hair, the heavier the body, and the larger the horns as the form changes from dwarf forest buffalo to northern buffalo.

Dandu *fly larvae. This insect also collects honey, which is delicious.*

A happy Baka with Dandu *honey.*

My share of the Dandu *honey on a phrynium leaf.*

Once honey is found, a small basket is quickly made from liana and lined with phrynium leaves. This basket is used to store the precious honeycombs. When filled, it will be lowered from a high tree.

Intense rain forest vegetation with flowering sapling.

Swamp and mud wallow with small track.

Baka camp.

Typical Cameroon forest buffalo with small horns and hairy ears.

One of my Baka porters—ready to depart for three weeks in the rain forest.

Safari and camp details: The first step of the journey is sometimes done by trucks. Our way is blocked by fallen parasoleiller logs.

Parasoleiller *tree—quick to fall.* The parasoleiller *is soft and used to build dugouts.*

Salt lick, deeply dug out by pygmy elephants, duiker, and other animals.

A happy Baka with his share of venison at the evening campfire.

Western kob antelope; rather scarce in the central Cameroon.

Crossing a larger creek above rapids.

Heaven help us! My gear is brought across a large river in a dugout from "medieval times."

Typical position of a Baka: ax over his shoulder, looking in the treetops for honey bees.

Venturing into remote forests requires experience, good geographic maps, and a functioning GPS unit. My Baka always admired the patron's "magic."

Very old traps—at least eighty years old. These were about fifty miles inside the rain forest with no paths leading to them today.

Small creeks often provide an easy trail.

Wild "mango" kernels are mashed and prepared as a rich paste.

Tired but happy after a two-day chase.

This old yellow-backed duiker with one broken horn is an unusual trophy.

Sunbathing forest buffalo.

Bay duiker—Cephalophus dorsalis.

The boat is off; the big trip into the unknown begins.

Me and my small Baka crew.

Peters duiker called with an ultralight electronic caller!

Hassan and the buffalo. This buffalo got caught in a wire trap and was gored to death by his brethren.

Scopes must be protected. An inner tire tube is effective and cheap to replace.

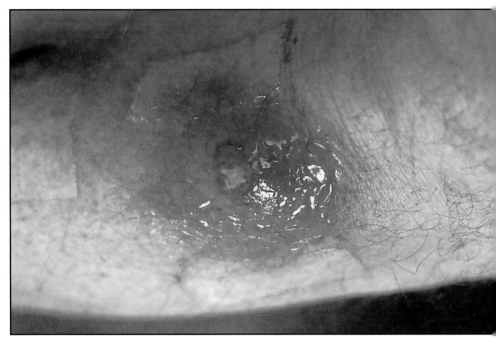

Tropical ulcers are the result of insect bites.

Author with bay duiker.

Black civet. This melanistic version is quite unusual. A civet is not a "cat" but a viverrid.

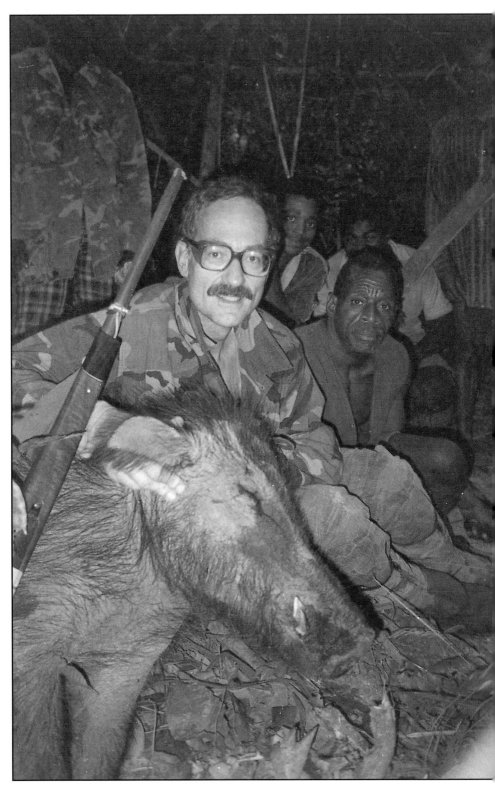

Giant forest hog.

Beautiful parasitic plant—Corne de cerf in French. The literal translation is "staghorn plant."

Warthog taken in central Cameroon.

A most discreet and almost strictly nocturnal water chevrotain.

Forest buffalo with their usual cow herons and oxpeckers.

Setting out to hunt in central Cameroon. "Desert Storm"-type U.S. military clothing is the best camouflage in dry areas.

The boat is wrecked in the middle of nowhere.

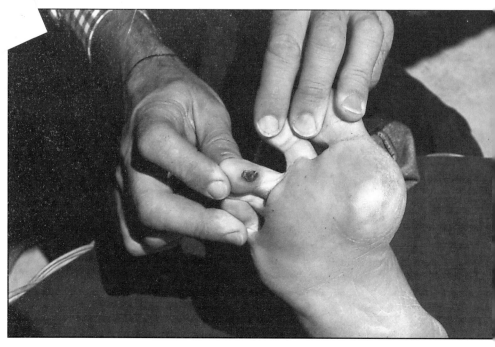

My expertise is often called upon to solve health problems. Here you see a sand fly egg, the size of a kernel of corn, in a man's toe.

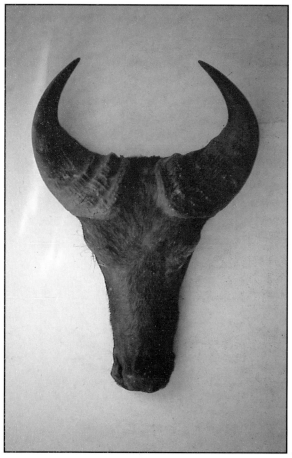

Very good forest buffalo.

Experienced hunters know what a challenge the red buffalo represents. It is barely possible for a few physically fit sportsmen to hunt them because they live in extremely remote forests, and it usually requires several long days of hard walking to reach their realm.

As a trophy, the red buffalo is not as physically impressive as the Cape buffalo, showing almost no boss (the enlarged thick bases of the horn melding together in the center). Typically, forest buffalo horns are thin, short, around twenty inches long, and set wide apart at the base with a backward sweep—an adaptation to its dense forest habitat.

It is difficult to differentiate between male and female, since the horns are very similar on this lightly built animal and the female's thinner form is difficult to distinguish. One hint is the color: Usually the bull will darken as he gets older, but sometimes old bulls show bright chestnut and occasionally cows are quite black. Who said hunting was simple?

The next year finds me back in this game-rich hunter's paradise. Again Paul is my guide. We are out for several days, but today no porters accompany us. The crew is taking a separate path to a lone camp where we will meet in the evening; at least that is my hope. Otherwise, I will have to camp on hard soil made miserable by fire ants, spiders, and myriad other aggressors that live in this incredibly rich insect biotype.

Our walk is relatively easy. We follow a well-hewn path from the village, then continue on a wide elephant trail. Many tracks indicate a strong population of the small but aggressive Pygmy variety. This year I feel more confident because I have exchanged the relatively light 9.3x64 for the powerful .458 Winchester Magnum. I can defend us more effectively should an elephant charge occur.

Hours later, as I trot behind my tracker deep in thought, fear becomes reality. Paul suddenly turns and climbs a big tree with remarkable speed. He would qualify for the Olympics if one of the events was tree climbing! At first I am bewildered, but then I understand. Certain distinct noises become louder and louder until they sound like a charging army. I would prefer a charging army. At least you can surrender to people!

A herd of at least a dozen elephant is trampling toward us with frightening speed, trumpeting, and breaking small trees. I see the tops of small trees bending toward me just thirty yards away. I deeply regret that I cannot climb like Paul, and retreat close to a large tree with my rifle ready. At this point I wish it were clip-fed and had a minimum of twenty rounds!

The first elephant partially appears in the dense foliage at fifteen yards, a small gray head with little tusks. Behind and at its sides more treetops bend. He is not alone: no time to waste. I quickly fire a shot in the air and pray for success. It would be ridiculous to kill this animal, and it would stir up trouble with the game department since he is not legal; his tusks are under the $10^1/_2$-pound minimum. Although a "Pygmy," he is still large enough to send me to the happy hunting ground!

Fortunately the report of the big bore is enough to change the animals' mind and direction. They change course, and soon everything is quiet again. Whew! Paul comes down after a prudent interval. We decide to take a break before continuing our stalk. I congratulate myself on my wise decision to "carry enough gun."

The noise has probably frightened off most game, but since it was just a single shot, some animals might remain. We cautiously move on. The forest gets denser, and suddenly we happen upon a typical scene. Around a spring in the forest is a hollow depression about twenty yards wide and eighty yards long with thick tangles of bushes, liana, grass, and other foliage as well as a trampled spot around a large, bright, red-ochre clay wallow.

We scan the hollow carefully. Fresh tracks on the trail leading in indicate that the wallow is a popular spot for game ranging in size from duiker to buffalo. Now it seems to be empty. Slowly and carefully we climb down the slippery path, gliding more than stepping on the muddy ooze.

Halfway down, the green maze covering most of the hollow's bottom comes alive and five red buffalo bail out. Fortunately they are not sure about our noise and pause at the opposite end of the depression. A stout bull tries to get our wind and momentarily rotates into a fully visible sideways position. Without hesitation, I draw down on its shoulder and pull the trigger. The impact of the .458 Winchester Magnum half-jacketed bullet at my point of aim raises a small cloud of dust. The bull turns clumsily and runs up the bank, but collapses in a heap halfway up.

I am very fortunate. The bull is extremely old and carries very attractively shaped, thick horns with a large boss and an interesting, uneven surface. Many hunts later this is still one of my best buffalo, and each time I look at this beautiful trophy I am transported back to that hollow in the forest. Hunting is more than the kill itself. It includes many wonderful memories one can recall again and again. Quick kills without effort are not memorable.

All this happened so fast that I had no time to think, and I am now worried about our porters. Marching separately does not work well. Hunting in remote forests can be very unpredictable, and even more unpredictable are the complicated machinations of the locals, even in the face of clear, unmistakable orders!

Paul just smiles broadly and waves my questions away. We will move on and reach camp within two hours; that should be enough time to send the porters back to cut the meat. But in Africa plans and reality are often two completely different stories. Amazingly, we're in synch, and the porters are lying around a cozy campfire at Paul's hunting camp. Upon our triumphant entrance with a buffalo tail, they are up and cheering. Minutes later they are en route with machetes to collect my bull.

I return to my private paradise every year and enjoy successful hunts for buffalo, elephant, and other game, but it is not until five years later that I am able to shoot my best buffalo. In my search for new, untouched hunting areas I move eighty miles northeast to a small village, hire a select crew of porters and a tracker, and set out through a dense forest for the Djerem River. After scaling a high ridge that acts as a watershed separating this area from another area that drains into a river nearer the village, the dense rain forest stretches for ten seldom-visited miles. The locals occasionally hunt the smaller drainage area but stop their trips at the ridge, which is two days away from their village—far enough to carry venison.

The pristine forest is home to some old elephant bulls, substantial populations of spiral-horned antelope such as bongo and sitatunga, and even the dark forest variety of leopard. It is April and the rainy season is beginning. Elephant are attracted to a one-mile stretch of huge trees that bear sweet figlike fruits. They seem to grow only in this area; the locals do not know of any other places where they grow.

Large creeks run across the forest that is home to a healthy population of buffalo. Several times I had encountered them at a mere ten yards, but did not want to risk shooting one because the report might scare the elephant and spoil my chances of finding a worthy bull.

My days of hunting are filled with rich adventure. Several times we follow the track of a single big tusker for days, only to lose him in a welter of other elephant tracks or when he gets our wind. Sometimes, after all the time and effort put into a stalk, we find that the ivory does not match the promise of the big foot.

After two exciting weeks we are running out of manioc flour (our basic food source) and have to return to the village some sixty miles away to replenish our provisions. Then I relied on local food purchased in the villages for my safaris. In later years I brought hundred-pound bags of fine Thai rice to the starting point of the safari and split it among the porters. It is easy to carry, gives a good ratio of weight-to-calories, and is easy for the *Patron* to ration. The amount required per meal for seven locals is approximately 2.2 pounds, or one liter. They like it the first few days, then complain about constipation, because they are accustomed to their high-fiber manioc diet. Rice is easily measured with one-liter cups, so the supply for the remaining days is easily calculated. The *Patron* also has to lock up the provisions and hand out the ration every morning and evening, or it will disappear. There is no enthusiasm among the locals for rationing provisions or keeping to a schedule; their concepts of both are very different from mine!

During those early days when I was learning how to manage a crew and organize my safari, I often had to wait for two days during most expeditions while manioc flour was prepared—a lengthy procedure. The manioc or cassava plant (*Manihot esculenta*) is a bulky bush with large leaves and brittle branches that grows to about ten feet in height. Its roots thicken, and in the second or third year, when they are arm-thick, they store enough starch to be harvested. Most species of manioc contain hydrocyanic acid, so the noxious roots are peeled and submerged in   running water for twenty-four hours. Then they are mashed and dried in the sun, and the white fibers are pounded to flour in a mortar.

The resulting fine white powder is poured into a pot of boiling water and stirred constantly with a big stick. The result is a sticky, gluey mass, that has no obvious taste.

It is low in calories and nutrients, but the locals love it. I have tried many recipes to make it taste better; the best one was to fry it crispy in thin layers.

Some decades ago the basic food in that region was millet, which is much richer and more nutritious. But the general education system was created, and children had to attend schools far away from their villages. They were no longer available to guard the millet fields, and the crop damage by birds was extensive, so manioc became the main food because it is easier to grow. Civilization has its downside.

We return to the village and wait for several days until this lengthy procedure is finished. After our provisions are replenished with new manioc flour we can venture out again. I have three months to hunt in Cameroon, so time is not especially critical.

During the first day back on the hunt, we are out of the big forest by noon and arrive at a clear spring on the steep, rocky slope of a 1,500-foot-high table mountain. Everyone relaxes in the coolness of a small orchard, but after a while hundreds of tiny black savanna flies plague us. They eagerly suck the salty perspiration from our skin and crawl everywhere, especially into our nostrils, ears, and eyes. I finally become so upset by these "sweat vultures" that I overcome my fatigue, take my drilling with the relatively small-bore 7x57R (.257)—this was before my "reduction" cartridges—and climb the remaining 250 meters to the mountaintop oblivious of the oppressive midday heat. I prefer to stalk at noon rather than be eaten alive by small flies.

There should be plenty of warthog (*Phacochoerus aethiopicus*) up on the flat top, which is sparsely covered by bushes and low grass. Although most carry small tusks, warthog are attractive to hunters because they are rare in central Cameroon. However, given the favorable biotope and remote area, they should be more plentiful.

The mammal books do not describe different species, but I found the form in central Cameroon to be about one-half to two-thirds the size of open savanna warthog.

I am relieved to find a cool breeze and carefully stalk the mile-long plateau. From time to time the bushes give way to a terrific view above the treetops of the adjacent dense forest, and there are no flies up here. The presence of many tracks promises a fruitful stalk, and this soon proves true. A huge warthog boar bails out of a bush and escapes so quickly into the grass that I can't even raise my gun. Too bad. We follow the fresh trail slowly for about twenty minutes until the plateau lowers toward one end.

Turning left, I step into a hundred-yard-long and fairly spacious rocky opening. Here water collects during the rainy season and evaporates afterward. At the rock's edge, some green, muddy spots provide water, wallows, and food. As I search the edges, my attention is caught by a dark rock under a tree at the opposite end. In the scope of my drilling that dark rock resolves into a stoutly built, dark-colored bull buffalo standing in the shade dozing. Its prominent dark horns are massive. He is an ideal forest buffalo bull.

This discovery seems to prove that this remote area experiences no hunting pressure, allowing the game to mature. I did not expect to find forest buffalo out on top of a hill at noon, but that's often their attitude, as I discovered on subsequent hunts. They like mountaintops because the steady breeze means fewer insects.

I am prepared to stalk plains game and have left my big bore with the porters back at the spring. I have some cartridges with full metal jackets loaded up to the safety margin and do not want to waste this chance. If the famous Karamojo Bell shot more than eight hundred big tuskers with his 7x57, sometimes ten a day, I should be able to collect my small forest buffalo. May the reader forgive me for daring to compare myself to him!

In any event, my drilling is extremely accurate, and I have all the time in the world to carefully select my shot. Unfortunately I can't get closer than eighty yards because three white herons and some oxpeckers (*Buphagus erythrorhynchus*) are sitting on the dozing buffalo's back. They stand watch and would alert the bull immediately if I moved in closer. I slip behind a tree with a Y-shaped branch and position the drilling firmly in this natural gun rest. Looking through the scope, I see the massive head facing me and position the crosshairs just under the eyes. Pressing the set trigger, I hold my breath and ease the trigger back very slowly. The drilling is rock-steady as the shot breaks and cuts the silence of a quiet noon.

The buff collapses immediately, but the "empty" savanna suddenly comes to life. Around the fallen patriarch twenty more buffalo suddenly rise and contemplate their immobile leader. Soon they begin running toward me! This is not a reassuring sight as I stand behind a woefully thin tree with a relatively small-bore gun in my hand, even though the drilling provides a quick second shot with buckshot. Fortunately the buff stop fifteen yards in front of my sparse cover and mill around uncertainly. Now I am able to watch them up close. Cows are yellowish and bulls are red, although some are dark brown. Two very small calves start moving toward me, but the herd veers off to the right. Whew!

My bull is on the ground, his legs bent under him in a sitting position—majestic even in death. He did not even hear the shot as the full metal jacket entered just below the eyes. He is a very old bull with a slight boss, unusually thick for forest buffalo. His horns measure $21^7/8$ inches and he will rank as No. 40 in Rowland Ward's *Records of Big Game*.

It is not easy to enter the book with *Syncerus caffer nanus* because some of the larger equinoctial subspecies of buffalo from the savannas of Nigeria, Upper Volta, etc., formerly were entered as dwarf buffalo. In any event, the book is not important except to confirm my luck in taking an outstanding animal. It is the "icing on the cake," but the adventure definitely counts for more.

Satisfied, I happily stroll back to my crew. They heard the faint report of the gun and expect anything from duiker to warthog. When I proudly lift the buffalo's bushy tail with its long, fine hair, they start yelling wildly. While my crew harvests the meat, I take care of the tail, extracting the bone and fixing it on a stick to dry. It is a very desirable item for swatting flies.

The area around the spring makes an ideal campground, and during the afternoon and evening we have a big party. Large fires roar, and delicacies are roasted. I barbecue the bones of an entire hind leg for twenty minutes on the embers until they turn black and become brittle. One stroke with the machete exposes the steaming, deliciously thick, yellow bone marrow. Not good for my cholesterol, but it is extremely tasty after a hot, hard day's walk. Everyone loses at least ten pounds on traditional foot Safaris, a highly desirable side effect for us Westerners!

The feast continues through the night. Other delicacies are heart, liver, and kidneys, and it's important to claim those fast. Otherwise they are gone in no time. The French have the right term for this food: *amuse gueule.*

My second tracker is an old Baya from a tribe in an adjacent northern area. He speaks only his language and always looks grim—probably toothaches—but as a tracker he is absolutely tops. Now he proves his abilities again by finding a crooked tree with large honeycombs full of dark, sweet, aromatic honey out in the savanna. Its taste is extraordinarily rich. Many flowers have contributed to the honey, and its aroma is like an herb garden.

The Baya are highly skilled trackers, and their tribe was highly developed when Cameroon was colonized. Unfortunately, much of their original tradition is now forgotten. While preparing a safari to central Cameroon, I found an old book by the German anthropologist Tessmann, who studied this tribe extensively some sixty years ago. He reveals interesting details about the culture and civilization of the once-superior Baya tribe.

Later I went on a three-week safari along the Pangar River with Bayas who showed no knowledge about or interest in the techniques of mining and melting iron ore, once a prosperous trade among their people. No one remembered the famous cults or brotherhoods, the names of their gods, or the myths of their ancestors. Skills such as wood carving and pottery were highly developed in the old days, but now only very simple designs continue.

As the night descends, the noise of the crickets becomes absolutely deafening for two minutes, before returning to normal. This is typical of gallery forests and savannas in central Cameroon. Farther south these crickets are found less frequently. My crew is eager to leave the next day and return to their village with large amounts of the smoked meat.

At dawn we begin a long, forced march. African days are short; it gets light at 5:30 A.M. and dark at 6:30 P.M. At first the walk on a long mountain ridge is easy; then it gets hot in the swampy depressions. An hour after dawn the next day we enter the village with flashlights in a heavy thunderstorm. Whew! Few hunting parties could cover this distance in one day, and I am the first white man to have hunted that forest and mountain. Pride in achievement often goes beyond the "kill" of a hunt!

I am relieved to reach the small village because I have been expecting Tord, a Swedish hunting friend. He couldn't join me for my three-month trip, but wanted to hunt with me for three weeks. Since he wasn't sure of his schedule, I had made arrangements for him to be guided safely to this village in the middle of nowhere. Upon arriving in Cameroon by plane, he would visit a friend in Yaoundé, who would make sure that he reached me.

It required courage and confidence to leave Sweden for a journey into one of the most remote regions of Cameroon to look for a crazy German doctor hunting many miles from the last bad track road. But no white man awaits me in the village. In any event, I have to stay at least two days while manioc flour is prepared. By then, perhaps my friend will have arrived.

I relax in my camper truck and pass the time by reading and feasting on fresh, sweet fruits such as pineapples, papayas, and mangoes, plus canned German food. Problems with food and porters keep me in the village longer than planned. My friend is seven days overdue, so I assume he won't make it. Rain falls softly but steadily during the fourth day, so I postpone departure once more and read comfortably in the camper.

Suddenly, a curly blond head pokes through the door. "Hey, Reinald, how are you doing?" I think of Stanley and Livingstone's famous encounter in the middle of the Congo during the last century. Of course, Livingstone wasn't sitting snugly in his 8,000-pound Unimog truck nibbling on delicacies from home!

After three weeks with no Westerners to talk to, I am very glad to have someone with whom to exchange impressions and opinions of Africa. We talk animatedly, and Tord tells me of his journey to date. He met my friend at the embassy in Yaoundé and enjoyed the unfamiliar life in an African capital so much that he stayed with him for almost a week before continuing north. Then Tord was handed over to Al-Hajj Yacoub who put him on the daily bush taxi to a small town on a bumpy track road some 250 miles north of Yaoundé.

I had positioned a reliable porter at the town's station who conscientiously checked for a white man arriving from Yaoundé. In Africa almost nothing goes as planned, but this time all went perfectly. My porter brought Tord over sixty miles of a terrible dirt road in a lorry. Courageous Tord! He left Sweden speaking only a little English and no French. He was lucky that I had to wait longer than usual for provisions. Still, I did not mind the delay after spending forty-five days in the bush.

I feed Tord well and give him some sweet kouri—Baya honey wine—to drink. Then we visit the chief, who organizes the traditional safari blessing for this evening. The chief and the elders gather, burn an herb over a calabash containing water and manioc flour, spit in it, then splash drops over our guns and us. Everyone in the village now firmly believes in our success. The ceremony is very important because it instills confidence in the crew and trust in the *Patron*'s luck during the upcoming safari. And if our luck is not so great, it is the fault of a stronger spell. Ah—Africa!

I carefully check Tord's luggage and remove all unnecessary gear. We have to minimize weight because everything has to be carried around for weeks. The more gear, the more porters; the more porters, the more manioc; the more manioc—well, we'd be here forever!

I also hire four new porters to replace others from the last crew. They were town folk, unaccustomed to rough hiking and heavy loads. The only other white hunter who ventured into this village some years ago would stalk out in the morning and allow his crew to make camp by noon. That Frenchman came back with only a few duikers after a week in the bush.

The villagers are still up for strenuous hunting because they want meat. Unfortunately, this ambitious attitude changed some years later; they became spoiled by other hunters and wanted the safari to be an easy adventure.

The next day we leave at dawn in a long, single-file line. All the locals are heavily loaded; I personally check their packs on a scale to make sure each weighs fifty pounds. Our speedy walk soon slows down and the oppressive heat and humidity take a toll on Tord, whose physical shape is not very good. He is overweight, and his long hair retains too much heat on his head, tiring him quickly. Seventy to 80 percent of excess body heat radiates from the head, so hats and long hair can impair physical condition.

Hiking times between pauses become shorter and the pauses get longer. Scientific research on athletes proves that rest aids recovery for the first five minutes. After that, further recovery is very slow. For faster recovery, it's much better to stop often for short pauses and use stress-reduction techniques.

We make camp at a crystal-clear creek after covering only half as much distance as five days ago when everyone was heavily loaded with smoked meat and trophies from the huge buffalo bull. Tord is demoralized and wants to return to camp tomorrow. Completely exhausted, he is afraid he will impede my hunting.

I give him some mineral pills and persuade him to cut his curly locks. He accepts without much enthusiasm, and I begin cutting. He wants to retain his good looks but I want a successful safari so I hack at his hair! Half an hour later he looks terrible with hair barely half-an-inch long. The Africans chuckle as they watch from their campfires.

I assure Tord that he will now release surplus heat easily and will not impede the hunt. He reluctantly agrees, but I am sure I will never be able to list him as a reference if I ever decide to barber full-time! Anyhow, most Africans think white people are ugly, and among many tribes it was customary to kill all albinos at birth. A few tribes allowed them to live and worshipped them.

The night is racked by a terrible thunderstorm spawned by the oppressive heat, but tomorrow's weather will improve. The next morning Tord feels better. He has recovered some of his strength, and it is easier to walk in the cool morning air. When it gets hot he is still able to continue and realizes the benefit of short hair. By evening we have reached the table mountain where I got my buff. Tomorrow we will enter the rain forest where it will be cooler, and the daily walking distances will be shorter due to the obstacles presented by the luxuriant vegetation.

We build our base camp here and hunt the surrounding forest and northern savannas. Tord gets into better shape every day and finds this pure hunting more and more enjoyable. During the sixth day we hunt a northern area with savanna densely covered with trees that reduce visibility to no more than sixty yards.

Our tracker watches the sky more than the bush. He is looking for oxpeckers (*Buphagus erythrorhynchus*). These colorful starlings are a basic brown with a red bill, yellow ring around the eyes, and yellow feet. They have a very unusual flight pattern. First, they climb with rapid wingbeats, fall, then climb again with more rapid wingbeats. If they spot buffalo or antelope, they literally drop down like attacking dive bombers.

Finally we spot an oxpecker. Our eyes are riveted when it suddenly swoops down almost vertically. This is the sign we have been looking for. Our confidence grows as another oxpecker arrives and dives at the same spot. Slowly we stalk downhill, trying not to make too much noise on the worms' sun-baked mud structures.

After a hundred yards we close in. The tracker, Martin, is point man. Tord is between us and we are now moving very slowly. There! Across a small draw a lone buffalo is grazing in the savanna with three oxpeckers sitting on his back. They live on ticks and also warn their host of danger by flying off. The buff's long tail constantly flicks to its sides to chase flies away.

Too many limbs in the line of sight make a shot risky, so Tord has to stalk closer. He doesn't want to risk wounding instead of cleanly killing the quarry he has traveled so far and worked so hard to locate. Due to rheumatic disease

94

he has problems bending over during a stalk and walks upright. This could be a real problem, but he manages to get closer by hiding behind trees. I remain in the rear and observe. He reaches a better position only sixty yards from his prey and quickly fires his .458 Winchester Magnum.

The bull collapses a bit too quickly for a shoulder shot, so Tord hurries close. A wise reaction, because the bull was only grazed near the spine by the bullet and is already getting up again. Tord quickly fires another shot to the neck, and now the bull is done. A good stalk, and his first buffalo! We are all relieved, and Tord feels great for not having given up. This evening the fires blaze up high again as meat is smoked and delicacies are roasted. Poor Tord is not allowed to eat too much of his buffalo since I am supervising his diet. In two weeks he will come out of the bush weighing thirty pounds less. You will not see this weight-loss program on TV!

My little companion—Luzie, a female German hunting terrier—feasts very happily on the meat and bones. Her belly is nearly bursting! During the last stage of our first expedition she got very tired but recovered back in the village. Now she is acclimated and enjoys the relative coolness of our base camp forest.

Newcomers often complain that the forest has little game, but a dog quickly reveals just how much game slips away unnoticed or hides without moving. When off her leash, little Luzie is constantly chasing something. If game is wounded, her help is invaluable. Once I wounded a large yellow-backed duiker (*Cephalophus silvicultor*) that we had to follow for more than a mile before she located him. Without Luzie this valuable and rare prey would have been lost, so I was very proud of my little huntress.

When we stalk savannas Luzie is kept on a leash. Otherwise she would happily follow the anubis baboons (*Papio anubis*) and almost certainly get mauled by them. They retreat quickly, then circle around to trap and attack their enemy. Luzie is accustomed to hunting monkeys, and upon hearing any noise, always looks up into the treetops.

The next morning Luzie has to remain in camp while we try another stalk. The day is hot, and the stalk is tiring. Hour after hour we cross forest and savanna, but our luck seems spent. We come across several good bucks, but they are always alerted too soon. No game for my good friend Tord today.

During one of my first safaris, a buffalo got me into more trouble than I had anticipated. We were stalking along a steep rock face, a place where I had often found interesting game. Animals seem to like the variety of foliage and grass available there. Suddenly we encountered a buffalo herd, which immediately became aware of us and quickly took off. One of the last animals was a big, strong bull, so I tried a running shot with my .458 Winchester Magnum and hit him too far to the rear. Uh-oh—problem time!

My crew refused to follow the wounded animal, even though abundant blood on the trail promised a short search. The dark blood indicated a liver hit, which usually results in the game remaining close by. After pressuring my tracker, Paul, he continued and we followed slowly. We became uneasy when the bull's trail entered a dense mass of elephant grass where visibility extended no farther than the end of the gun barrels. Slowly, with many a pause to listen intently, we moved on. A sudden charge would be extremely difficult to handle, so Paul walked behind to allow me adequate room to shoot.

We breathed a sigh of relief when, after another two hundred yards, the bull's trail made a sharp bend into a gallery forest. It was more open now, but sometimes we still had to crawl under branches and trees. From time to time Paul grabbed his amulet, or *gri-gri*, as it is called in Cameroon. It contained special magic against buffalo and had been made by a highly respected Pygmy medicine man. Still, Paul preferred to play it safe and stay behind my gun!

Suddenly I recognized a spot of the bull's skin through the foliage to our right. He stood sideways and was now stalking us, but his light color gave him away. The rifle came up in one swift motion, and two shots were fired in quick succession. The bull collapsed.

It was one of my first buffalo, so with the self-confidence of a novice I handed my rifle to Paul and asked him to back me while I approached the bull from his rear with my knife. I was accustomed to killing dangerous game with my razor-sharp knife and had done it many times with huge wild boars in North Africa. My Muslim friends always became terribly frightened when I did this, but I had never had any trouble before.

As I stood behind the bull and stooped to stab his heart, he showed me a buff's amazing courage and strength by rising in one quick motion, causing me to ride him like a rodeo cowboy! Fortunately Paul was steady enough to drop the bull with a clean shot! "Ride 'em cowboy" in darkest Africa!

Buffalo are thought to be the most dangerous game and are responsible for the highest number of fatalities among hunters. My friend Gotthard, a companion during nine safaris, once had a close encounter. We always split up in the field, going in separate directions for the course of the safari, so neither of us had a back-up rifle.

After several days Gotthard encountered a very big bull head-on in a remote savanna. He had to fire his .458 Winchester Magnum at its chest from eighty yards at a slight angle. The bullet did not hit a vital point. The bull lowered its head and charged from that distance. Gotthard had no cover except some small scrub trees and had to rely entirely on his rifle. The second shot didn't slow the bull down, but the third round finally brought it down only three feet in front of Gotthard! The huge trophy bull made the Rowland Ward book as No. 42.

Everyone regards wounded buffalo as extremely dangerous, but the hunter must also be very careful when approaching a downed animal. Never step between the legs of a supine beast. As long as twenty minutes after a buffalo dies, reflexes can cause the incredibly muscled legs to twitch abruptly, easily smashing a human's legs. This type of injury in the deep bush could be a death sentence.

A buffalo hunting video surprised me when the professional hunter (PH) shot a bull, then immediately stepped between its legs while talking about how to hunt these animals. It was supposed to be an educational video! It is not cowardly to be extraordinarily cautious around buffalo. Maintaining a healthy respect for this quarry will help to bring you back from a safari in one piece.

But back to my hunt with Tord. A week later we arrive back at the village, a lean and energetic Tord marching proudly ahead of a long file of heavily loaded porters. We are heartily greeted by the villagers, and nearly every hut receives a large load of smoked meat. The women expel a typically shrill whistle, created by the tongue and upper gum being closed and vibrated (as if rapidly pronouncing a highly pitched letter *R*). That evening a big party starts and does not end until dawn. The drums thunder, local wine and brandy flow, and dancing and laughter abound. Successful safari: joyous conclusion!

Chapter 4

The Holy Grail–
A Safari into an
Unknown Area

We plod monotonously along a small path that mean-
ders through the forest. I plan to explore a vast area close
to the Congolese border, southwest of my previously hunted
game-rich regions. During the preceding season I sent a
fellow hunter there with a detailed map and instructions to
check out a vast river drainage full of swamps covered by
thorny raffia palm. He did very well, getting a sitatunga, a
forest buffalo, and heavy ivory weighing 35 and 40 pounds,
but early luck kept him from venturing as far as he could
have. Now it's my turn to push my crew to their physical
limits in pursuit of the Holy Grail. After six safaris in these
forests, I have a dependable crew who know my intentions.

At first it was difficult to get the Pygmies to work because they are not accustomed to structure or time con-
straints. At one point on the trail I waited for over an hour
to collect the stretched-out file of my Pygmy crew, but the
rearmost porters still did not show up. Intrigued, I retraced
my steps down the elephant trail expecting a disaster. Instead, I found my porters sitting happily under some big trees
cutting small nuts with their machetes. So much for reaching a distant swamp in record time!

For the first two days we follow a small, deeply beaten footpath that links several villages. "Village" glorifies these agglomerations of four to six huts, but the path used by merchants on their way to the Congo has enough fast traffic at times to make them seem like cities. The merchants hire porters to carry expensive goods—clothes, petrol, and toilet articles—to the Congolese villages. The villagers pay for the goods with "cheap" gold dug out of the mineral-rich Congo.

During our first night we stay in one of the small villages. The chief proffers one hut for me and another for the porters. In the evening a large, old, beautifully carved drum is beaten hard, and everyone dances until late in the night. There is no shortage of palm wine or the highly concentrated brandy, *hha*.

Earlier that day two Pygmies had arrived from a Pygmy settlement at the Congolese border to the south where they had participated in a funeral for a renowned medicine man, Martin Ango, of the Baka group Likemba. Pygmies from a hundred-square-mile area had attended this feast, where they drank and danced for months.

The famous medicine man had cured many Pygmies over his relatively long life of some forty years, hence their reverence. Unfortunately my tracker, Lazare, who had worked for me during four previous safaris, had also attended and was unavailable for this safari. Too bad. He was an extremely valuable and knowledgeable hunter, and I sincerely enjoyed his company.

The two Pygmies bring me bad news: Lazare died last week after an evening of palm wine. Naturally, they attribute his death to bad magic. They think he was poisoned by a woman claiming money for some lively nights. It could have been anything from common tetanus to an incarcerated hernia to Ebola virus. Ebola is quite common among the locals, but they often survive the dangerous disease because of antibodies in their blood. In Central Africa around 13 percent of Bantu villagers carry antibodies and among the Baka Pygmies it's around 35 percent. Ebola is the name of a river in Zaire's north, but its namesake virus is common throughout all equatorial forests from Gabon to Zaire. It is transmitted through monkeys, mainly chimpanzees (*Pan troglodytes*) that get it from ticks or other animals such as rodents. It is a nasty disease that is often fatal.

What a shame about that invaluable man. I still have an old, heavily used hand drum at home that he carved many years ago. I will keep it to remind me of my wonderful companion on several outstanding hunts.

On the afternoon of the second day we leave the path and slowly penetrate a less-frequented trail that becomes nothing more than a meandering game trail in places with occasional duiker and pig hooves imprinted in the mud. Late in the afternoon we stop by a clear creek to camp. Within minutes the dense undergrowth is whacked away by powerful machete strokes, and a cozy place miraculously opens to accommodate my mosquito net. I keep busy building a rest for my rifle with my luggage. I still need to sight in my new red-dot scope.

My departure from Germany was hasty, so I was glad when my gun finally showed up, even though we had to postpone our hunt three days waiting for it. Finally my new .460 Weatherby Bullpup arrived and freed us to hunt. It enables me to fire "reduction" shells, but the aim is one hand to the right and two hands low! I silently praise the bipod, which gives solid support in front. The back of the rifle rests on one of the drums I use to protect my luggage from water and other damage. It's easy to remove the bolt to accommodate the bore sight and adjust the red-dot sight by using a spot marked on a large tree some forty yards away.

Ten shots later the sights are dead on, and the reduction cartridges have kept my shoulder from being pounded to a pulp by the big .460 rounds. Also, the muzzle brake effectively reduces 60 percent of the recoil; I now have full confidence in my new rifle. Two days of fast marching with heavy loads have taken their toll, and tonight everyone retires early.

The next day finds us on the trail again. At noon I take a Global Positioning System (GPS) reading to decide how much farther we will go before veering off into unknown forest. By 2 P.M. we are at the chosen spot and leave the trail. From now on we will follow game trails using machetes to cut our way. A small compass on the wristband of my watch keeps us on course.

I am seldom able to get a fix with my GPS unit. I am usually able to take a position reading only two or three times a day: A huge fallen log might provide a cutout arc in the sky, or a sharp creek bend might allow an unobstructed view of a small rectangular strip of sky. It is not easy to find the requisite opening in the dense canopy, even with a premium model equipped for parallel reception.

The two methods of getting a fix with the GPS used to be parallel and sequential. The parallel system used one receiver for each satellite, and four satellites were required to calculate a three-dimensional position. A parallel system worked better under a canopy because it picked up the satellites faster. The sequential system used only one or two receivers. If two receivers were used, one picked up a satellite and the second was switched between the three remaining satellites. If one receiver was used, it switched between satellites. This degraded the signal-to-noise ratio and required a strong signal. Under a heavy canopy of trees, you would often lose "lock."

A quality GPS set is definitely a must: Twelve-channel receivers give much better and faster position readings. Also, modern units have menus with helpful hints and display bearings only if they are accurate—a very important feature because storing wrong coordinates could be fatal in remote regions. Good GPS units are very exact and will help prevent uncomfortable nights in the bush and loss of precious hunting time. Sometimes the woodsmanship of the locals is not very good, and they may lose their bearings in new areas. I have often brought my crew back to camp with my GPS unit.

Together with a GPS unit, a detailed map (1:200,000 or smaller) and a compass should be carried. The topographic maps of *Institute Geographique Nationale* in Paris are available in Yaoundé and show latitudes and longitudes.

Without protest the crew follows my directional hand signals. They are accustomed to my guidance and probably think it is black magic, but they know that it works. After acquiring a GPS fix, I gather the trackers around me and explain the mechanism. They stare at me with blank expressions and probably don't understand anything—even after many years. But it is an established ritual, and gives them confidence. Truthfully it helps me too!

During foot safaris in open country one covers about two or three miles an hour, even while humping ninety-pound loads. However, in the dense bush that might be the straight-line distance of a hard day's walk.

Soon we hear the familiar shrieks of chimpanzees, and my tracker tries to call them in for a photo by emitting a series of duiker calls. The rising and dying squealing usually attracts chimps very quickly; they rush right in and yell like madmen. These chimps must have had some bad experiences with locals because they immediately fall silent and slip away. No further sign reveals their presence, so we continue our march.

Half an hour later my tracker Jacques stops abruptly, hands me my .460 Bullpup, and motions me to get ready. He makes the sign for gorilla by compressing his brows with forefingers and thumbs, making them protrude—a prominent feature of a male gorilla.

In the rain forest everyone is afraid of gorillas because they are numerous and often attack. Usually it is
only a mock attack to scare humans away and allow the
females and young to retreat. Sometimes the aggressor is
a single old "silverback" gorilla, named for the prominent
color of an aged male's dorsal hair. These giant mammals
are extremely dangerous. Having lost the dominance fight
in their bands and been cast out by the new leaders, they
wander about alone, their toothaches, rheumatism, and
bad temper adding to their aggression toward humans. The
hunter must be prepared to defend himself because an old
silverback is a ferocious killing machine. Of course their
aggression is also caused by the Pygmies and blacks hunting them for their fat. All black tribes praise the gorilla's
meat and fat and pursue the animal mercilessly: "The power
of the beast is in the meat!"

Fortunately the group wandering toward us is peaceful, and they quickly retreat after realizing our presence.
Before retreating, they attempt a wild charge, bashing trees
and yelling wildly to give the females and young time to
escape. Still, one can never be completely sure, and I feel
quite uneasy even with my big bore ready. It would be difficult to explain to the game department that a gorilla was
killed in self-defense.

Game officials know that the Pygmies love gorilla meat
and use their skin for traditional leatherwork, so they mis-
trust hunters who down apes for any reason. A proud Pygmy
always carries a small gorilla-leather pouch on a cord over
his shoulder containing necessary items such as a flintstone,
iron, and hemp to start a fire.

After several minutes the gorillas vanish like ghosts
and the forest is quiet again. My porters have run off, so I
whistle as loudly as possible to get them back. For this
purpose I carry an alarm whistle that is also helpful in an
encounter with an elephant herd. Game regard the noise

as natural and do not react by panicking. Slowly the Pyg-mies and Bantus trickle back.

Originally I had wanted to take just Pygmies with me but ended up having to hire some Bantus from the village as well. (Bantu is the ethnic name for all the tribes in the Congo area.) The Bantus gathered and created all kinds of difficulties to force me to recruit some of them.

There is animosity between the two ethnic groups. Bantus treat the Pygmies as their slaves, and although the Baka are becoming more self-confident, they have yet to free themselves from the yoke of the traditional relationship.

The Baka live on the Bantus' plantations and work for them. It is extremely rare for a Pygmy family to have its own plantation, which would be easy because land is free and ba-nana, manioc, and many other foods are easily grown. How-ever, it would require regular work to first clear woodland, then the quickly returning jungle. Planning and routine are not among the Pygmies' strengths.

Now the Bantu villagers are uneasy. The rain forest far from their village seems dangerous to them, and this gorilla attack confirms their apprehensions. This will make it easier for me to maintain the balance of power between the two ethnic groups. The Bantu will regard the Baka as more valuable because they know how to handle these dangers. It is safe to say that Africa is more divided by ethnic and tribal divisions than by political boundaries. Unfortunately, it is also safe to say that in many states democratization leads to tribalism as the local politicians of large tribes gather more followers and dominate the less populous tribes.

Soon we are on our way and continue until nearly 3 P.M.—time to make camp and find meat for the pot. It is useless to call duikers during rest stops close to hunted ar-eas. They are wary of sounds made by a column of walking men and will not respond.

By now, most of the porters are accustomed to their wilderness routine, so our camp is soon set up near a tiny creek with clear water. Still, I need to exercise my authority and prod several lazy ones who prefer to sit and relax instead of working.

I fix a lightweight rope across the small rectangular clearing, place a plastic sheet on the ground beneath it, and hang my mosquito net covered with a tentlike sheet of Tyvek for protection against the morning coolness. I stuff my precious cot into this white "hut" with an inquiring look at the small spots of sky visible through the close canopy.

The sky is blue, it is not too hot, and there is no wind. It looks as though it will not rain, so the large plastic sheet is set aside. If it starts raining tonight, we can always pull it back over the rope.

It is wise to lay down a plastic sheet or at least cover the earth with large phrynium leaves. Otherwise small white termites come out of the ground and quickly eat the fine mesh of the mosquito net. They love all fabric, especially plastic weave. While lying in bed at night one can often hear them rhythmically attacking the fabric.

Once I killed a huge boar at dusk and had to camp near a swamp infested by clouds of mosquitoes. My poor Baka were soon sitting around large, smoky fires slapping their backs rhythmically with leafy branches to chase the bugs away. I grinned and slept nicely under the mosquito net, but only until 4 A.M. when I bolted upright and began slapping frantically at the mini-monsters. We anxiously awaited daybreak so we could escape this dreadful location. The termites had found my mosquito net, which was hanging on the ground, and eagerly chewed large holes in it. This opened heaven's gates for the invasion of all flying objects.

Presently, the camp boy is busy covering a spot on the ground with large leaves and hanging my recently filled water bag for my evening shower. He hands me my bottle of drinking water so I can add disinfectant. I open the locked rice container and hand out tonight's rations. It is a bothersome chore to unlock and relock this container every day at dusk and dawn, but it's the only way to ensure that provisions last until the end of the trip. If the cook helped himself, he would just take a little more of the seemingly inexhaustible supply each day.

Finally we are set up, and the tracker, one porter, and I leave to hunt. The crew hopes we will be successful; they are hungry for meat and expect me to provide it. Thetrophies do not mean anything to them except unnecessary additional loads.

We walk for about a mile, then hide in some dense bushes. After loading my rifle with a reduction shell and camouflaging my treacherous white face and hands with a headnet and gloves, I am ready. Jacques calls out in a series of high-pitched squealing cries, sounding almost like a suffering rabbit. The ground is wet, good for hunting elephant and stalking but not good for hunting duiker. The first tiny blue duiker (*Cephalophus monticola*) just whirl by and almost pass between my legs. They move too quickly for me to aim and shoot, especially since I had made the mistake of choosing an "ultra dot" brand variable 3–9X scope with an optional red dot for my new .460 Weatherby Magnum Bullpup rifle.

Reduced to its lowest power during close encounters, a scope with 3X magnification still does not provide a wide enough field of vision. I regret not having kept the red dot from my last rifle and switching it to this one. Otherwise the Bullpup with its short and extremely practical thumbhole design is definitely advantageous.

More stopping and calling follows. Four blue duikers rush past us, but we have no luck. I begin to think that today a shotgun would have been better; then I remember that about ninety percent of all duiker encountered during my last safari would have been too far away for a shotgun. There's always a tradeoff when you're on foot safari with minimal gear. Still, I prefer *my* way!

Jacques really wants to stuff his stomach with meat and drags me through the forest until dusk. We barely find our camp in the dark. He has to shout the monkey call several times—a noise that does not make game suspicious. It carries far, and the porters in camp respond with the same call to guide us home.

I am relieved to get back to camp and undress for my shower. It's important to stay completely covered until after dark. During the afternoon hours tiny mosquitoes called *mut mut* fly low to the ground and suck at any exposed soft skin. They are just barely visible against the light. If bitten, your lower extremities will itch terribly at night after heating up in your sleeping bag. If scratched too much, the open bites often become infected and result in so-called tropical ulcers—large suppurating wounds.

In Cameroon one must dress differently than one would in southern Africa, where most people wear shorts and are lightly clad even while hunting. For Cameroon 100-percent cotton BDU clothing in Woodland Tarn pattern are the best bet. The summer field jacket works well as a shirt, and BDU Jungle Boots provide the best protection and the most comfort because they dry easily and their air vents ventilate your feet at all times. One often has to wade in waterways, and these boots pump water out in small jets as one walks.

The new issue jungle boots with speed lacing are very comfortable, and their padded collar provides even more comfort. Tucking your trouser legs into them and adding gaiters will keep out ants and even fine sand particles suspended in the water. Small grains of sand in your socks will cause friction and result in blisters. After many years of experimenting, I have found the old wrap-around woolen gaiters that British troops used for so many years to be the very best. They are hermetically sealed, meaning that all entry points for ants and sand are blocked. Passing through a horde of ants is a most unpleasant experience. They bite everywhere, and many times my entire crew and I curse together in a kind of war dance while quickly stripping to get rid of the biting monsters. Too bad there were never any girls with us!

It is difficult to find true British gaiters outside Great Britain, but one can purchase the wrap-around gaiters used to protect horses' legs in a saddler's shop—a place that sells riding gear. It may not be the cutting edge of fashion, but it beats those blasted ant bites!

Cold water from a plastic bag provides a refreshing shower that revives me. I don my lightweight camp clothes and enjoy my provisions. The crew has to content themselves with rice and a sauce of oil and tuna while I enjoy Black Forest ham on rice and dried fruits for dessert. It's good to be the *Patron*!

There are social classes in the jungle. All my crew got an advance before leaving and could shop for convenience goods in the only retail store. Hausa tribesmen from the north nearly always operate such stores. They control the majority of trade, while Bamoun tribesmen from the west control most clothing and transportation businesses.

A small short-wave radio provides the latest news, which is sometimes very helpful, as illustrated by the following:

Once we came out of the bush after four adventurous weeks of hunting in one of the most remote areas of central Cameroon. A coup d'état had taken place, and the army's counterstrike had caused hundred of deaths but saved the president. The entire country was in an uproar, and three counselors to the rebels were being sought—Arabs, which to black Africans means "white" people. And here we were, three white hunters with wild beards, rifles, and all kinds of equipment. We got through it only by keeping our cool!

Next day we get an early start and my crew is convinced we should advance deeper into the forest for successful hunting—meat for the pot. Jacques leads the way and soon comes across a large elephant path. It is almost like a forest freeway or "autobahn," and he advances quickly. We cover a lot of ground, and by noon everyone needs a long rest.

Suddenly Jacques leaps aside and starts whacking frantically at the ground with his machete. A small green-and-yellow snake (*Causus rhombeatus*) coils up and tries to escape by searching among large dry leaves for a hole in the red-ochre ground. Too late—it is cut in two. I rescue the head, then start skinning the small reptile while my Pygmies shake their heads and laugh. The *Patron* is crazy to touch that poisonous animal. I put the head and skin in a PET bottle filled with one-half denatured alcohol and one-half glycerin. It will be perfectly preserved and tanned by the time I return home. The alcohol will draw the water out of the tissue and replace it with glycerin. This method prevents rot, and the skin will soften and retain most of its beautiful color. The color in reptile leather fades almost entirely if tanned in the traditional manner.

Now I can relax and make myself comfortable. My hip is aching, so I prefer to lie down and elevate my legs on one of the one large fifteen-gallon barrels I use to carry light but breakable and water-sensitive items. That helps a lot, and after an hour's rest I am ready to go again.

These barrels are ideal for luggage, especially during the rainy season. They are completely watertight and their screw-top cap can be locked with a padlock, so no beetles or any other insects (or natives) can enter. I even use one to check my rifle into airline cargo. This keeps it safe and arouses no suspicion. A large, lightweight, ten-pound, twenty-five-gallon drum is much lighter and much more secure than a weapon case. We all know that the greatest danger in airline transport is theft of firearms, and traditional gun cases are a dead giveaway.

By now we are far from the main path, but signs of human presence are still everywhere. We even pass a decaying camp made by Pygmy hunters, instantly recognizable by their round huts made of cut sticks pushed firmly into the ground with the tops interwoven and covered with large phrynium leaves. All game trails leading to the camp are barricaded with the tops of cut-off trees to keep a leopard (*Panthera pardus*) from sneaking in. Pygmies fear that leopard are lurking about at night. I used to chuckle about this, but later changed my mind. These "forest" cats are smaller and darker than the larger and lighter open savanna variety of panther. They are all nasty customers, no matter what shade their coats are.

Now I question my decision to explore this area, which looked very promising on the detailed map. Three days earlier I'd sent a friend to my old game-rich hunting grounds that are laced with swamps and frequented by buffalo and elephant. I almost begin to regret my decision to come to this new area, but stop myself. This is unexplored territory, and explore it I shall!

Although my friend does not speak French, he can easily hunt my old grounds accompanied by my experienced and well-trained crew. He would have had a very difficult time pushing a reluctant crew into new territory to search for big game far away from their stomping grounds.

I muse during the monotonous march until Jacques stops abruptly and excitedly motions for me to get ready; another gorilla is moving toward us. I cock the hammer as Jacques points out a grayish spot thirty yards farther ahead next to a tree.

Suddenly his tone changes: "No, it's an elephant coming toward us!" I quickly eject the reduction cartridge and

111

chamber a regular big-game cartridge up from the magazine beneath it. Unfortunately, it is a 500-grain half-jacketed bullet, good for side shots at the chest. I have no time to pull a solid from my belt and load it. The elephant is moving steadily in our direction and is now barely fifteen yards away. I can clearly see its short but extremely thick tusks. Normally I would wait for longer tusks, but at this distance and since it will be the first bull with my new Bullpup rifle, I do not hesitate. We're in an ideal location to save all the meat, so it's an easy choice.

Silently praising my big bore, I lift the Bullpup and as the cross hairs settle on the third wrinkle of the forehead, I pull the trigger. Instantly the huge bull falls to his knees. Even with a half-jacketed factory bullet, the .460 Weatherby Magnum has enough power to penetrate and knock down this colossal animal. My ears are ringing. The 162-dB noise, measured in 2,000-Hertz frequency, is absolutely deafening! Usually I close my ears with foam plugs, but this time it was impossible. I barely had enough time to chamber the regular cartridge.

Behind the fallen elephant appears a second, smaller bull. The Pygmies call these young bulls *mossemée,* while my huge animal is called *semée.* This *mossemée* may be smaller but it is still big enough to wreck me and my entire crew.

He disappears to the left and waits a few minutes for his friend but finally departs. For safety's sake I fire another bullet behind the ear, and with a heavy shudder the fallen elephant dies. Whew! That was a completely unexpected encounter. At these close quarters it could easily have ended in the bull's favor. A swift charge would have put him among us with disastrous results.

My crew closes in and starts yelling joyfully about the mountain of meat. For half of them it's their first-ever close-up view of an elephant. I am not quite as happy and wonder whether I was too hasty. Perhaps I should have waited before filling my only license for a big one this season. El Dorado still lies quite a distance ahead of us. Still, if it proves as good as anticipated, I can always hunt it next time.

The bull has beautiful long hair on his tail, so I quickly sever and secure it. There's no time to lose because the crew want to pull hairs as souvenirs and good-luck charms; the fine hairs can be woven into beautiful bracelets. I have such bracelets made in Istanbul, Turkey, where one of my friends is a goldsmith. He braids the hairs very nicely and positions $1/3$-inch-wide golden rings under them for more stability. I've worn one every day for the last eight years, and the stabilized and protected hairs have not suffered in the least.

Basically elephant hair is easy to braid. The secret is to soften them first by putting a half dozen strands in a solution of one pint warm water and a soupspoon of ammonia for ten minutes. Then the hairs are clamped in a vise, and knotted together in three loops following a method used in North Africa. The basic weaving principle is to move the middle sling through the outer sling to the right and then the new middle sling through the outer sling to the left. After each pass, the arms are spread wide to pull the crossing hair tight. After weaving, the hair is oiled with any vegetable oil. Africans firmly believe that elephant hair protects the wearer, and from what I have seen at big-game conventions, so do the hunters.

Distant thunder interrupts our celebration, so we quickly make camp about two hundred yards away. A small creek provides water, and the sparse vegetation allows us to clear a place rapidly. I attach the rope to some trees, and the large plastic sheet creates an instant six-yard-by-six-yard shelter. The thunderstorm misses us and the heavy wind gusts announce rain, but the only sign of rain is the distant thunder. This respite gives me time to clean my rifle and go through my usual camp routine. I enjoy German bread and French country sausage with lots of garlic together with a hefty dose of muscatel wine. The drink serves as a silent salute and a tribute to the fallen jungle monarch.

I had the crew dig a trench ten inches deep around the upper part of my tent. This proves wise when it pours cats and dogs at 4 A.M., and the improvised ditch sends the overflow around my shelter, keeping me snug and dry. My Bantus did not set up shelter and get pretty wet, while the Pygmies stay dry in a nice shelter of bamboo and leaves. Village people!

Today is rest and recreation for me but a heavy butchering day for my crew. I cut my hair short to allow heat to radiate out more easily; then I shave my skull completely à la Yul Brynner! No social encounters for the next fortnight, so it does not matter if I look ugly. The hair will grow back before I return to civilization. I feel much better afterward and in the days ahead I will be much better off bald. Another idea for future safaris: It helps get rid of the heat that saps strength and endurance.

My new summer field jacket is still impregnated with a protective wax lining and does not absorb much   perspiration. I wash it and rub the inside with a pot-scouring sponge to roughen the ripstop cotton fabric so it   absorbs perspiration better.

At noon, when I finally start to relax, we get invaded by ants. They attack on a wide front. Fortunately one of my old porters, Emanuel, has just returned with a load of fresh meat. He springs into action and places large amounts of ashes and burning embers in a line around my spot to barricade me from the ants. He makes several trips from the fires of the meat-smoking tables to the battlefield around my spot, but at last he is triumphant. The ants beat a retreat and look elsewhere for prey. One minute we're faced with earth's largest land animal and the next with one of its smallest. The variety of Africa is quite remarkable!

That incident proves I made the right decision in hiring Emanuel. He is an agreeable, quiet porter who worked for me during several previous expeditions, but I didn't want to bring him this time because he has an infection that complete clouds his left eye. I was afraid of complications and doubted that he would be able to carry his load during a long expedition. But he worked quietly and carried his load well. Now he proves his value. Every day he approaches in the morning and the evening and sits a bit off from my tent, waiting with a broad smile for another treatment of eye ointment.

Now Emanuel is making a new handle for his ax. Pygmies buy or trade for rectangular 2-inch by 18-inch pieces of steel. They carry these blades of tempered high-carbon steel in their baskets and if a handle is needed, they cut a small tree with a strong side limb. They slice the V thinner, cut it in the middle, thrust the blade into this opening, and bind it tightly with rope, which is intricately knotted. The finished ax is extremely heavy and accurate. Usually used to cut down trees for extracting honeycombs, it now serves just as well to cut up the fallen giant: Jumbo's hide is two inches thick on the back!

I enjoy a nice relaxing day topped by a long siesta. Distant rolling thunder alarms me from time to time and announces rain. I look inquiringly at the blotches of sky visible through the close canopy, but the rain does not arrive in our camp. This is perfect weather for hunting big game—quiet stalking and ideal tracking conditions. I recall stalking quietly just thirty feet behind an elephant in falling rain on more than one occasion. Under these conditions minutes seem like an eternity.

The rain finally arrives and it pours cats and dogs until the next morning. Night is a good time for rain because then we are sheltered. Again the shallow trench leads the invading water away. One is well advised to carry a cot during the rainy season. Besides keeping ants and spiders from walking across your face and hands at night, it guarantees a dry spot if unexpected torrents of rain should invade your shelter.

I want to leave today to explore the swamps in the forest ahead, but it is still raining. Departure can be postponed for another day since I already got my elephant. From now on it will be leisurely exploring and hunting smaller game.

Another lazy day passes with plenty of exotic food such as elephant trunk, feet, and heart. Elephant foot is delicious but requires long cooking. The easiest way is to dig a hole in the earth about fifteen inches deep, cover the foot with large leaves and earth, then build a fire for smoking the meat just above the hole. A day later one unearths the foot and eats the fatty tissue inside the skin with a spoon—food of the gods!

I try to use the rest period to train a bright young Pygmy to take position fixes with the external antenna extension of my Scout GPS. I send him up a tree for a better, wider view of the sky, but it does not provide a fix because he is too close to the canopy and has only a sideways opening of about 45 degrees—a bad angle for satellite fixes. The unit computes and computes but does not achieve a fix. The cheaper units I used in the past would show a fix, but the coordinates were often miles away from the real position—a very dangerous situation that can lead to failure and perhaps even a fatal end. "Lost" here has an entirely different meaning than it does in civilization!

In the evening I pack my equipment and food for the upcoming trip. We will return to this base camp in about a week after our explorations. Two Pygmies and two Bantus will remain here and smoke the meat. After four days they will also pull out the tusks and hopefully keep them safe.

If there is no time, one has to cut out the tusks, and the first one-third of their length is buried deeply in the skull. It is amazing how exactly the Pygmies place the blows of their machetes or axes to avoid injuring the ivory. Each stroke hits the same spot.

116

I realize I have brought too much food from Germany. Bad planning, but on the other hand an additional porter does not cost much and is happy to earn money and receive meat. My porters will be glad to help clear out my portable delicatessen, although my table fare is as foreign to them as elephant stew would be to my brethren back home.

The next day we start out early and proceed toward the swampy rivers on the map. At first we have it easy in a relatively open forest—not much cutting is required. We walk on game trails, switching here and there to maintain direction. But then we have to climb a small hill and veer to the north for half an hour to bypass a thick, thorny maze of bushy palm trees. To get back on course we move to the southwest for about an hour and ford a small creek. Another hour west, and a fallen tree provides a small opening in the canopy for a fix.

We are on course and have approximately four miles to go to reach the first of a series of swampy rivers. Anticipation is rising: I expect to find miraculous game-rich meadows and large trampled openings with salt licks and rubbing trees for elephant. Game is dispersed throughout the forest, but tends to congregate near the swamps.

The anticlimax comes soon enough. We reach a well-hewn path leading to a six-month-old Pygmy encampment with the usual round huts. From there a large path leads north along the swampy river, which is probably difficult to cross. Trees and branches have been cut down to facilitate travel on the original elephant path. This hunting path is regularly used, which means no decent hunting in unexplored pristine forest—my favorite kind of place to hunt.

We proceed due north at a quick pace. The Pygmy elephant tracks from the previous evening cross our path, and large, fresh leopard tracks are visible several times in the mud. The leopard traveled on this path last night for a long period of time. We also encounter red-faced "mandrill" baboons, the first I have ever seen in the rain forest. *Papio mandrillus sphinx* is a rare sighting.

Suddenly Jacques stops and motions for us to be quiet. He is excited and sure we are close to elephant. Slowly I continue with him while the porters look for easy-to-climb trees. But we soon realize that a family of gorilla has fooled us again.

I have ample time to watch a female gorilla sitting ten feet up in a tree, feeding on leaves and berries. Another half-grown gorilla on a closer tree spots us. With a plaintive howl he jumps down and retreats into the forest. The female follows immediately, then both sit forty yards from us and scan the forest. I freeze and my Woodland Tarn camouflages me so well that they cannot detect me. For fifteen minutes I watch them through the rifle scope, which I have cranked up to its highest power—9X. It is interesting to see the female caressing and comforting the smaller one. Then a huge male with very prominent eyebrows joins them. The Pygmies aptly signify gorilla when they compress their eyebrows with forefinger and thumb.

All three gorillas sit together, looking around, then groom one another by digging in each other's fur with their black fingers—a fascinating sight. Too bad I didn't bring my camera with the big telephoto lens. Last year I got some beautiful photographs of forest buffalo and Pygmy elephant. I even caught a sequence of a big buffalo bull and an adult Pygmy elephant bull around the same size, quarreling over a mud hole. They looked like two drivers back home arguing over a parking spot.

Finally I get tired of watching and retreat silently. The porters have been relaxing, and we join them for a well-earned rest. Everyone is chewing on smoked elephant meat. I pull out packaged cheese and crackers and enjoy a light snack.

We continue along the open path with long strides, still heading north. Shortly after 4 P.M. we reach yet another three-week-old camp at the end of this forested "highway."

I have never seen such heavily traveled pathways in a good hunting area, so my hopes for this supposedly game-rich and unexploited sector are falling drastically. Perhaps the difficult terrain ahead will present natural barriers: One should never cease to hope!

With hindsight, I now realize our luck encountering the elephant under perfect conditions three days ago. I was right in deciding to shoot. This eases my current disappointment, but I still recall the game-rich country I usually hunt and envy my friend, Wilhelm, whom I had sent there. Not even duiker come to the call—too much hunting pressure; and I love duiker hunting so much! They provide great satisfaction for their small size.

We descend the forested ridge into a valley and cut our way through thick bush until we find a dry, level place to camp. In a short time the hostile thicket is cleared and shelter is built quickly. My GPS unit shows we are just 3½ miles north of our elephant camp; we walked quickly and steadily nearly all day but made a wide arc.

The lightweight cot provides excellent respite after our strenuous march. I enjoy the sounds of crickets, owls, and night squirrels until I fall asleep. I do not need an alarm clock. My interior alarm goes off at first light the next morning; anticipation undoubtedly helps. I waken the crew and get them to start the lengthy procedure of boiling their rice. Their response is not very enthusiastic. They definitely love to sleep in!

My breakfast is simple: I pour some cereal and a hefty mixture of nuts and dried fruit into a cup, add some sugar and instant cocoa, then fill the cup with water. I munch slowly through it and start my daily routine of putting on my hunting clothes. I conclude by slipping into moist boots and thoroughly attaching the old British woolen wrap-around gaiters. Protected from the legions of nasty insects, I make a thick foam and shave with the hot water my camp boy Francis brings me. If I grew a beard, it would itch and become an insect condominium.

Next I update my electronic diary. I have plenty of time since it takes almost two hours for my crew to get ready to leave. The Pygmies are especially expert at dawdling because they are not keen to leave the cozy fire. Finally everyone is ready and in a long single-file we head west, then southwest. Around 9:30 A.M. we enter a fairly large camp built around a year ago. Clearly, an elephant was shot close by. Part of a tree lies on the ground with a large hewn-out rectangular hole. Pygmies used it as a receptacle for fat, and only elephant would provide enough fat to fill this log's bowels.

Now I'm really disappointed with this supposedly virgin hunting area: Four Baka camps in four miles is way too much hunting pressure. It was a mistake to invest so much time in this shot-out area!

We turn around and cut our way northeast toward a swamp where my partner shot a sitatunga and a nice buffalo last year. Unfortunately I had left the GPS coordinates in my luggage back in town. This way is tough. We advance slowly, and Jacques has to do a lot of cutting.

We try to call in duiker, but the zone is overhunted. My crew looks sour because they did not bring smoked elephant meat with them. I had told them to put some in their light loads, but they were confident that I would be able to supply plenty of meat as usual. They probably wanted to save the precious elephant venison to take home.

By noon my tracker is exhausted and badly in need of rest. All afternoon we endure the same ordeal: cutting, bending, cutting, duiker calling, cutting. It really is a grueling day. Twice tiny blue duiker run through the bushes. Even in overhunted forests they respond to the call. Their survival technique is speed, and it still works; I can't put the cross hairs on them. The absence of game tracks and the ever-present cut foliage prove that human visits here are frequent.

As I reach desperation point, a third blue duiker sneaks up and falls to the dull thud of the reduction shell. Now we have camp meat plus a nice mount for my taxidermist back home. I take out my Damascus knife, a beauty that I almost don't want to carry on expeditions. My good friend Rob Charlton of Damascus USA made this one, and its practical uses are immense. The steel is so sharp that apart from the esthetic pleasure of looking at its elaborate pattern, it is extremely handy.

My Pygmies always stare at my knife in awe and often ask to borrow it for minute work. I need to keep a close eye on this treasure. I think I could easily exchange it for the chief's young and beautiful daughters! Hmm, it *has* been a long trip!

Now my knife acts as a scalpel for the careful skinning in preparation for a full mount. I have to do it myself because the locals are not accustomed to such demanding work. I have taught several porters and they do it right after some practice, but sometimes they get careless and just cut up trophies. A few days earlier my camp boy cut up a beautiful "gold cat" (*Felis aurata*) and wrecked the attractive spotted fur.

Evidence of severe hunting pressure is confirmed as we look for a place to camp later in the afternoon. We hear the rhythmic sound of ax strokes some distance away, and my Pygmies carefully approach their shy brothers. If we rushed in, the other Baka would run off. That does happen, but Jacques convinces them we mean no harm, so they slowly return to their campsite.

A pitiful, half-starved horde of Pygmies gather around us. They have been hunting this patch of forest for the past two months and have already been much farther north. Three hunters, their wives, and a bunch of small kids with two dogs and a puppy—they are hunting elephant with three worn-out single-shot shotguns! A good way to reach the "happy hunting ground" in the sky ahead of schedule.

Out of each shotgun barrel protrudes the wooden handle of a lance with a fine small blade. The Pygmies strip the pellets from a shotshell and use the powder to propel the spear. The hunter sneaks up under the elephant's belly and fires his lance into it! Then he follows—sometimes for days—until the huge animal becomes sick and weak enough for the final kill.

During the past two months neither this horde nor another one across the swampy river have gotten lucky; they have lived poorly on nuts, honey, and occasional wild yam roots—just enough to survive. A small child screams bloody murder as it notices a 6-foot, 5-inch white man with a shaven head! Since the Bantu are not much bigger than Pygmies, I must seem like a giant to him! After presenting the wives with a pound of peanuts, we camp far enough away to avoid being disturbed by crying babies with night-mares about hairless albino monsters.

It is difficult to wait another hour for darkness so I can undress and shower, but a large river is close by and legions of *mut mut* are avidly searching for food. I do not want to be their evening feast, and am rewarded for my discipline with a refreshing cold shower at nightfall followed by a sound sleep to regain my strength.

The following day we hold a war council and decide to retreat. If two hordes of Pygmies wandered around here for two months without finding big game, it's a safe bet we will have no luck. Better to march back toward town where a friend is due to show up; we can help him hunt elephant in another forest. My crew has told me many times about a great stretch of forest close to their villages. I had always been too fixated on far-off game-rich regions to explore there, but now it's time to check it out. In any event, I already have my bull.

We take the horde of Pygmies with us, at least the men; their families are too slow but will follow at their own speed. At first we cover a lot of ground quickly, but my camp boy, Francis, develops a severe pain in his left shoulder. Three months ago he fell off the back of a truck and fractured his shoulder. All the cutting and clearing with the heavy machete has been too much of a strain. He gives his load to the other porters, which is not a problem since most carry light loads. However, walking is painful for him. He moves slowly and rests frequently. I find hard, contracted muscles on his upper arm and massage them to loosen the cramp followed by strong anti-rheumatic medication and a sling for his arm. We don't make good progress because he has to stop and rest quite often.

Jacques and I go ahead to stalk duiker or other game, but that hope is in vain. The porters just take advantage and dawdle. It's frustrating to wait an hour here and there for my crew to catch up—especially since the injured camp boy caught up to us quite a while ago.

In the afternoon Jacques moves along with considerable speed. He wants to reach elephant camp by nightfall and feast on heaps of nicely smoked meat. As usual, my Bantu crew members go slowly at first, then end up running like hares; these villagers can't organize their time. The Pygmies act differently. They also want a portion of the food ahead but move quickly at the outset.

Now we are almost running along our previously cut path and arrive at dusk to find the elephant cadaver stinking. It is alive again with thousands of grayish maggots, streaks of ants, and clumps of flies. Putrid clouds rise from inside the thoracic cage. Somewhere I read that the biomass of all the ants exceeds that of all other animals and humans together!

I'm quite happy about our return. I quickly rebuild my plastic sheet tent on the same spot vacated days before and organize everything else. Our camp guardians have been busy and proudly present me with the attractive tusks, pulled out with the help of their knives. They are not long, but are very thick, beautifully stained, and weigh 28 pounds each.

I feast on Black Forest ham and German bread. From some distance away we hear the imitated monkey call; the wives of the horde, slowed by the children, are just arriving in the pitch-black night. Their husbands respond and call them in. An hour later everyone is happily reunited around a fire and chewing up a storm! Yum—real food! The Pygmies are so content that after an hour or so they start singing their polyphonic chorale with everyone, big and little, participating. I am awestruck and regret having left my small tape recorder in the village. The sound of their natural harmony is one of my most treasured memories of the Dark Continent.

Baka music is quite famous, but it's rare to hear the real thing. Acute hearing is vital to their survival in the rain forest, and perhaps this contributed toward development of their superior tonal abilities. At home in the village the guitarlike *aiita* is played with virtuosity. Its soft sound offers a sharp contrast to the hard-hit drums and to the ecstatic dances.

Finally my guests tire and everyone stretches out to sleep. Unfortunately there is no sound *anything* with Pygmies. They sleep in their thin clothes on a bed of phrynium leaves on the cold ground, so they invariably waken every few hours to throw new logs on the fire—another reason to sit and chat endlessly at full volume. I would think they would have nothing left to discuss, but even after weeks together in the small, closed community of a safari crew, they never stop talking!

I nod off again after angrily shouting several times for them to be quiet. At first I always tried to have their camp at least fifty yards away from me, but as soon as I had designated both camp sites and started to build my tent at a safe distance, all the Pygmies would happily unite some ten yards from my spot and start building their huts. They want to be under the constant protection of my rifle. I used to laugh about this and their efforts to block game trails leading toward our camp with the crowns of smaller trees facing away from camp.

Tonight I finally understand: My tracker sneaks under the tarp, pulls urgently at my hand, and whispers anxiously. As soon as I awaken from deep sleep and figure out what is going on, I start to fumble for my rifle. A deep growling noise sounds as if it were just a few feet away! This ranks right up there with things I'd rather not wake up to.

A leopard is stalking us! It is probably the owner of the large tracks we found in the mud. He must have been attracted by the smell of rotting meat. Fortunately my torch and loaded rifle are ready. I get into my boots and roll out from under the tarp. I move slowly toward the noise, scanning each and every bush with my flashlight. I glimpse bright eyes for an instant; then they disappear. The leopard is silent for a moment; then the growling begins again a few yards away. Fortunately, the animal retreats and I follow, coughing loudly and making noises to ensure that he is scared off.

As we pass the elephant carcass, white clouds rise into the slightly chilly night air emitting an appalling stench, but I don't feel at all cold. I think the leopard is gone now, but we move around for a while and throw sticks into the bushes before returning to the camp.

Now I know why the Pygmies are afraid of these cats. This one was clearly stalking our camp. It is unfortunate that they are protected and can be shot only in self-defense. Years ago one of my former trackers in the Mouloundou region shot an elephant. Afterward he built a camp and went looking for water. When he returned to the elephant after dark to cut the trunk for a stew, he found a huge, growling leopard sitting on top of his elephant chewing at the flanks. He killed it as it crouched to leap at him.

Twice in 1989 I was fortunate to encounter the beautiful, dark forest leopard. Both encounters took place in bright daylight during a safari north of the Lobéké swamps. Unfortunately their numbers are rapidly dwindling due to the use of wire snares. If the leopard finds a duiker in a snare, it will prey upon it. The hunter will then set snares around the half-eaten antelope. The odds are quite high that the leopard will step into one of these the next night. Leopard skins and skulls are frequently offered on the black market.

After this exciting episode it takes me a while to fall asleep again. My former confidence in quiet nights disturbed only by invading ants is lessened. "Things that go bump in the night" takes on a whole new meaning when the "bumpee" (me) and the "bumper" (old spots) are going one-on-one in the darkness of nowhere! Finally I rely on my magic rifle and relax.

The next morning we take it easy and sleep longer. Again the crew happily chews smoked meat, and I feast on a fatty chunk of the heart: The fat is light, has a high melting point, and tastes sweet.

One rain shower has followed another almost without pause, preventing us from packing. But today it's dry, and for a change the Bantus want to move first. They want to head home with their loads of valuable meat, but their camp has been invaded by maggots creeping out of half-rotten, improperly smoked meat; there are even raw pieces still lying around. No wonder many complain of diarrhea. Their camp is a mess. I can talk hygiene until the cows come home, but the natives will still blame their diarrhea and the rains on bad spirits or magic.

By 10:30 A.M. we've broken camp and are heading back to the village. The Pygmies happily stay behind with their bellies swollen almost double. They will have some fine days of stuffing themselves before carrying the rest of the meat to Martin Ango's funeral party, probably trading it for high-powered "fire water."

Our day is not very pleasant. We should be in the dry season now, but Saint Peter sends us light rain again and again. All day long we wade through mud and across swollen creeks. Everything is dripping wet. Fortunately we can store sensitive items such as food, salt, cameras, and ammunition in the watertight drums. Rain was always a nightmare during previous safaris when we used surplus duffel bags lined with plastic bags. They invariably became soaked, along with their contents.

The valuable Baka porter, Jean Paul, is just a shadow of himself and drags along slowly. He suffers from dreadful diarrhea—not surprising considering how they care for meat in this warm country. Oh, those yummy microbes and maggots!

We meet two Baka on their way back to the funeral. They bring wonderful news: My friend has downed a huge elephant close to the village, and everyone has left to participate in its processing. Great! We each got our most desired trophy early. However, I will not see my friend for another two weeks. He has continued hunting deep in the forest and has had his crew carry the beautiful 70-pound tusks out of the jungle for thirty-five miles. I send a message urging him to take extreme measures in safe-guarding valuables. Better safe than sorry.

That night we camp close to a large creek swollen with foaming runoff. The fires blaze higher tonight to dry our wet clothing. As usual the crew complains about mosquitoes, but I am safe in my net and sleep soundly.

Another rough day lies ahead. We have sixteen miles to go before reaching the village, and I have picked up a case of diarrhea—not pleasant during a tough march. It was probably caused by my camp boy not boiling my tea water sufficiently. During this safari his formerly excellent work has fallen off significantly, and I will have some words with him back in the village. Now it's a monotonous march through mud. I don't mind long distances at the beginning of a hunt because I anticipate the upcoming adventures. However, walking back is boring because there is little to anticipate.

In one of the tiny villages along the path there is a treasure stored in the council hut—a huge war drum, at least fifty years old and beautifully carved. Carefully bound liana vines keep a tight grip on the skin, which resounds magnificently. The skin for big drums has to be thick, and the best material is the solid hide of the colorful bay duiker (*Cephalophus dorsalis*). For the past three years I have bargained with the chief for this drum—so far in vain. He refuses to let it go because the villagers believe it brings them luck—too bad for me.

In the next group of five huts we happen across a fetish ceremony. In the middle of a 50x60-foot rectangular area of trodden clay a small fire burns. Beside it sits a pot filled with various roots and covered by a small wildcat pelt. Two drums lie next to it. One is the typical long drum with a hide over one end; the other is a hollowed-out cylindrical tree trunk with a slotted opening that emits a high-pitched sound when beaten with sticks.

When I photograph this arrangement, a wild-looking fetishist comes running out of one of the huts. He angrily protects the magic pot from my camera. I am accompanied by a large crew and carry my Bullpup with its impressive elephant bore across my chest, so he dares not act aggressively. The other villagers are crammed into the hut and were probably in the middle of a ceremony. If the rite should fail to reveal a thief or destroy a bad spell, it will be my fault. My crew looks a little worried, but they are reassured when they see me grinning. To them my magic is more powerful than the fetishist's ceremony.

During one of my first visits into this area a newly recruited tracker told me, after a lot of persistent questioning, about a very distant swamp with a half-mile-square place "where the elephants dance." He had visited the place as a child some thirty years earlier. One of my porters told how he went there once, and his hunter ended up killing a big bull. They soon discovered it was a mistake to reveal such things to the *Patron*, who was intent on finding El Dorado.

We had a tough four-day march to the swamp, which was about thirty miles farther along, but it proved to be "game heaven." It even had a small isolated population of dwarf harnessed bushbuck in the middle of the rain forest! But more important was a small mineral lick at the swamp's east end that I decided to convert into a salt lick. We camped an hour away from the swamp to avoid spooking its inhabitants. Each time we went there we found buffalo, bushbuck, female sitatunga, and sometimes elephant peacefully feeding and bathing. Before we left, I wanted to go there to pour some salt in the mineral lick.

The dwarf harnessed bushbuck I observed were only about half the size of the established dwarf bushbuck (*Tragelaphus scriptus scriptus*) of central Cameroon, which I have taken. The central variety are smaller than those in the savanna regions of northern Cameroon, so it seems likely that the ones we found in the swamp are yet another subspecies.

The salt-lick idea wasn't working out as I had hoped. We had to walk north, and the swamp was an hour south. The trackers flatly refused to go there and then return back again. I had already pressed them to walk long and fast to find that swamp, so I didn't want to push my luck. Suddenly I had an idea. I told them I had to perform a magic ceremony in the swamp, and there was no further discussion. Magic ceremonies are not questioned, especially when conducted by someone as protected against witchcraft as I am, the proof being that I seldom need a second bullet.

I sent the heavily loaded crew north and rushed back to the swamp with two Pygmies carrying five pounds of salt.

Usually it would be unthinkable to waste such a precious item, but for the sake of sorcery this was not a problem.

When we arrived at the perimeter of the swamp, I left my Pygmies and crossed to the earth lick. I loosened the earth with a machete in a shallow spot directly at the foot of an eight-foot-high rock wall and poured the salt over the soil, adding water so it would dissolve and penetrate into the ground. I did some hocus pocus, spreading my arms in a praying gesture and bending down for the Pygmies' benefit. Then I moved back toward them, trying not to sink through the bouncing grass stems and half swimming on the swampy ground. When I was almost there I turned back and sang a German hunting song. It was terrible to begin with and even more frightening when sung by one who is completely tone-deaf!

The Baka were deeply impressed, however, and to intensify the effect, I told them to not to tell anyone about this ceremony and that no one should come anywhere near this swamp for at least a year; otherwise someone might be struck dead by the powerful spell! By then I would be able to return to an undisturbed game haven.

The magic apparently worked, because three days later I downed a fine elephant bull. When I returned to "my" swamp the following year, no one had been there and the shallow earth lick had turned into a giant cave with a ceiling so tall that even I could stand upright in it. Of course I did the same thing again and provided the game with more nice salt.

Each time I visited that lick I shot a good bull three days later, so my Baka knew their *Patron* had strong magic and there was no reason to fear a local fetishist! My fame spread so far that on my next visit I had a private volunteer army of ten spear-bearing Pygmies to accompany my regular porters with no expectation of pay except their share of meat.

But back to my current hunt. We move on after a brief rest. My BDU Vietnam Boots are wearing out after their seventh safari. The leather is weak and small holes show. Not a problem since I have a new pair of BDU boots with speed lacing and padded collar back in my luggage train. But for now I hope these will survive our remaining twelve days.

The fast march takes its toll even after days of acclimation and I now have itchy spots just under my ankles—too much friction from the socks. Before the spots turn into blisters, I rest and apply a Band-Aid to the reddish skin. Now the irritated skin is protected and I experience no further trouble. I always keep Band-Aids in my pockets for many purposes, the most important being to cover the muzzle of my rifle to prevent water and dirt from entering the barrel.

The monotonous walk drones on and my mind wanders. Sometimes a vision of sweet cake with a gracious portion of cream crosses my mind, but mostly I think and make plans. Our hectic Western routine does not allow for this kind of personal brainstorming. I think about today's hunting, but my thoughts soon wander toward ways to improve my equipment and techniques. I carry a small handheld computer in my daypack, and at rest pauses I note some of the worthier ideas. I always emerge from the forest with a bunch of new projects, a large diary, the fodder for many faxes, and a "to do" list. The Baka are accustomed to my writing now, but at first they gathered around to stare at the display with its magical row of strange hieroglyphics.

The last segment is very tough. We limp along in the dark and arrive around 8 P.M. at the small river bordering our village. It is deep enough to require a ferryman and a dugout. After loud shouting the ferryman arrives plastered to the gills on palm wine and decides to take advantage of the situation—a white man arriving at night. He demands two-and-a-half times the normal tariff. I offer him a total sum for all my people based on the normal tariff. This is fine with him. Under the influence of alcohol he just hears the big sum without realizing that it's only the regular fare and not his anticipated windfall profit!

My luggage is brought to the County Commissioner's house, where I relax with food and drink. My crew stays in the village with friends and family, and I make small talk with my host until I nearly fall asleep in the armchair.

I retire to the guestroom and gladly strip off my smelly hunting clothes. Tonight there's no shower, just a sponge bath with a bucket of clear water, but even that is marvelously relaxing, as are cookies, sweet wine, and R & R under the mosquito net on my cot. What a difference to be in a dry room again—it's almost surreal. I usually sleep well in the forest, but tonight's rest is heavenly.

The next morning dawns dark and eerie under a yellowish sky. Distant thunder announces torrential rain. I am fortunate to be under a real roof. I did well to press the gang to march fast in the dark last night. Half an hour later the sky opens up, and a terrible thunderstorm sweeps across it. Lying on my cot watching the rain through a door is much better than sitting miserably cold and soaking wet under a quickly opened tarp in the jungle. A big *Parasoleillier* tree in front of the house is heavily hammered; they sometimes fall over during storms, but this one has solid roots. This is a perfect day to relax. Tomorrow we will set out again. A friend is scheduled to arrive today, and perhaps we can find him an elephant in that area my crew has described so often.

The commissioner's family takes good care of me, and I enjoy Madame's delicacies. Chicken and red wine are welcome changes from the past fortnight's monotonous and sometimes meager fare.

At noon a beaten pickup truck arrives, and my hunter friend steps out. He is on schedule, which is not usual in this part of the world and on these terrible track roads. We arrange his gear: I double-check all necessities and weed out unnecessary luxuries, watched intently by my crew.

Early the next morning a small truck takes us to the village from which we will depart. Twenty eager young guys from the huts demand to get recruited, but I refuse even though I would like to replace half my crew. They are   exhausted but desperately want to continue in order to get paid and receive meat.

Many locals say I am hard on my crew, but that is not always true. I keep all members of my original crew in spite of the small loads that require just two-thirds of the porters at most. I also succumb to the old chief who pleads with me to hire one of his offspring as a cook.

The rice was calculated to last for the entire expedition, but we are definitely short. Some provisions disappeared the night we arrived in the village three days ago. In the village of the district headquarters there is a small shop operated by a woman and owned by Al-Hajj Yacoub, the *Fulbe* merchant. The clever guy has his fingers in every pie and is now busy purchasing cocoa. The cocoa in this region is renowned throughout Cameroon because the villagers allow the beans to ferment for two weeks, which adds a great deal to the quality. In other regions the farmers spend just two days fermenting. Here the price for a pound of cocoa beans is 500 francs CFA. (The CFA franc is related to the French franc (FF) at 100 CFA franc for 1 FF. One dollar U.S. equaled 515 CFA francs in 1996.) Cocoa from other regions costs 20 percent less.

The store's provisions are scanty, but amazingly rice is available. I'm able to buy just five pounds, along with some cooking bananas and boiled manioc sticks. Then I discuss the price for a dugout and a boatman (fisherman) to take us across a small river. He will also need to await our return. The fisherman is amenable, so after some glasses of palm wine we agree on a price and start moving.

By now it's noon and we walk fast. Some Bantu porters are still missing but that doesn't matter since we have too many people anyhow. My tracker proceeds moderately; apparently last night's palm wine has not yet evaporated. Also he has not put on his amulet to protect him from attacking animals.

After an hour's walk we enter a forest populated by game. Two blue duiker (*Cephalophus monticola*) and a crested porcupine (*Hystrix*) are hanging from foot snares. Two of them still show signs of life, so I kill them quickly with single strokes of my machete to spare them more suffering. They would not survive even if I loosened the snare. This device causes too much shock and other damage. My natives just look on: They have no feeling for suffering animals or for human suffering apart from their own families and possibly their tribal brothers.

The missing porters join us, and some are still so hung over that they yell at us for daring to leave without them. This emotion is directed at me and I must not tolerate any lessening of my high standing, so I give them a thorough dressing down. That sobers them up a bit, and the quick pace helps the alcohol evaporate.

At 4:30 P.M. my tracker declares that the river we need to cross by dugout is too far away to reach before nightfall, so we camp at a clear creek. This often happens in an area unknown to the *Patron* but well-known to the crew; they make up facts about the region to suit their purpose. The next day I discover that the river was just an hour's walk away. We could easily have reached it before dusk and built camp by nightfall, but the tracker wanted to rest and possibly feared the mosquitoes there, so he just lied to me. This often happens, but usually the excuse for camping early is that there is no water ahead, which is seldom the case in the rain forest. That excuse is hard to buy, so I usually push on and we always find water.

I did the chief of the last village a favor and hired his son Yves as cook. That proves to have been a wise decision, and the evening passes very pleasantly. The next day we take our time and start slowly, but it soon gets exciting as we repeatedly cross fresh elephant trails. My friend is eager to follow them immediately, an idea that my crew cheers. Even my tracker swears there is a decent *kamba* (elephant bull) in the small group. The "fly in the oint-ment," of course, is the *Patron*, who knows that these tracks were made by the undesirable Pygmy variety of elephant.

Naturally, they just want meat close to the village and would be delighted if my inexperienced friend shot the first animal in a hurry because they care nothing about the ivory. Anyhow, he is under time pressure because his schedule is very tight.

I exercise my authority and motion them to continue toward the river. It would be ridiculous to kill one of these Pygmy elephant. Their tusks would barely weigh the 10.4 pounds required by game law. The crew follows me, but there is some grumbling in the file of porters. Same guys from yesterday—there could be more trouble.

An hour later we reach the river. We have to wait again, since the owner of the dugout has not shown up yet. He was supposed to leave his hut yesterday and join us during our march. I'm sure he preferred to pass the night in the village with his wife after taking an advance on his pay from the local seller of palm wine or, more likely, the villager who makes a very fine high-percentage booze.

Today my tracker carries his *gri-gri*—the amulet that protects against animal attacks. It is a string of threaded, dried liana fibers from which hang several smoke-dried pieces of wood of various lengths and a leopard tooth. I try to persuade him to sell it to me, but he categorically re-fuses. I do not give up, and the other Baka try to help me. After a while he becomes unsure and tells me he will think about it. I increase the cash offer and add to it one of my small plastic containers. That offer is very attractive, and he is now wondering whether to accept. He says he will let me know when we return from the hunt. I would love to have this unique piece for my collection because it is quite rare.

My porters find the hidden dugout, and two of them set out to get another boat that was hidden a month ago. We sit and relax in the fisherman's hut; he shows up half an hour later. After another half-hour my two porters come running back quite excitedly. They went downriver and saw two elephant on a small island! They looked closely to see whether the ivory would match the *Patron*'s expectations and tell me that it protruded at least an arm's length from the jaw. This is definitely a worthy bull as another twenty to twenty-five inches are inside the jaw. My friend is fired up and foresees a quick end to his quest for an elephant. I have my reservations, knowing that in the imagination of inexperienced people animals are often much larger than they are in real life.

We quickly enter the dugout with the tracker and float downriver. The bulls are gone, and the oppressive, humid midday air promises a hot, tiring stalk amid clouds of hungry, aggressive horse flies and their nasty brethren—the tsetse—twin pains in the neck. Imagine a flying insect with a cigarette in its mouth that is snuffed out on your skin; that's what a bite feels like. Carefully, to avoid making any noise, we land and leave the boat.

We soon find a sizable elephant wallow filled with thick, brown mud, and the tracks reveal that there really is a huge bull! Slowly we follow the big round footprints on the island through a network of large and small trails. They lead us back and forth as the animals wander, and it is difficult to tell whether they were made before or after the bath. These elephants could be very close. This island is very narrow, perhaps seventy yards across, but about 800 yards long with a small, deep river flowing around it.

Our stalk must be undertaken during the worst time of day. It is close to noon, and we run the very real risk of bumping into standing, dozing bulls. The noon-till-three

Baka tracker, Bosco, poses proudly with this treasure.

Huge boar—red bush pig.

After six weeks in the bush.

*Old yellow-backed duiker came to the call. Its meat was full of filaria worms.
I lost my appetite that day.*

Two days later we leave in Indian file, with all porters heavily bent.

Good Peters duiker.

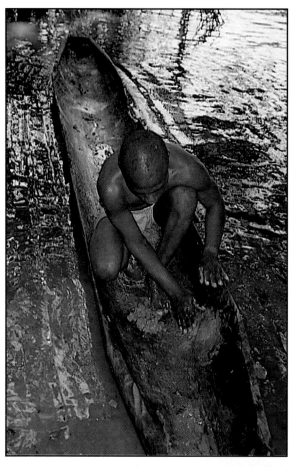

Repairing a dugout.

Relaxing in camp.

Tonight the fires are blazing to smoke the local delicacies. It's four days of tough walking to the next village.

A powerful animal needs a powerful caliber: .460 Weatherby Magnum.

Serving as a porter among my crew was a witch doctor returning home. Notice his nose; it was bitten by a gorilla! He sold me a very beautiful Baka amulet.

Pygmy elephant.

veryone is happy.

The beehive high in this tree presents no problem for the Baka's axes. A liana provides a "security harness."

Tracker Sumano and a nice kob de buffon.

Baka village—typical hut with a good microclimate inside.

If you move, you capsize.

The Baka use burning amber to start a fire. They carry it for hours on the march.

A pair of US jungle boots with tight fitting gaiters. A must to protect oneself from ants and sand washed into the boots while wading for hours in small creeks.

Rose ivory can be beautiful.

The pygmy elephant bull and the buffalo bull quarrel over a mud hole. Each one wants to drink the saline mud.

This buffalo trap is seldom used these days. It is placed near water holes in the savanna in central Cameroon. Once it catches around the buffalo's foot, the hunter can easily follow the spoor left behind.

The western sitatunga—an elusive ghost—is one of the most difficul game animals to bag in the Cameroon.

Left to right: Good buffalo, kob de buffon, *and bongo in central Cameroon—three lucky strikes.*

The trackers and porters are even happier than I, for they know that meat will be abundant in their distant village.

River crossing.

The bark of this rare tree is considered magical by the Baka.

This rose ivory is from a medium bull.

caly, white-bellied
nteater.

ar in the rain forest we
meet two Baka hunters.

A giant is down. I have mixed feelings: I feel sorry but I am also happy.

Forest elephant in a clearing.

afternoon siesta is a common elephant habit. Cautiously we move at a snail's pace and even turn the leaves to prevent treacherous sounds from our clothing. Sometimes we have to kneel and crawl under low-hanging liana and branches—a bad position for a quick shot if a sudden elephant charge should occur. Why couldn't this stalk have taken place when they were distracted and feeding noisily? I really should have pressed my crew to continue yesterday afternoon.

My confidence drops after a while, but my trigger-happy friend wants to search every single thicket on the island. He is still hoping to find the bulls, but I am skeptical. The large tracks are too far apart for a slow-walking elephant, and they slide forward a bit, typical of an escaping bull taking long strides.

We discover that the bulls have exited the island at the far end and crossed deep water toward the shore near the village. We gather for a conference. The tracker thinks we have no chance because the bulls probably got wind of the two porters; the idiots should not have paddled in close to look at the ivory. I disagree. Many times upset elephant will just walk several miles and then stop again to feed, but the tracker points out that they went into a very nasty swamp.

It would be best to collect the crew and walk around the swamp's perimeter, trying to cut the bull's tracks where they leave the impenetrable thorny thicket. It is likely they will recross the river at night and retreat into the vast uninhabited forest on the other side. We hold a war council and decide to gather every one, cross the river today, then continue downriver tomorrow on the opposite side in an attempt to cross a fresh track.

The crew is not pleased by the decision; they wanted a fine camp by the riverbank with lots of fishing while the *patrons* slave away at elephant tracking. But that is not my technique, especially since we do not have much time. I prefer to walk with the crew, keeping a considerable distance behind the tracker and hunters, and camp here and there to avoid unnecessary trips back to base camp.

The tracker and I are deposited with my friend on the opposite riverbank; then the ferryman returns to bring the crew across. That will take at least two hours, and while waiting we can try to call duiker to provide meat for the pot. The locals have promised that this forest is game-rich, but I am suspicious. This whole project sounds very much like "operation meat" to me: Just have the *patron* stumble around near the village to provide meat.

There is little sign of animal activity here. Only blue duiker move through the jungle at our call, and they are either extremely cautious or run swiftly through our limited field of vision. We cannot shoot and give up by evening. To compensate we find a beautiful open forest gallery for our camp with a clear creek running through it. Its isolated trees with thick, long leaves must produce some toxic substance that prevents the usual undergrowth. Instead the dry ground is covered with leaves.

Yves is again busy on my behalf and provides very satisfactory services. After dinner I set up my little Walkman and speakers and play a tape of Pygmy music from Zaire. I am curious how my Baka will react to the sounds of a distantly related tribe from the Ituri forest. Within minutes they are all gathered around and listening intently. From time to time they chat animatedly. They understand most of the songs and are enthusiastic. They want me to play these songs for their wives back in the village.

There is an unexpected side effect from playing the tape. One song is accompanied by rhythmic slapping in the water, and this sound inspires an unidentified animal to come running up and stop abruptly under a bush just two yards away. My flashlight reflects off two greenish eyes, but the animal disappears quickly. This reminds me of one evening when a water chevrotain ran through our camp, passing literally between our legs! It happened so fast and everyone was so surprised that no one grabbed the animal.

Unfortunately this peaceful evening is disturbed by rising tensions between the Bantu and the Baka. The Bantu start the hostility. The Pygmies are very peaceful, and they also carry almost all the heavy luggage! The night is hotter than usual, so I lift the Tyvek cloth hanging over the mosquito net and sleep just fine.

The sky is dark and overcast, but no rain seems imminent, so I organize my crew to set out by 7:45 A.M. Porters with tarps and rope walk close behind me in the event of a sudden downpour. There is constant thundering in the distance, but it's not until around 9:45 A.M. that a rising wind signals imminent rain.

In a minute the rope is tightly secured between two trees and a tentlike structure is set up using the tarp. We sit comfortably on the drums and wait. The sky is dark, and peals of thunder roll over us. It rains cats and dogs, but we are safe under the thin polyethylene tarp and wait it out while nibbling on our provisions.

At 1 P.M. we continue. The Bantu villagers want to rest some more, but since the rain is over, I ask why. I also ask them bluntly whether or not they want to continue. If not, the village is still close—they can reach it today. I advise those who decide to continue that it will be tough going. We are entering a dense and seldom-visited forest and will likely follow elephant tracks as quickly as possible from dawn until dusk. There will be no time to fiddle around.

This was not the response they expected, so they close ranks and think that their solidarity will pressure me. But that does not work. I get tougher and appeal to their conscience to make the right decision. Finally they agree to continue, and we march quickly to make up the lost time.

After three hours we have already crossed the tracks of a medium elephant bull twice—one my friend would be content to get. But I am still hoping for Big Foot from yesterday's stalk on the island.

Again we try to call in a duiker. Hunting is getting better so human pressure is apparently lessening. One bright chestnut Peters duiker (*Cephalophus callipygus*) sneaks close. My pulse accelerates: I want it badly, but the animal remains well hidden. He is visible for a moment, and my reduction cartridge sounds. He is gone in a red streak, and the Pygmies chase after him with their spears. It can't go far after a hit in the chest.

The Baka return after a fruitless chase and my confidence fades. I try to track the animal and retrace my line of fire. *Oh-oh*—a thumb-thick liana was in the bullet's path, but in the dim light was not visible in the scope. The liana is shredded and the duiker is gone. No stew again.

I try in vain several times to get a GPS fix. There are not many satellites above this unexplored equatorial region. If a little war should open up close to this part of the world, there would be more satellites in orbit. I am unsure how deeply into the forest we have progressed. The detailed map shows several creeks, but it's impossible to tell which of them we've passed. Without help from the GPS, a detailed topographic map is of very limited value.

In the openings created by large fallen trees grow special bushy trees called *bapteria*, a soft wood that breaks easily. While clearing a place for a GPS fix, one must take care not to touch them (except momentarily while cutting) because they are home to an especially vicious black ant. The queen hollows out branches of this soft tree and lays eggs inside. The ant colony then occupies the entire tree and ferociously attacks all invaders. The locals call it the "tree of the adulteress." Until recently unfaithful women were tied to these trees to suffer long, painful deaths. Whew—probably not many adulteresses around here!

It's 4:15 P.M. and we face a large, deep swamp. I try another fix in a swampy opening but give up after fifteen minutes. Not enough satellites are visible, and the futile effort just eats up my batteries.

Camp is set up in a dense strip of still-wet vegetation. There is not much space for three level sites (Bantu villagers and the Baka always camp separately), but after a while everything settles down. The shower bag is filled and securely tied to a tree, and the ground below it is covered with large phrynium leaves. Now I can relax.

Yesterday evening I handed out a tin of tuna as a little sauce for my crew; tonight it's a tin of liverwurst. Not much, but it adds a bit of taste to the rice. The cook does his best and is relieved by the fishing success of several porters; I always carry hooks and fishing line in my hunting equipment. Now everyone is smiling over a huge pot full of fish. Good—a delicious change.

My tracker worked extra hard today, cutting our path nearly all day long. He gets a fine perfumed cigar, and I am rewarded with a broad smile in return. Baka love tobacco and hashish. During the rest stops a familiar spicy smell often drifts toward me.

A very pleasant night washes away the tension and relaxes us. The next day we move out early, still in high spirits after having eaten well. We proceed in our chosen   direction often zigzagging to avoid nasty swamps. At noon it gets easier. We encounter large elephant paths and cross fresh elephant tracks several times. Upon examination, the tracker whispers *koumba* (elephant cows) or *likoumba* (small elephants). Where there are many female elephant, a bull will not be too far away. They wander in from time to time to see whether a female has come into heat.

I realize that the villagers are getting restless again. It's difficult to get them moving. Twice we seek shelter from a thunderstorm and quickly set up the tarp, but each time it misses us. Around 2 P.M. we reach the lower part of a large creek. This is the river I have been looking for.

A GPS fix is possible where a bend of a creek allows a view of a small stretch of sky in a 90-degree angle. The reading shows we are farther ahead than I had realized. This creek is the goal I had set in the village, but was not sure we would reach. We have crossed the fresh tracks of several elephant herds plus the two bulls, all moving toward the river. Not bad, and we still have time. I alter the original plan to follow this big creek up to its source in a distant forest, and instead start to circle away from and then back toward the river. I am very tempted to explore that forest, but it must wait for another safari.

A nice camp is quickly built in a relatively open spot. Tonight I have more space and air. I set out to hunt duiker with the tracker and a Pygmy, Edouard. Edouard calls and I am amazed by his superior technique. Both men chuckle, and the tracker admits that his calling is useless compared to Edouard's.

The same tension manifested in camp between the ethnic groups appears in all aspects of daily life. Nowadays the Pygmies are kept like slaves close to the Bantus' villages. They accept all kinds of goods, food, and marijuana from the villagers to whom they are deeply indebted. If a Bantu needs a laborer, he calls a Baka from his hut. There is no need for the Baka to be so dependent; everything grows so easily—even their beloved marijuana.

We enjoy our stalk and chat during stops. The relationship between Edouard and me is good. His calling draws in a Peters duiker. A bullet drops it immediately, and we now have a fifty-pound animal with tender meat. We move on, but can't call in any more duiker. Old Pygmy huts explain why—hunting pressure.

By 5:30 P.M. we are back in camp, and my camp boy brings bad news: There is just enough rice left for four days. Something is wrong. We got additional provisions in the village, so we should have enough food for six more days. It turns out that the very first day the villagers ate all the cooking bananas and manioc that were supposed to provide another two days of food in addition to the rice ration. Now we have a serious problem that will cut short our precious days of hunting.

Yves serves some delicious fat catfish on rice that cheers me up. However, this good cheer doesn't last long because ants invade everywhere. I have to retreat from my nice camp into the humid night, accompanied by derisive laughter from the villagers' camp. That does not please me: "Wait," I say to myself, "He who laughs last laughs best." My Baka, Edouard, steps in and with the camp boy brings embers to build a kind of burning Great Wall of China around my camp. The invading ants are finally beaten back and I pass a good night.

The next morning I ask my camp boy, who also acts as a crew foreman, whether I can reduce the rice ration by one-fourth since everyone has had lots of meat and catfish. That would give us another day of hunting. He readily agrees and hands out the reduced ration. This provokes the final crisis.

The Bantu threaten to desert and walk back to the village. They think I need them since we still have heavy loads to carry. Being pressured makes me even angrier. I explain the situation and ask them three times either to continue or to leave. They refuse to continue, even when I ask them individually. They stick together, confident I will surrender.

OK, that's it. I let them go. We will reallocate the loads among the Baka, who are devoted to me after four safaris and remain loyal. The deserters get a cup of rice for the trip, although it's not necessary. They know a shortcut and will be in another village tonight; we are not that far from civilization. I refuse to pay them now. That will happen after my return, and will they be surprised! My camp boy also has to leave to take care of the ivory from my bull. That might be the reason for their mutiny. He goes back to elephant camp; they stay—unfair.

It takes some time and many heated discussions before they depart. I prepare my equipment and divide it among the remaining six Baka. The tracker, Jacques, carries the rucksack left by the camp boy, and I now have the dubious pleasure of carrying my heavy .460 Weatherby Magnum. Fortunately, it weighs two pounds less than a normal Weatherby and because of the Bullpup design, is carried across the chest, balancing the weight on the shoulders. There is no long barrel sticking out, which would invariably get caught in the maze of vegetation as the bearer bends frequently and twists under branches and liana. The Bullpup hangs conveniently down in front.

It is not so bad once I get accustomed to it. It's like my early safaris when I always carried my own rifle. I stopped that ten years ago when I switched to the powerful .460 Weatherby Magnum and suddenly had a long, heavy, 12-pound smokepole to deal with instead of my relatively lightweight .458 Winchester Magnum.

We are eager to put some terrain between the Bantus and ourselves. They started harassing the Baka and left quite angry. Apparently they had expected another end to their uprising and felt uneasy about the outcome.

We find a "bridge" made by a crooked fallen tree and cross the slippery trunk carefully. Once on the other side, we head downriver. The going is very tough; poor Jacques has to constantly whack a path in very dense undergrowth. After two difficult hours through swamp and dense undergrowth, we cross a nice bull's track headed toward the creek, and an hour later game trails lead us to another bridge formed by a fallen log. But this one is not natural: It's man-made. On the opposite riverbank we rest and eat. The Baka have smoked meat and some rice in phrynium leaves from the morning's ration, and I devour slices of cheese.

The sky is fairly open, so I take a quick fix with the GPS and review our plan. My Baka are hindered by the heavy loads, so we change our route. Instead of the wide circle, we will cut right toward the big river. I still hope to cross the track of Big Foot from the island. Fortunately my friend does not lose confidence and stays relaxed.

We advance slowly, zigzagging through dense bush. An hour later the tracker stiffens and motions for absolute quiet. He perceives some noise and is unsure of its nature. Then he gets excited; it's the typical grunting of pigs. Just my friend and Jacques move on, tiptoeing through the foliage.

The constant low grunting signals the Cameroonian variety of bushpig. The bright red pigs are a good sign of reduced hunting pressure. The Baka love them for their thick layers of highly esteemed, delicious sweet fat and hunt them hard. They stalk and spear them wherever possible.

My friend sneaks up, and after a while the dull sound of a reduction load shot reaches us. Unfortunately, it was very dark in the dense undergrowth, and all he could see was a constantly waving tail. He shot at what he thought was the black rump, but a black stump was in front of the boar, so there is no delicious meat for us. Not only the Baka look disappointed. I also love that sweet juicy fat!

An hour later Jacques stops and listens intently. Now we can hear it too, a whiplike crack some distance away. That's typical of only one animal—the mighty elephant moving through the dense forest and breaking liana here and there.

Have we finally found a bull for my friend? The porters are left behind to find secure retreats high up in solid trees. We load standard cartridges in both .460 Weatherby Magnum rifles and proceed slowly. Anyone who wants to hunt elephant with me must have a .460 Weatherby Magnum; it's life insurance and guarantees getting a wounded bull even under the worst circumstances. These days huge tuskers are rare—a chance may present itself in one out of ten safaris—and it would be stupid to waste the chance of a lifetime by using a caliber suitable for open savanna country, but

145

not dense cover where close encounters and last chance situations are entirely possible. This is not bravado; the .460 is more than enough gun if used properly.

In this dense bush it's extremely rare to get an ideal position for a safe shot on a bull. There's no way to move around silently and try to get the beast into view from another angle. Also, if it's wounded in the evening and has to be followed the next day, it will be lost if it rains overnight. The tracks just vanish, but with one or more .460 Weatherby Magnum bullets in him, he won't go far! I normally do not use more than one or two cartridges on an elephant.

We look for the path of least resistance to get near our prey. Some three-hundred yards later we cross a single track. It is not large, but is deeply imprinted in the soft soil. The three toenails are very clearly marked in front and look slightly deeper. The tracker points to this sign with sparkling eyes and hisses, *"Kamba-semée!"*—probably a huge bull with valuable tusks.

He tears off his clothes and with bare chest and legs dives under obstacles. Now he makes almost no sound because the leaves no longer rub against any textile except his torn shorts. We follow, far clumsier in our ripstop cotton clothing and not nearly as agile.

Fresh droppings stop us. Jacques puts his finger into the horselike but much bigger black balls, then throws some upward triumphantly: Hot, we are close. For another ten minutes we follow the track through some extremely thick Aframomum plants. The elephant pushed a tunnel through these cornlike plants, and we sometimes have to crawl on our knees to follow. This is an awkward position for a charge. The shot would have to be at point-blank range and a real stopper; otherwise the song would be "Bury Me at the River's Bend." We sigh with much relief as the Aframomum ends, wipe the plants' resident ants off our jackets, and continue in an upright position.

146

We are now on a steep, slippery slope, and we slide more than walk. It's not easy to trail this bull; fresh tracks of other elephant crisscross and lead us astray. Suddenly Jacques leaps aside, and we have the bull in full view at ten yards. He has stopped feeding and is aware that something is wrong. His head moves slowly from side to side, and his long trunk swings to and fro while his liplike nose curls in and out. He tries to get the wind of a potential aggressor.

Full of tension, we evaluate the brown-stained yellow tusks. They protrude about thirty inches from the jaw and are of moderate thickness: a medium bull, not too bad nowadays and just right for a beginner. My friend is uncertain. He will have another safari at the end of the season and is in no hurry. He also considers the steep rise in trophy fees, which have just doubled to $2,000 U.S. Finally the bull decides. His trunk curls up above his head like a giant snake, and in one swift motion he takes off at full speed, passing just ten feet to our side. We duck under a branch and run in the other direction. My friend will try for a bigger bull. Well done—I would have made the same decision.

Jacques looks disappointed. He envisioned a huge pile of meat close to his tribe in the village and could care less about tusks and trophy fees. We rejoin the porters and continue toward the river for another hour. It is time to camp. The sloping ground makes it difficult to find a level place, but we finally clear a small spot. My jungle boots look terrible; a large tear gapes at the inside of the right instep. I hope to reach the village, then travel home in my shiny new pair—the only shoes I have now!

Tonight is much cooler, and through the leaves of the canopy a clear sky and shining crescent moon provide a new feeling in the jungle. The locals confirm that a cold spell usually sets in around Christmas.

Next morning we move in the direction of the river island. The porters are tired now; so we had best proceed home. Five-hundred yards after leaving the camp my foot catches in a liana and I fall headlong to the ground. Jacques rushes to help, but I still retain some instinctive falling techniques from Judo training in my student days. The danger in falling is becoming impaled by previously cut or broken trees whose bases stand like spears along the path—nature's "punji sticks." A severe sprain, dislocation, or bone break would be a terrible but relatively manageable mishap.

By 10 A.M. we step back into our camp from three days earlier. Our circle is completed and we encountered only one bull. Where are the two others, and where is Big Foot from the island? He either did not cross the river or remained close to it. Irrelevant questions since we would need a fresh crew to check the area thoroughly. I was not tough enough, and should have changed the entire crew at the beginning; the locals don't have the stamina for long treks, but I didn't have the heart to refuse them work. They wanted the job and the meat, and worked well during the first safari. Most of them are with me for the fifth time.

I am their only hope for earning money to buy clothing, shoes, and pots because their Bantu masters "pay" for Baka services in food, booze, and marijuana. Whenever I arrive in a village to begin a safari I am greeted by approximately fifty stout Pygmies, so I am happy when friends accompany me and I am able to organize their crew for them, employing forty-five or more villagers. It is a big boost to the local economy since their pay is funneled directly into the market for goods. Also, the trophy fees are paid into the chronically deficient local treasury. Do-it-yourself hunting in Cameroon really enhances the value of game.

It is a shame that this paradise will be destroyed in a few years. A new license for professional logging companies has been issued, and they are already cutting large track roads into the pristine forest. Worst of all is a new one-hundred-mile road that will bring the once-remote forests within a one-day march, undoubtedly resulting in heavy poaching. Greed will destroy the last refuge of wild African game forever: Shameful.

The World Bank has set aside a one billion dollar credit to "save" the rain forest, but development projects are also heavily financed. One project involves surveying the elephant populations by cutting long lanes into the forest to check elephant tracks, also providing easy access for poachers. Can't they use fine-tuned military heat sensors to scan for elephant? Such a large target releases a mountain of heat.

Such development maddens me. Traditional foot hunting provides the locals with money, food, and the animal parts needed for their dance ceremonies and other rituals. The best development aid is to give them a life of dignity. They cannot cope with massive development projects over short periods of time and will probably end up living in diseased slums, impoverished and addicted to alcohol and drugs.

These sobering thoughts, among others, make the march on our old well-hewn path go quickly and by late afternoon we are at the river. We pass a fifty-by-one-hundred-yard clearing on a steep slope where underlying rock allows only grass to grow. Now it is yellow and waist-high. We crossed it on our way in, and Jacques told me he frequently encounters buffalo and giant python snakes here on the sun-baked rock. We enter carefully, but the clearing is empty.

Halfway through, my attention is caught by a three-foot-wide trampled path across the grass. This relatively fresh-looking track leads toward a group of bushes down on the riverbank. Jacques pays no attention and is leaving the grassy clearing and entering the forest. I whistle softly to catch his attention and motion toward this promising sign. He shrugs his shoulders and makes the sign for buffalo.

As I look down toward the scrub, I see some tops shaking. There is game! Jacques also sees it, so we sneak down along the track. My gun is ready but I am taken by surprise when a huge crocodile splashes into the river and swims rapidly upstream. There are some rapids and the river is foaming; the reptile is hidden and a shot is impossible. The fifteen-foot-long croc floats upriver for a while near the opposite shore. It would be easy to kill, but we would never be able to recover it. The length and girth of a croc this size must be seen to be appreciated. It is huge!

The return march is tough. My Baka are like horses that smell the stable and want to get home. With lithe grace they duck under every obstacle while I wind my long body through the same barriers, often getting stuck. On top of all this, it's hot and I have the heavy Bullpup dangling across my chest. Is this miserable or what? "Hey," I think, "I could be returning empty-handed" (or empty-tusked)—and that ends my mental complaining!

I breathe a sigh of relief when we reach the fisherman's camp around 5 P.M. and cross the river in his dugout. It's rotten and has only about an inch of freeboard, so we dare not move much. These hollowed-out trees are very unstable. It is rumored that more people are drowned in these forest waterways than are killed by snakes and other animals.

The fisherman is accompanied by his father, an old man with a white beard. It's rare to see old people here since most locals die in middle age. They are Bantus and upset to see us coming out of the forest four days early on account of the deserters. In a long speech the father blames several older Bantu porters: They should have had the wisdom and foresight to consider their responsibility toward their families before staging a mutiny. He has obviously gained the wisdom that comes from years of experience. It's not often the villagers get so much pay for relatively easy work, so why not endure six more days and return with pay and presents? He is especially incensed with one man—a relative of his with three wives and six children—who can never provide a decent life for them.

On the opposite bank we proceed farther into the forest to escape the ever-hungry mosquitoes and find a beautiful spot to camp in a big, leafy, open area. I am tired, but accustomed to the eleven-pound rifle by now. One of my first projects at home will be to lighten this gun; it's an easy job and should have been done by the maker, as ordered. Since its muzzle brake is super-efficient, recoil is no problem. I tested the brake at home with a .375 H&H Magnum, and it reduced the original recoil by 47 percent. Anyhow, in the fever of the chase, one hardly notices recoil.

I record these thoughts in my handheld computer for further evaluation and action back home. On this beautiful night I regret that my safari is coming to an end. One waits so long and anticipates all the adventures; suddenly it's here and gone, but I'm already planning my next safari.

The next day consists of a monotonous march toward the village. At 1:30 P.M. we arrive and relax in the huts. I have my Bullpup on its bipod in front of the hut I am invited to use, when suddenly a car pulls up and I look out the door. Cars are seldom seen out here in the back of beyond.

A young tourist, apparently Japanese, steps out and starts taking photos. As he turns and sees my dangerous-looking bipod-mounted-Bullpup with the big bore and my friend and me looking militaristic in torn and dirty Woodland Tarn jungle fatigues, he pales and jumps back in his car. He is apparently scared to death by the fierce white mercenaries or CIA agents preparing to move into Zaire! The Congolese border is not far away, and Zaire is in an uproar due to heavy combat with the Tutsi rebels.

My last top-priority job is to secure my tracker's talisman. He had promised I could have it once we returned to the village, where he would no longer need it for protection against the forest's beasts, and could start the lengthy task of making a new one and filling it with magic.

When I arrive at his hut he hands over the magic necklace and I examine it with dismay: Only a few of the beautiful ornaments are left because the clever guy removed the best ones. I growl and make it clear that my money and the precious plastic container will pass hands only if the necklace is complete. Very reluctantly, he pulls out the valuable *gri-gri* and adds them to the necklace. It must work, for it has protected him from an angry jungle denizen—me!

Now we both have our treasures, and the necklace will find an honorable place among my trophies. I am especially proud of a beautifully inlaid, ninety-year-old iron spear from central Sahara presented to me by an old Tuareg camel driver I had hired several times to accompany me on hunts for Barbary Sheep—aoudad (*Ammotragus lervia*). He had killed two aoudad with that spear, cornering them after long chases.

I once hired a porter who was an old Baka, very revered by the other Pygmies. He wore a magnificent necklace with all kinds of magical talismans including strips of otter skin. With a great deal of difficulty and the combined help of my Baka crew, I managed to persuade him to sell it to me after three safaris. I presented him with a folding German army knife with an extremely sharp sawblade. Besides its good steel, it was very attractive with the German eagle on the handle. I returned the next year, expecting him to have made another beautiful *gri-gri,* but he simply wore my knife on a string around his neck. It was apparently magical in itself. For these people all objects have their power, and this knife appeared extremely powerful to him.

Today my Baka all receive gifts for performing above and beyond the call of duty. They are eager for future employment and want to know when I will return. I assure them they will be on my next payroll. One stout guy is very happy after being presented with my torn Jungle Boots. I wonder how he will manage my size-twelve boots;

his size-ten feet will have to grow! One man's worn-out trash really is another man's treasure.

A lorry picks us up late in the afternoon, and we arrive at the commissioner's house by nightfall. We are pampered with stewed elephant trunk from my bull, garnished with fresh mushrooms, and Spanish red wine to drink. Life can be so beautiful!

The next evening we return to the Baka village with the commissioner and his wife, and are rewarded with a ceremonial dance. The full moon makes the splendid setup look unreal. A huge drum is brought into the clearing, and the drummer begins a rhythmical beat. Another Baka wanders over and strums soft melodies on the *aiita*, accompanied by melodic songs. He finishes half an hour later, and the drum beats harder and hotter as they get into it.

Suddenly something is moving and clattering about in the bush. It stops and starts again several times, and tension rises. A ghostly silhouette jumps out: It's Alphonse, one of my trackers, wearing a thick raffia apron with tails of colobus monkeys and nutshells that dangle and sway to the movement of his hips. A high ringing sound intrigues me. Where is it coming from?

Around his ankles are thick rows of nutshells that rattle as he stomps on the ground. The big drum beats the rhythm of his ecstatic dance, and the women sing incessantly with high-pitched voices. Alphonse dances toward me, advancing closer and closer in a vaguely threatening manner. Should I retreat? He was always one of my most cheerful and friendly companions. Alphonse cannot want to harm me even while in a trance, so I stand my ground. He stomps up just short of body contact, then retreats slowly with a stern visage.

Later I discover the source of the high metallic ringing noise: Alphonse complains about burning sensations when he takes a leak, so I discreetly lift his apron and find a small bell. It looks like one of our alpine cowbells. How did it get to this Baka village at the edge of the world? For them it's a major treasure.

The ceremony is a fantastic and worthy climax to yet another adventurous safari.

Chapter 5

The Big Threat

The palaver seems endless. Apparently the village chief enjoys his superior position because he talks incessantly about only one subject—his superior position! Our safari seems to be at a dead end after only two long, hot days during which we walked some thirty-three exhausting miles.

Slowly the details become clearer. I want to cross a distant river in a certain place, but there is no fisherman there with a dugout to ferry us across. The only place to cross the river is thirty miles upriver from that location. We just came from there. But the only fisherman there seems to be out of town, and no one knows where he hides his boat. In Africa, a possibility always miraculously surfaces after a while, so I keep smiling and inquiring.

The good citizens of Cameroon like to create panic in a white man in order to profit or to act up for the fun of watching a white man suffer. In this region the local authorities are very reluctant to help white hunters because of the crude behavior of some professional white hunters (PH) around ten years ago.

A Spanish PH refused to allow the villagers to participate in harvesting the meat from elephant kills. His crew was allowed some meat, but the rest was left to rot. What a waste of precious protein, and how unjust to the locals, whose forest it was! He probably feared the never-ending quarrels between himself and the villagers over the best portions, but with some organization and supervision the meat could have been divided fairly and benefited the local population. I always allow everyone to participate.

Suddenly a porter arrives from the village and tells me that the fisherman has returned from a hunting trip. I will find him a mile south in his hut. I thank the chief for his "help," end the futile small talk, and hurry to meet the ferryman.

A stout young man cheerfully greets me in a smoky shed and offers his services for an exorbitant price. I cheerfully refuse. Finally he agrees on twenty dollars to take us to his camp, transfer everyone across the river, and be available at the river three weeks later for the trip back.

We start right away and reach the river in three hours. As usual, things don't work out as I had planned. Most of my Pygmy crew does not show up until late afternoon. They had found a tree with small nuts and happily gathered around, collecting and cutting the hard shells all day long. They long for this tasty food with high nutritional value, but our time to reach a very distant swamp is limited and precious. Their "fast food" stop cost me a lot in wages and time.

It's hard for Africans to understand white people's timetables and tight schedules. I plan nearly everything based on past experience with safaris and travels while they simply walk along and see what the day will bring. Perhaps they are wiser, but right now it drives me crazy to have lost half a day's hunting on the game-rich bank on the other side of the river. They have had nuts but will have no meat in the evening pot.

My equipment is ferried across and I camp alone on the other bank. My little camp boy and tracker look somewhat worried, fearing leopard and other dangers, but I am happy in a quiet jungle camp beautifully situated in an open forest on a high bank. Large game trails promise exciting days ahead. I enjoy a short stalk and hear some antelope fleeing, but don't see any game. What a wonderful respite next to a roaring river without endless chattering in the middle of the night.

Yesterday's scolding worked well: The camp boy took care of breaking camp early, and everyone is ready to go at 7 A.M. We have a good start to our safari into an unknown land.

For years I had tried to reach a distant region far from my usual hunting grounds, because all the big-tusked elephant we shot came from that direction. On the   detailed map I had located a perfect biotype with large swamps, but none of the Pygmies knew anything about that sector. They had never ventured so far, and neither had anyone they knew. It appeared to be totally untouched. In previous years I had been unable to reach it because it was too far for a three-week safari. This time I prepared everything beforehand, chose a different route, and allowed an additional week.

My Baka were advised about my goal well in advance and agreed to follow me. Normally they do not dare to venture into unknown zones. All kind of excuses are brought up, ranging from cannibals to dreadful beasts. With me they have no such fears since I have guided them safely several times with my magical GPS: Our hunting success has always been high, with plenty of delicious meat to feast on. I even have four spear-carrying volunteers who accompany me without pay just to get their share of rice and meat. Now I lead a small horde of sixteen men and two children in a stretched-out single file into unknown country.

Today it's hot, and many small hills with dense vegetation take their toll. Perspiration runs freely and the Baka moan about the steep, slippery slopes, but luck is with us.

As the tracker and I walk silently in front of the crew, a bay duiker suddenly moves across the trail. This is a relatively rare sighting. Usually bay duiker are nocturnal, and seldom respond to a call.

In one swift motion I grab the rifle from my tracker's shoulder, cock the hammer, and fire. The duiker runs off clumsily, and a distant thud indicates it has fallen to the ground. I do not hear this faint sound, but the Baka with their infinitely superior hearing note all such signs and report them. We follow the blood trail, and I bend over to examine a huge male. The bright chestnut body contrasts nicely with the pitch-black dorsal stripe. It's a beautiful animal with large, round horns.

My crew cheers happily about the meat, and it is soon cut up and wrapped in large leaves. The natives do not need plastic bags; nature provides everything, and they still have the skills to utilize these gifts. My tracker, Gilbert, shoulders the rifle and takes the lead again. It's quite handy to have a five-foot Baka in front. I can easily look over his head and, if necessary, grab the rifle that he carries flat over his shoulder.

During my early safaris I proudly carried the big bore myself, but gave it up after buying my first .460 Weatherby— a heavy, unevenly balanced cannon. The heavy barrel pulled the front down, and the sling swivel was fixed too far back. When shoulder-carried, the rifle invariably slid backward. I resolved that problem by fixing a better balanced swivel stud on the barrel. Still I prefer to have it carried by someone else in front. It's difficult for me to bend and twist under tangled twigs, roots, and liana with a heavy, unbalanced rifle that gets stuck in the vegetation.

Gilbert is very skilled at finding his way. He instinctively seeks out the path of least resistance through nearly solid vegetation. His bare feet enable him to feel the flat ground where elephant have walked and follow the path.

There are no major branches across an elephant trail; they are cleared by the ambling steamrollers. We more or less follow a large elephant path in our hike along the waterway.

The large stream is bordered by steep hills, and all the game use the same trails along its bank—the paths of least resistance. Gilbert does not like to cut vegetation, preferring to duck under the obstacles, and I have no choice but to follow. The difference is that at five feet he bends easily and at six feet five I am on my knees. This painful exercise results in a quiet stalk and has resulted in several hunting successes, so I endure.

Here and there fresh elephant tracks double our pulse rates and we follow excitedly to the next muddy ground to check the size, but they are always from small animals. At noon we get a nice surprise as we approach some large rapids. For some distance now we have heard the water roaring. This conceals our noise, and we are suddenly in the middle of some bushpigs. The bright red animals are busy turning over leaves on the ground searching for worms, beetles, and ants.

I get a good hit on one animal with a 185-grain jacketed hollowpoint bullet from a "reduction" shell; he collapses and drags himself into some cover. The Pygmies move in eagerly with spears and dispatch the red boar, causing it to die quickly with loud shrieks. This incites the other pigs to rush back to help the wounded animal—typical behavior. Is it instinctual to defend our own kind from danger? They mill around, grunting, in the cover of huge phrynium leaves until they get wind of us and disappear with a series of characteristic snorts.

We are lucky to have downed the boar. Bushpigs are very hardy animals and, if not mortally wounded, can take off and travel long distances. It is not just my Baka who love the fat meat! Shortly a nice fire is burning, and the liver is roasted for lunch. The pig is divided up with its skin intact, and everyone happily wraps some fatty parts in huge leaves. The "take out" bags are ready! It will be a good dinner and an animated evening.

My decision to try to reach these swamps seems to have been a good one. We are still a considerable distance away, but already game is abundant. An hour later we have a close encounter with a huge gorilla. He sits in a tree and chews peacefully on some nuts. The old silverback male is alone, apparently an outcast. When he becomes aware of us he jumps down and escapes, yelling wildly. He smells very badly, especially his droppings—round, green balls like horse droppings. It's rare to find big males in trees because they usually feed on the ground. Human presence seems minimal here; only a few old cuttings testify to long-ago visits.

By 3 P.M. Gilbert tells us we are at a creek area named Lakya. There should be a swamp nearby, and he smells elephant, too. He thinks we should camp here and look around. Nothing doing! This sounds like operation "camp early, walk the boss around, and come back in the evening to a cozy fire with nicely roasted fat pig meat."

After several safaris I know my tracker. He can be a son-of-a-bitch who likes to impose plans best suited to Sir Gilbert, not necessarily those that would ensure the success of the safari. I just shake my head and make the crew walk for another hour under constantly rolling thunder. Rain threatens and we finally camp near some rapids. Since rain is very likely, I tie a rope between two trees and fix the thin plastic tarp across it. Now it can pour.

As I begin to skin the precious skull of my huge duiker to preserve it and the rest of its bones for my mammal collection, my camp boy cheers me up: "*Patron*, you must be tired. Relax and leave this task to me. I am still young and can work."

Hmmm, does that mean I am an old dodderer or that he is an eager helper? I decide on the latter and happily relax. I have to update my diary, so I pull my well-protected palmtop computer out of a tightly sealed waterproof drum and write.

Dinner is absolutely delicious. We all enjoy the tasty meat, and the rice absorbs the abundant fat nicely—a nightmare to a cholesterol-conscious physician. Is bushpig the good or the bad cholesterol? Tonight I don't care as I gorge on the tender morsels. Yum!

The air is warm under the tarp. I don't need any covering or extra clothing at night because the mosquito net does an excellent job of protecting me from angrily humming nocturnal visitors. I place a candle lantern with two reflecting mirrors outside my bivouac and continue reading and writing. It's neat to watch the flying nasties kamikaze into the flames. Fortunately the thunder vanishes and no rain disturbs the night. The distant roaring of the rapids lull me into a deep and pleasant sleep.

I am rudely awakened at 5 A.M. by the ringing of my alarm clock. What a jolt on a lovely morning in the rain forest! But it's vital for the sake of my goal. I doubt Hemingway's claim that he never missed an African sunrise because its impossible to witness a sunrise in the rain forest. Still, "the early bird catches the worm."

I have to press the Baka to get them going. They love to sleep in, and it takes time to boil rice; it's not their favorite task. My camp boy brings me hot water. I prepare a nice cappuccino and use the rest of the water to shave. I usually tackle my stubble every fourth day.

Once the Baka are ready, I gather the trackers and lead personnel around me and open the map. As always, it is a mystery with seven seals to them, but they like the ceremony and are always deeply impressed. I take a fix with my Scout GPS and am quite content. We've made more progress than anticipated.

Our goal is still far away, and I am not convinced we can cross thirty miles of hilly jungle in the time frame allowed by provisions and my vacation time. The map shows that across the hills is a higher valley, which turns in a large loop and has no drainage for the accumulated water so swamps with thorny raffia palm thickets occur for some ten miles. It should be a game paradise.

No Baka in my crew has ever been there, and no one in the last few villages had any information about these swamps. Perhaps they really are a last white spot on the map. I promise everyone a bonus of five days' pay if we reach this El Dorado. It should be easy if the large elephant trails continue. Today we will leave the river and cut across the hills to avoid a large riverine loop.

By 7:45 A.M. the long file of sixteen Africans sets out, lance blades glittering. I make sure no one with a spear walks in front of me. During these long walks one often thinks deeply. While monotonously placing one foot in front of another and thinking of other things, it's just too easy to get the wrong end of the spear in your face. Miles from anywhere, one cannot be overcautious. Also, God only knows what lovely microbes live on those blades!

The luggage is transported in wooden frames carried by porters with the help of strips of bark positioned across their foreheads. No wonder the Baka have   special skull shapes: Even the children carry their loads with forehead bands. Everyone still has some meat in leaf baskets dangling at their sides.

Two hours later we hear the typical cawing sound of herons (*Bubulcus iris*). We must be near a grassy swamp opening where these birds usually gather. The tracker moves ahead very carefully; my rifle is cocked, and I am ready to switch off the safety. Soon a beautiful scene unfolds.

To the right stretches a 100-by-200-yard-long grassy flat, and ahead a large 30-foot wallow is dug out under a big tree, filled with light, liquid-brown mud. Around its edges the fresh tracks of elephant, buffalo, pig, and duiker attest to the spot's magnetic attraction for all game. Animals rid themselves of lice and ticks by taking mud baths. Even a large python (*Python sebae*) visited last night. We try to follow its track but have to abandon it on the dry ground farther on. Python is near the top of a Baka's wish list—much "magic" in the ingestion of its flesh.

My horde is enthusiastic about a special tall herb and spreads out to collect it. It smells like lemon balm, but for them it has intoxicating properties. They tell me they used this herb in the old days, before the Bantu villagers sold them marijuana.

Everyone carries a large supply of the herb as we continue along the river on elephant trails. After an hour we cross a clear creek, and Gilbert wants to follow it uphill. He has never been here but insists it is Lakya creek. A GPS fix and a search of the map coordinates show that Lakya is still ahead and this creek soon ends at a steep slope, so we continue along the river.

By noon we reach a dry wallow and take a break. When Gilbert disappears for some urgent call of nature, the second tracker, Jean Bosco (a porter on my first hunt in Cameroon), hurriedly motions us uphill. Competition! Gilbert reappears and protests loudly. He leads his followers in the original direction. Just as we get to the top of the hill, two excited Pygmies sent by Gilbert arrive and claim to have seen the fresh tracks of two good elephant bulls.

Bosco takes a shortcut, but, as so often happens, his way turns out to be a poor choice. It ends in a precipice, so we have to climb back up the hill. The heavily loaded porters work hard for their pay on this expedition. Finally, soaked with perspiration, we reach Gilbert forty-five minutes later to discover that he has exaggerated again; the two tuskers are small Pygmy elephant with minute tusks. Gilbert is not reliable about sizing up elephant; he just wants to eat elephant meat and cares nothing about trophies.

A small opening in the canopy allows a GPS fix. We are only four miles from our last camp and lost a good hour following these elephant. Now it's time to cross the hills. The elephant seem to do the same—a heavily beaten trail leads uphill to a picturesque pass and into a small creek that has cut a deep canyon into the precipitous slope. Rocks line the steep escarpment, and twisted trees and big ferns form an unreal countryside.

The three- to five-yard-wide creek carries clear water over small gravel, and is littered with elephant droppings. This is a main elephant trail, but the last jumbos to walk it were small ones, judging by the size of the tracks and droppings.

Suddenly Gilbert freezes as he goes around a bend and motions for me to join him. He makes the typical elephant gesture, pressing his hands, forefinger thrust outward, at the sides of his upper lip to indicate long, forward-swept tusks. I quickly eject the reduction shell and load a regular solid, then peer around the bend. It is just a small Pygmy elephant with toothpicklike tusks. Gilbert should have realized that at first glance, but he just sees the "inner value"—the pile of precious meat and fat. This tracker is worthless.

I want to make the elephant run off since he blocks our passage through this steep canyon, so I cough and rattle metal. The stupid elephant trumpets loudly, turns around, and charges! Oh-oh, the last thing I want to do is kill such a small one in self-defense. My horde has already scampered up the steep slopes and sits there safe in some treetops, contemplating the show below.

I decide it would be wise to join them and start climbing frantically, but in vain. The slippery clay does not provide an easy escape route, so I turn around and face the charge. Fortunately the elephant thinks it wiser to retreat and rushes up a canyon to the left. Now I have time to tackle the climb and manage to haul myself upward by clinging to roots and liana.

When I am safely up the slope on a small plateau and relaxing, the stupid elephant comes rushing in again through the bushes. He apparently feels well concealed in the forest and secure enough on level ground to attack humans who intrude on his territory. It is frightening to hear a beast weighing several tons crashing through dense undergrowth straight toward me, especially when visibility is just twenty feet. He may be a Pygmy, but not a foe to mess with.

Now I have to stop his charge: I fire a shot in the air, reload rapidly, and know that i may have to kill him with the next bullet, or be trampled or gored. This is why I do not take anyone elephant hunting who has a caliber inferior to the .460 Weatherby.

The deafening 160-dB noise of the .460 rolls through the bush, and for a moment I can't hear anything. Will he keep coming? The trees no longer move; then I hear him moving off. Whew, that was tight!

My tracker rushes down from his perch and sets out to follow the elephant, smiling happily. I stop him and ask what he is doing.

"Oh, I am going to see where the elephant falls. You always kill with one or two bullets."

"No." I explain that I shot in the air to scare it off, "It isn't hurt."

This is not the answer my tracker was looking for. His broad smile quickly fades along with his vision of happy days around a steaming pot and piles of elephant meat on the smoking table. Everyone looks at me reproachfully. This white man is hard to understand: He wastes a precious cartridge *and* lets a mountain of meat go.

We continue our descent to the creek and thirty minutes later encounter several small elephant. Fortunately, they are not in an aggressive mood and disappear silently. It's amazing how noiselessly these huge animals can move.

At 5:30 P.M. we are still in steep terrain, but manage to find a small level spot to camp. It's not easy to clear a space for my cot, but Ferdinand and my camp boy eventually manage. I enjoy a refreshing shower, clean my rifle, and hit the sack early to the crickets' loud song. It was a tough day with a lot of climbing under hot and humid conditions. I am getting older.

I sleep soundly until a dull thunder wakens me. I quickly jump out of my cot, dress in daytime clothing, store my night clothes and other gear in watertight barrels, tighten the rope, and motion the Baka to pull the tarp across it. We just manage to finish when a heavy rain starts. The water falls like thick ropes and the drops bounce high off the muddy ground. We quickly get dirty up to our thighs. Half an hour later the rain ends, and a clear sky peeps through openings in the canopy. Huge drops still trickle from wet leaves, so we wait, eat breakfast, then leave at 7:30 A.M.

The slope becomes less steep, and after ten minutes on the large elephant path we are at the bank of the river we left yesterday to avoid the large loop. The GPS confirms that the shortcut saved us a day's walk.

Still, it's another tough day. Twice we have to climb very steep slopes because rocks block the trail at the riverbank. Game trails always seem to lead right to the summit, then follow well-beaten paths along the ridge. By 11 A.M. we reach the first of three major rapids blocking all dugout traffic. We have lunch and relax. Every Baka produces a delicious piece of smoked ham and enjoys it. Me, too. I hope we find bushpigs again! To some people, P.E.T.A. means People for the Ethical Treatment of Animals. To me it means People Eating Tasty Animals!

By noon we are moving again in tough, steep terrain. Shortly before 2 P.M. the porters want to camp close to a clear creek, mainly because of Gilbert; he sees a lot of small fish and wants his kid to catch them for a feast. Too bad for him: Big boss has other plans, so they all have to keep moving for another hour. At 3 P.M. we reach a larger creek and camp in a nice open forest glade.

I am not too happy with my spot, which is very close to a large snake's hole. A python slept in a five-by-four-foot cave under a big tree's roots last night. Will it come back? Not a pleasant thought while falling asleep. My Baka said it wasn't dangerous since the smoke would frighten the snake away, but they camp farther away and put me next to the cave. Maybe I should push them less tomorrow—if there is one!

We set out half an hour later to hunt duiker. It does not look promising. There are no duiker tracks, only fresh elephant spoor. On three other safaris, I shot good bulls on afternoon duiker hunts close to camp.

I am tired by the long day's walk, and now I have to bend and crawl through the undergrowth on hands and knees. To avoid making noise, Gilbert refuses to cut a single liana, or is he punishing me for making him work longer than he wanted to?

Twice we call blue duiker in, but the first one just runs by and I miss the second head-on at forty yards. Bad luck. The second tracker, Bosco, declares very seriously that it's no good to hunt duiker today because it's Sunday! I guess he got indoctrinated at a missionary school. "No Hunting on Sunday" is the law in North Carolina, according to my knife-maker friend Rob Charlton, but not here, thank goodness!

The string of bad luck has reached camp, also. When I get back, my little camp boy looks like a beaten dog awaiting a scolding. They filled the precious shower bag too full, and when it was hung, the rope snapped. The bag bounced on the ground and was torn in half. They repaired it with straps of tire inner tube, but now it holds just half as much. Three gallons of water is still enough for a shower, so I just laugh it off.

Before leaving the city, I always buy about ten 2-inch-wide by 7-foot-long straps of inner tube. The porters love it.

It speeds up the morning packing and helps in repairing all kinds of equipment.

For dinner I am served dry rice and upgrade it with raisins, dried fruit, and sugar—tastes good. But the best is a big spoonful of my special mixture of Bavarian butter and honey. If butter is mixed with honey it will not get rancid because the honey acts as a preservative. Before antibiotics, honey was widely used as a medication for rashes and infected skin wounds. The sugar in the honey dries them out so they heal quickly.

The next morning we follow the beaten track along the river until about 10 A.M., when the narrow waterway widens and turns away from our direction of travel. Now comes the moment of truth: From the map I figured we should strike out across the forest from here to reach the mystic swamps. For most of the remaining distance we can hike on the ridges of some hills. The other possibility would be to follow the river until we find the swamp's drainage, then try to follow it upstream. The latter is chancy and possibly time-consuming since the undergrowth along the drainage might be extremely thick. I finally decide to cut straight across, using the lightly wooded ridges as much as possible.

First we ascend a steep hill to the crest. My guess proves right: There is a large, easy-to-walk game trail. We step on duiker droppings repeatedly and try to call them in, but all efforts fail. The only creature we see is a black snake curling around a hole twenty feet up a huge tree. It is not the usual thick, twelve-foot-long black snake, but even this young six-foot reptile is fast and disappears quickly. These black snakes are probably not the "tree cobra" (*Thrasops jacksonii*), described as reaching a maximum of seven feet long. Also, the tree cobra has a thin tail, while these have short, thick tails. Thick or thin, I stay out of their way!

By noon we are in a narrow valley with luxurious vegetation. Exhausted, we have our midday break at a small crystal-clear creek. A horde of greater white-nosed monkeys (*Cercupitheaus nictians*) move close in the treetops to feed on nuts, and I accede to the porters' pleas to kill a big one for their pots.

The Baka use their break to swarm into the forest. Soon one yells triumphantly and calls the others for help. He has found a beehive of *dandu*—dark brown, slightly bitter-tasting liquid honey from small, stingerless bees. They nest in particular trees that often develop hollowed branches. My friends collect a big pot of the precious liquid. I get my share and save some in a small PET bottle. This will be delicious with the dinner rice.

Closely resembling the *dandu* is *molingi* or *mupalé*, another liquid variety of honey from small black flies that also nest in trees. Both beehives are often revealed by a small black trail from the minute entrance in a dent on the trunk.

Ntibà is a black honey from small, stingerless bees. Another very special honey is *moko*, found below ground. One has to dig down three feet to find a round form shaped like a hornet's nest with an interior honeycomb structure containing liquid honey from small flies. The "real" honey most familiar to me is called *poki*, and its beehives are found above the ground in hollow trees.

The small creek provides an easy path, so we follow it until we hear the rushing sounds of a little waterfall where the creek enters a crystal-clear river in a dark canyon. A GPS fix shows that we are in the next river system toward our destination. The small river is shallow and provides many hours of excellent walking—at least for me. The Baka, especially Gilbert, do not like it very much. The water feels cold on the bare feet of heat-spoiled Africans.

It is amazing how the Pygmies can walk barefoot in such a hostile environment. A variety of thorns of all sizes are everywhere, and from time to time my tracker stops to extract one from his foot—a hair-raising sight! White people with soft feet could not do ten yards. The natives have developed very thick skin. What a contrast: "Civilized" people need to develop a "thick skin" to manage in our modern society while the Baka need thick skin only on their feet!

The scenery in this canyon is breathtaking. Long vines hang from crooked trees, and small sandbanks are covered with a broad variety of plants. We advance quickly. Sometimes we have to climb the steep walls to avoid deepwater holes among the rocks—ideal places to hook catfish. In one place we come across a sapling chopped down around eight years ago. A fisherman probably came up from the bigger river, which can be crossed on foot during the dry season, even in its wider section.

At 2:30 P.M. Gilbert finds another beehive and wants to camp there to chop down the tree. This is fine with me, but he can make do with half the crew. The rest have to continue with me to camp farther on.

We have encountered elephant tracks all day long, but now we find a really big footprint; unfortunately it's a week old. We finally enter an open forest and set up camp on a slope with two level spots. When all the work is finished, the other half of the crew shows up. Apparently there was not much honey in the tree, but that may or may not be true.

The ever-suspicious Gilbert, who does not want to bypass a beehive, may be part of the reason for the tale of little honey. He would happily eat it all himself unless obliged to share it with others. His character is different from that of the other Baka. They are always content and quiet, share all food, and help each other. Gilbert is frequently quarrelsome and insulting to the others; he always tries to get the best for himself.

Tonight he declares himself worn out, so I leave for the evening hunt with Bosco, Salomon, and two porters.

I am not keen on hunting with Bosco after a hard day. He is as flexible as a snake and winds under and around all obstacles effortlessly, while I invariably get caught and end up cursing in a tangle of liana. I happily let him carry the heavy Weatherby. With that gun it would be much worse for me and, as a beneficial side effect, it slows Bosco down!

Here and there he stops to listen for sounds of game, especially elephant. The Baka's hearing is incredibly acute. Tonight Salomon calls duiker, allowing the screaming call to artistically rise and fall.

The duiker either approach carefully and circle until they get our wind—a characteristic foot stomping revealing their presence—or they run through such close cover that no shot is possible. My Baka are hungry and motion me on and on. Finally I see a red spot in a small opening at thirty yards and down a nice animal.

The other game seem to ignore the dull thud of the reduction shell that resembles the sound of a falling tree. I could shoot several times without disturbing other game. Once I even killed a red bushpig while a huge elephant bull continued to feed fifty yards away.

During my safari in December 1996, a friend was following a promising elephant track when a sitatunga suddenly rose out of some bushes in a swamp. To hunt a forest sitatunga is extraordinarily difficult, and the chances of bagging one are very low. As a measure of difficulty, it is much easier to get a decent elephant!

My friend shot the sitatunga with a reduction shell, and after the compulsory photos of such a rare prey, continued following the elephant's track. In the next creek bottom less than 600 yards away, he found an old bull with a tremendous set of tusks peacefully feeding. It was nearly black and the tusks weighed 44 and 45 pounds, a tremendous set for a forest elephant. Needless to say, he now praises reduction shells.

By 5:30 P.M. we are back in camp. My clothes are soaked with perspiration and smelly. If tomorrow is hot and sunny, we will make our noon stop at a creek and I will wash them. For now I immerse my head in the clear, cool water of the creek, then proceed with my evening tasks—reloading the reduction shells and cleaning my rifle—before enjoying German sausage with lots of fresh garlic.

I am safely under the mosquito net relaxing on my cot when it suddenly starts to tremble. A deep humming sound increases and decreases. An earthquake in the rain forest of Cameroon! My garrulous dwarfs are suddenly completely silent. It is a while before they start talking again, this time in subdued voices.

They ask me about the phenomenon because they think it is caused by the white man's magic. How in heaven can I explain plate tectonics? I try for a while, but it just causes more confusion. My Baka finally conclude that there is even more magic on earth than they ever imagined.

Dinner comes from a four-star restaurant: The porters fished in a deep pool and caught enough small catfish to fill a big pot. It is delicious on rice. Soaked dry fruit, raisins, and my butter-honey mixture on rice make a luscious dessert.

The next morning the always-friendly Bosco has parental problems. He has brought his twelve-year-old son along to instruct him in big-game hunting, and to ensure that he will have a servant. Metul refuses to bring him water from the creek and runs off into the bush. Daddy is furious and yells. He suspects Metul of having smoked some of the wild dope they collected in the swamp. So, Baka have troubles with kids, too—a consolation of sorts. I wonder, what is their equivalent of "Just Say No"?

Everyone is keenly interested in the conflict, and this infuriates Bosco even more. Finally Metul is brought back by another Baka and walks at the rear under his dad's reproachful glances.

I gather the crew around me and explain today's plan with the help of the map. First we will follow the creek up to a large bend; the time needed to reach this spot is difficult to predict. The canopy around camp is so dense that I cannot get a GPS fix, so I'm just guessing at where we are. After about two hours of hiking in the creek we should reach a fork, where we will follow the right waterway. After about an hour we should come to another tiny fork. From there we will climb a hill and continue straight ahead for some hours on a plateau until we descend into the next drainage. By then it will be time to camp. All sixteen Baka watch me with big, awestruck eyes. No one has ever been there before, and I am telling them how the area is structured!

Our departure is delayed by Bosco's family problem, but we manage to leave by 9 A.M., walking in the creek. Gilbert is upset and wants to climb the steep slopes, but has to follow my orders. No suffering on slopes or bending under branches. It is also easier for the porters in the creek bed. The old tracker carries a piece of burning wood to warm him in the chilly morning air. I do not like it much since he trails a long line of stinking smoke and I have to walk in it, as he must be well aware!

As I stroll in the ankle-deep water, I see a sudden movement in the grass of a sandbank and grab the rifle. Before I am able to cock it, a huge "giant lizard" (*Varanus niloticus*) weighing at least eight pounds scampers off into the forest. Our search for it is in vain. These very tasty reptiles are as fast as greased lightning. It happens again half an hour later. The lizards are common here, an indication that no hungry Africans are around. Reaching a maximum length of around seven feet, they are aptly named.

At noon we reach the big creek bend shown on the map, and an open sky allows a GPS fix that confirms my guess. We have a nice rest in a beautiful setting—long weeds hang from the branches, leafy parasitic plants grow on bizarrely bent trees, and the gravel in the creek glitters as if dipped in gold dust. These minerals are worthless, but gold and diamonds occur in this zone. Many jungle creeks contain precious deposits, and sometimes Baka find valuable stones. I regularly turn gravel over but so far without luck, discovering only ordinary quartz. However, in central Cameroon I once hit a small bonanza and gathered three ounces of gold.

Now it is time to tackle the ordinary tasks and wash my smelly clothes. They will dry enough in the sun to wear afterward. In this hot climate it is agreeable to wear cool, moist garments and they dry quickly.

I am confident we will reach the mysterious swamps. We are making good progress, and the crew is still in high spirits. Without these "old hands" who have worked for me for three to five safaris, I would have no chance.

We splash upriver through the creek all day long, passing marvelous scenery that is much more fascinating than the monotonous rain forest. I am glad to be wearing my British army gaiters, simple 4-inch-long strips of loden cloth wrapped around boots and trousers. They effectively keep out the fine sand particles that end up in one's socks and rub the skin raw. They also keep out ants, which we encounter in large numbers on the trails. Silently I thank my friend Achim for this valuable tip.

A muddy streak trailing our way in the clear water reveals the presence of game upriver. We motion the porters to stop, and they follow quietly at a distance while Gilbert and I stalk carefully ahead. After some one hundred yards a black patch of skin in the undergrowth and familiar grunts betray a giant forest hog, another rare trophy. The .45 caliber JHP XTP bullet fired at his shoulder throws the boar to the ground. It strikes the spine, which lies lower in pigs than in other game.

I am overjoyed about this exceptional animal, but the crew is not as delighted. They would much rather roast a fat bushpig than a meager giant forest hog. The old male's tusks are fine, but there is a big difference between the "monster" boars of Kenya and the West African subspecies that is much smaller. This boar looks funny with his large, flat, flexible nose and long thin hairs that stand upright from his skin. I save the jaws and the small tail as trophies.

The Baka cut the boar into pieces and pack it while I move ahead and take a GPS fix. We are almost at the fork, and now the GPS shows its usefulness. On the map the fork is very prominent and both branches of the creek are of equal width, but in reality the right branch is just a trickle and quite hidden in the undergrowth. I certainly would not have recognized it as our turnoff point without the GPS unit.

Unfortunately I've lost my compass, just a small stick-on model but it was sufficient for orientation and basic direction. It was convenient to wear it inside a breast pocket and occasionally glance at it to check direction. No big loss—I have another small compass on my wristwatch and a larger one in my luggage.

Our little creek leads us steadily uphill. By 3 P.M. we reach the last fork and leave the creek to climb straight uphill. Gilbert turns his head, and with a confident look in his brown eyes asks whether we will find water ahead. Their faith gives me an eerie feeling. What if the GPS fails or all compasses are lost?

I assure Gilbert that we are almost on the top of the hill and there will be water on the other side. They move on without hesitation, and soon we walk atop the plateau. I forgot to fill my water bottle earlier but during a rest the Baka supply me with fresh, clean water by tapping a special liana with a lightly twisted bark. They cut an eight-inch-thick piece about an arm's length long, and as soon as the other end is also cut, a trickle of clear water flows out of a spongy layer under the bark.

Once I shot an elephant in an extremely dry region and wondered how we could camp near the kill. My crew from the northern Baka tribe just laughed and showed me these liana. Within minutes they had a fire going, a pot full of water gathered from severed pieces of liana, the elephant liver removed, and a nice lunch cooking.

Another variety of liana provides caoutchouc, a thick, gluey, milky substance that sticks to clothing and stains it black after it dries. Even in this remote zone, now devoid of human habitation, there are man-made scars in the bark of these caoutchouc or "rubber" trees (*Funtumia elastica*). The spiraling cuts date back eighty years when pressure to collect the precious sap must have been high. Little dwellings are scattered throughout the forest, and an old colonial map shows a major path going through this area. A valuable commodity for use in tires, rubber (*Hevea brasiliensis*) is now harvested on plantations in Asia.

We cross many elephant trails and two huge wallows with bright red-ochre mud. The surrounding trees are covered very high up with the clay, since elephants rub their hides on them. Some of the clay is still wet, meaning elephant were here around noon. The height of the clay indicates the size of the animals, and these visitors were small.

By 4 P.M. we reach a roaring creek on the descending slope and camp on a small, more or less even spot where two slopes meet. Quick and efficient work by the camp boys clears a space, but the area is small, so we all have to camp together. The landscape is picturesque, since the creek has to find its way through craggy rocks that are quite rare in the rain forest.

After today I enjoy my crew's full confidence. All my predictions have proven true, and even my rough timetable panned out! The odds are high that we will reach our goal within two days.

176

The repaired shower is already hung, so I change my daily routine and shower before dusk. Punishment follows promptly. The tiny *mut mut* mosquitoes feast heavily on my legs, and the bites itch terribly. Still I'm somewhat consoled by another delicious dinner featuring the pig's heart with sweet fat on rice.

The roaring creek drowns the chatting of my crew and mixes nicely with the cricket's song. I sleep well until 5 A.M. when another storm brews. As I jump out of my cot, a small click catches my attention: The compass on my wristwatch slipped out of its plastic base and dropped onto my rifle. Lucky again. In the mud I would not have heard it. Later I'll glue it back onto its base. This seems to be a bad time for compasses. Perhaps I should ask my little friends to put some magic herb on the fire.

The camp boy quickly pulls the tarp over the rope while I don my clothes and pack my equipment. The rain is light and steady, ideal for hunting and promising a cool day. It is most welcome since the map shows some steep slopes and high hills to climb today; they surround our goal—the swamps.

At 9 A.M. we continue due east in the creek. Gilbert hates the cold water and walks slowly. He is weak today because he ate too much meat and fat last night and is stricken with diarrhea. The "big shots" among the Baka greedily hogged all the fat, and the younger ones, who did not get much, are now grinning over their discomfort.

We leave our creek at a beautiful waterfall and begin to climb, following a wide elephant trail that is almost a highway. A huge fallen tree has opened up the canopy sufficiently to provide an easy GPS fix that confirms we are exactly on course.

By 11:30 A.M. we cross the fresh track of a lone bull elephant. While the two trackers follow it, we linger under a large tree where my porters detect a hole with a potentially large beehive. Half an hour later the trackers return, and one assures me that the bull will have nice tusks. Knowing his craving for elephant meat and fat, I am skeptical but have to check it out. I foresee problems with those waiting at the beehive. They will not want to share any honey with the "big shots," who did not pass on much pig fat yesterday. Always conflicts and problems!

We follow and push hard on the bull for about two miles, but I find its track too small. Bosco also thinks it's only what the Baka call a *mossemée* or young bull. This bull is heading somewhere and walks at a considerable speed. If he would start feeding we could close in very quickly, but at its hurried pace it would take us one or two days to catch up—not worth it judging by these small tracks.

We give up and wait for the crew, who are supposed to follow promptly. As feared, this turns out to be another mistake; it takes ages for them to arrive, and judging by their contented expressions they have fed well on honey. Felling the huge tree to cut out the beehive was time-consuming, and of course they tell us the honeycomb was almost empty so there is nothing to share.

The tracker becomes very angry, and a rapid discussion flares up. He yells for quite a while, but the youngsters don't take him seriously, which makes him even angrier! Sometimes I think it would save a lot of time to take a load of honey as part of a safari's provisions and hand some out on special occasions. On the other hand, the Baka badly need the vitamins and enzymes in this delicious forest honey.

My GPS fix reveals that we have only six miles to go to reach the swamps. We have already covered fifty miles as the crow flies. Not bad. Time passed quickly today. It is already 3:20 P.M., almost time to camp since the routine takes about an hour and the crew has to gather firewood. But we should cover a little more distance, so we hike across the hill. The tracker is so angry that he wants to walk the crew till nightfall, but that would exhaust them too much.

At a small creek I begin looking for a nice spot to camp, and by 5 P.M. I call a halt. Now it's time to enjoy the scenery and the sounds of crickets and birds one neglects during tough marches. I am getting excited! Our goal is close, and with a bit of luck we should reach it tomorrow.

That night I get diarrhea and cure it immediately with doxycyclin. It isn't any fun to repeatedly drop your pants and get a sore bottom on a hard trek. Personal hygiene is very important when one has to walk long distances and perspires profusely due to excessive heat and humidity. Anyone suffering from raw legs should have a small flask filled with a mixture of 10 percent boric acid and talcum powder to prevent such problems.

This morning we get an early start and are out on the march by seven. We walk across relatively open rain forest for half an hour, then come across a larger creek that I recognize from the map and hike in it toward the swamps. Gilbert protests; it is too cold for his feet, but he has to follow. It's the fastest and most direct way.

One cannot undertake this kind of expedition without a good command of French and a comprehension of the African mentality. Gilbert, and to a lesser extent the other tracker, Bosco, both need a firm hand. Giving them free reign would not result in a successful hunt.

This is beginning to seem more like a honey expedition. The forest is so remote that we come across beehives almost daily without even searching for them. By 9:30 A.M. we have found a promising hollow in a large tree with bees swarming in and out. It's *poki*, the "real" honey. It doesn't take long to fell this monarch. On both sides the sharp Baka axes bite in, and fifteen minutes later it collapses with a loud crash, dragging smaller trees with it. My little fellows have struck it rich. The beehive contains numerous honeycombs with about seven pounds of dark, aromatic honey. I get my share and place it in a small PET bottle. It will make a delicious dessert with rice this evening; it upsets my stomach if I eat it straight.

For another half-hour Gilbert suffers as we splash through the clear water. Then we climb a ridge, find a nice wide elephant trail, and head toward our goal. This area looks extremely promising; many fresh elephant tracks crisscross our path. Unfortunately one huge track visible in the clay is about three weeks old. He looks like a real "granddaddy" of a tusker. Later we find a mark high up on a tree where he rubbed his hide and peeled off some bark with his tusks. From the height of the mud and the dents made by his tusks, he is huge and carries long ivory. This could be my dreamed-of Big Foot!

Suddenly we come across human cuttings on the trail. This is discouraging; we are not the first to visit these swamps. But the signs date back six or seven years when this remote area was heavily hunted, probably by poachers from the Congo. We find several elephant skulls, all big and once bearing large tusks. All the kills date from around the time of the cuttings, so someone apparently struck a bonanza and went home with heavy loads of prime ivory.

At 3 P.M. we reach the swamp. Rainwater is trapped between two parallel ridges for many miles with no drainage. This creates waist-deep mud in an enormous two-mile-wide by twenty-mile-long thicket of raffia palms. At this time of year it is impossible to cross, except at certain narrow spots where game regularly move using fallen logs as bridges. Still, it is a terrible mess.

After a rest break we look for a place to camp. Later today we will check out the immediate vicinity. Tomorrow will be the big exploration. The camp is probably temporary, so we just clear some spots on a slight slope.

When we set out to explore, the trackers are even more eager than I am to check out this El Dorado we have expended so much effort to reach. Half a mile later, it gets exciting: We are sneaking along twenty yards above the swamp on a steep slope when suddenly a commotion in the water and a mighty splashing betrays large game. Three large gray shapes move off hastily. The elephant either got our wind or heard us.

I approach a small outcropping on the slope and see two animals in the rear at thirty yards. They are just Pygmy elephant cows. The lead animal is not visible, so I retreat hastily. I do not want to tangle with these aggressive little devils. Of course Gilbert wants me to rush in and kill the first one: "*Patron*, it is a big bull!"

I approach slowly from the other side of the slope and spot the third elephant from behind. It is no bigger than the other two, so it cannot bear good tusks. But it trumpets wildly and charges head-on, fortunately in the other direction where Bosco and the porters are sitting safely in trees. They watch the animal passing at ten yards and confirm that it was also a small cow. Gilbert has very limited value when it comes to judging tuskers.

We continue to stalk along a clear trail on the edge of the swamps when a nice sitatunga bull is suddenly staring at us from about forty yards away. I still have the regular cartridge in the chamber and try to change it without making noise. The bull stares at us for a moment and just as I am ready, he disappears in a split second—my fault for not switching back to a reduction shell sooner.

A moment more and he would have been mine. I could easily have taken him with the .460 round, but it would have been idiotic to drive a crew of sixteen heavily loaded locals across hills and through creeks day after day, then spoil the silence of this remote game paradise and possibly scare away Big Foot with one loud shot.

Discipline pays at the end; at least that is my hope. We move on and come face to face with a second sitatunga bull, but he has heard us and stands camouflaged in the raffia thicket intently observing us. A head shot is the only possible option and I dare it hesitantly, but he takes flight with a loud splashing and a massive splintering of bamboo. Upon inspection, we find shattered bamboo branches in the line of flight: The bullet got deflected. This is not my day. Even duiker calling fails, so we go "home."

Exhausted, I enjoy a cool shower. Ferdinand, the second camp boy, has made me a small table out of some tree branches. My GPS reveals we have covered sixty miles in the past ten days. That is, of course, as the crow flies. We meandered many more miles through the rain forest, actually closer to eighty miles—a fantastic distance in a jungle with no human path or trail. I address the crew, compliment them on their endurance, and confirm their bonus. Ten days, eighty miles—at home less than an hour on the autobahn!

During the next few days the porters can rest while I set out with a small crew on a two-day reconnaissance. Both trackers, one camp boy, and three porters join me as I circle the swamps. Our survey commences well: By 8:30 A.M. a young Peters duiker passes in front of us and drops at the dull sound of the reduction shell. We have tonight's supper. Duiker hunting sounds easy, but it isn't. My friends have often returned to camp empty-handed because one has to react very quickly. In most cases the target is just a faint red spot behind leaves that vanishes in an instant. One of my favorite game animals, duiker provide entertainment way out of proportion to their small stature.

If the animal drops to the shot, one has to be on it as quickly as possible to secure it. In some cases it's just stunned and may get back up and escape. The Baka, who are afraid of everything, believe a wounded animal can have bad magic and change into a dangerous beast. They do not dare grab a duiker because it could stab them with its small, sharp horns. They don't realize it's sufficient to put a boot on the rear legs to immobilize the animal, then dispatch it quickly and humanely.

Time after time we cross fresh elephant tracks, but all are small. A huge gorilla standing upright watches us for a moment through the foliage only ten yards away before it silently vanishes. It is another stinky guy and we almost have to hold our noses. My Baka deeply regret that their stupid white *patron* does not shoot it.

The Baka hate gorillas and want to devour each one they see. The meat and fat provide strength, passed on by the animal's powerful magic. The skin is also very desirable for making the small pouch that every Baka carries on a thong over his shoulder.

Suddenly the tracker in front of me takes off, running as fast as possible. I take off after him since this always signals an ant invasion on the trail. They attack ferociously and bite everything they can find. Even though they can't enter under my pants, they move upward quickly on clothing and attack under the jacket. Their sting is awful. Gilbert has already stopped and undresses hastily to rid himself of the pests. Many times the tracker gets caught because he is looking around and not watching the ground. The ants come in many varieties, but the huge black ones that bite and inject venom are particularly bad. Large, painful, lumps pop up immediately. Don't ask me their Latin name, but it should be *Bitus Africanus horribilus!*

Near 10 A.M. the tracker stops and listens intently, then motions me to follow him. He has heard bushpigs. We follow for a while but scare them off. I want to return, but Gilbert presses on and we finally locate a nice boar. Too bad. I already have one—my limit—proof that the hunting permits in Cameroon are quite restricted these days, something else the Baka cannot comprehend.

Ere, one of my best porters who is accompanying me for the fifth time, complains of a headache. I examine him and diagnose a severe malaria attack, then unpack my first-aid kit. The diagnosis is not difficult since his forehead is hot as a bonfire. I did not bring my big medical kit on this reconnoitering trip, but fortunately I have two spare Chloroquine pills from my own supply. They prove sufficient, and by the next day he is free of fever.

Through infection with plasmodium the locals acquire a temporary immunity that prevents malaria attacks for some months, but when resistance lessens they get new attacks. I always carry a provision of locally purchased Nivaquine pills. Malaria-stricken porters get double doses three times daily for two days. Regular treatment would last for five days. Otherwise I give them two doses (400 mg) of Chloroquine, followed by 200 mg six hours, twelve hours, and twenty-four hours later.

We cross a hill on our big loop and hit another large swamp with raffia palm thickets. It's no fun fighting swarms of black horseflies on a hot and humid day, so we retreat up the hill and move sideways above the swamp till we cross a small tributary at 12:45 P.M. Good spot. We will camp here and stalk until evening.

As we build camp, Gilbert whistles and signals us to be silent. He hears elephant and runs toward the noise like a madman. We soon realize this is idiotic; it's a very small animal. Then Gilbert changes direction, and we move toward a faint trumpeting sound. Again the clay reveals just a small track, but we follow. It might lead to a huge one, which has happened to me several times in the past, so we check it out.

Sudden noise signals monkeys, but my Baka start to run and shout "*bobo*" (gorilla). I stop and smile, but the smile vanishes as all hell breaks lose. The gorilla is charging, and my rifle is with my fleeing tracker! I take advantage of the

A new ax handle is made.

Camp! Safe haven to relax.

Manioc flour is made in huge amounts for us and twenty porters.

Valuable food—big elephant bowels, one inch thick.

Magic is everywhere, and the chief gives his benediction to our weapons.

The Gaboon viper is slow but very deadly.

Blue duikers.

Cooking is important; Bake
traditionally cook their food i
phrynium leaves!

We proceed in our chosen direction even if we have to zigzag often to avoid some nasty swamps. It gets easier by noon.

large swamp. It took some seventy miles on foot to reach this sanctuarium.

From time to time we find old ivory during our safaris. Heavily eaten by palm rats and other rodents, the ivory is even more beautiful as a piece of nature's artwork.

Good forest buffalo taken in central Cameroon.

Gorilla droppings—lowland gorilla are everywhere.

Valuable cargo in a rotten dugout.

Good forest elephant with oxpecker.

Competition is fierce; the Baka crawl in the belly.

The carving-up begins: First the thick hide is taken off, then the stomach is pierced.

Nice rose ivory and tools to cut the meat—spear, blade, and ax.

This stone, found in a crocodile's stomach, is considered magical and is highly prized by the natives.

This lucky Baka dug out a big nyam root, which is welcome food.

Typical forest ivory.

Anatomy of elephant skull.

Ready for departure with my Baka crew into the rain forest-three weeks into unexplored forest.

Submerged logs provide natural bridges in deep creeks.

Beautiful rare flower in the rain forest.

A reminder of colonial times decorates this eighty-year-old rubber tree found forty miles from any road.

Beautiful wood drum from a local chief.

*aka weapons for hunting
*lephant. The spear is jammed
*nto a shotgun with no pellets
*n the cartridge and shot at
oint blank range.

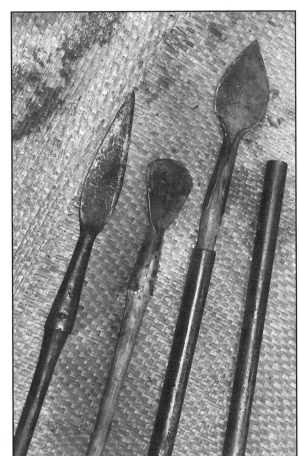

*This typical forest elephant
as excellent tusks.

The No. 1 Peters duiker in Rowland Ward's Records of Big Game, *vol. 22.*

Forest roads are often impassable in the rainy season.

Jungle cat shot in the middle of an elephant herd in the rain forest. It was focused on the feeding elephant instead of my stalking.

Elephant droppings are necessary vehicles for the distribution of seeds. For certain trees and plants this is their only chance to spread and grow.

Snakes are everywhere bu rarely seen. Here is the deadl green mamba.

This shower is a luxury on a foot safari.

We found an old elephant jaw and cut out the teeth for souvenirs. This Baka is using a typical ax.

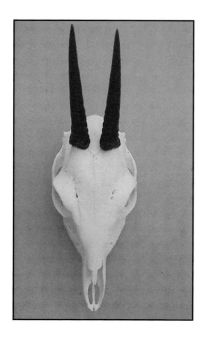

1

2

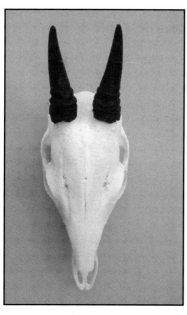

3

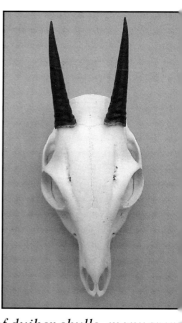

4

This and the following pages show a variety of duiker skulls, many were collected by Reinald von Meurers on hunts in the Cameroon. They may be seen in the Jungbauer collection in Germany. Note the interesting differences in skull sizes\formations and horn figuration. 1. Southern bush duiker—Sylvicapra grimmia—male, Zimbabwe. 2. Blue duiker—Cephalophus monticola—male, southern Cameroon. 3. Red-flanked duiker—Ceph. rufilatus—male, Central African Republic. 4. Bay duiker—Ceph. dorsalis—male, southern Cameroon.

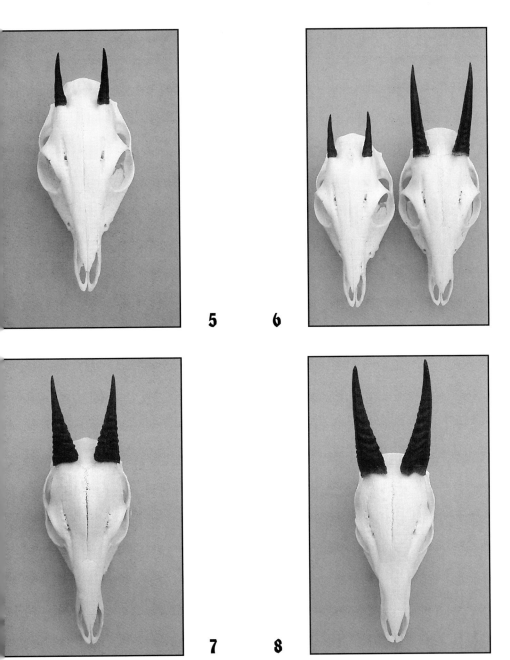

5 **6**

7 **8**

The above are all forest duikers from the Cameroon. 5. Bay duiker–Ceph. dorsalis–female, southern Cameroon. 6. Bay duiker–Ceph. dorsalis–southern Cameroon; left: female, right: male. 7. Gabon duiker–Ceph. leucogaster–male, southern Cameroon. 8. Peters duiker–Ceph. callipygus–male, southern Cameroon.

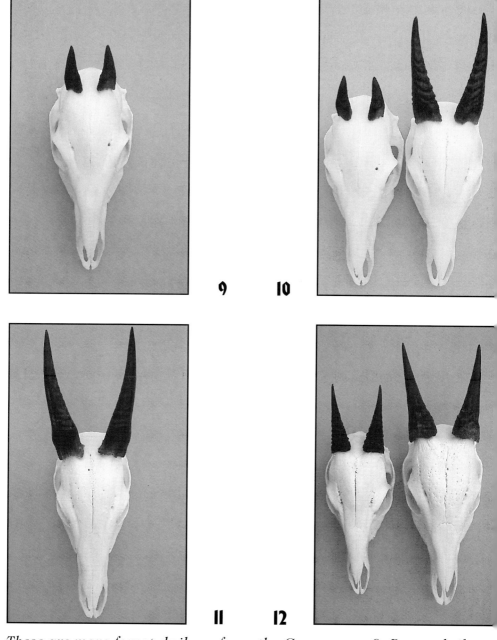

9 **10**

11 **12**

These are more forest duikers from the Cameroon. 9. Peters duiker–
Ceph. callipygus—female, southern Cameroon. 10. Peters duiker–Ceph.
callipygus–southern Cameroon; left: female, right: male. 11. Peters
duiker–Ceph. callipygus–old male with exceptionally long horns, south-
ern Cameroon. 12. Left: Gabon duiker–Ceph. leucogaster–male, south-
ern Cameroon; right: Peters duiker–Ceph. callipygus–male, southern
Cameroon; both animals are approximately the same age.

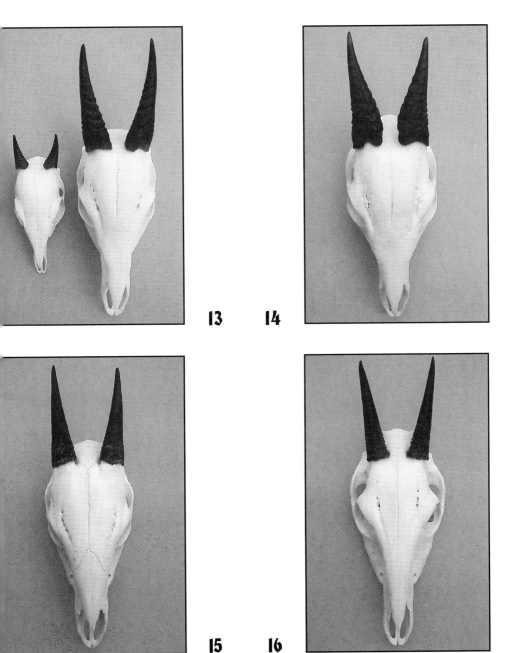

The above is a comparison of duikers from West and East Africa. 13. Left: Blue duiker—Ceph. monticola—male, southern Cameroon; right: Peters duiker—Ceph. callipygus—male, southern Cameroon. 14. Harvey red duiker—Ceph. harveyi—male, Mt. Kenya. 15. Abbott duiker—Ceph. spadix—male, Mt. Kilimanjaro. 16. Yellow-backed duiker—Ceph. silvicultor—male, southern Cameroon.

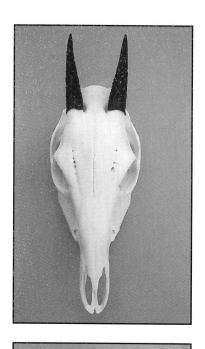 

17 **18**

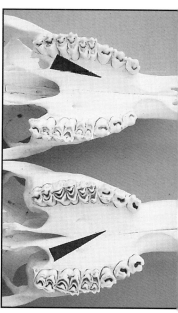

19 **20**

Africa has three "giant" duikers that are much larger than the rest: Abbott,
yellow-backed, and Jentink duikers. 17. Yellow-backed duiker, female, Central
African Republic. 18. Comparison between the largest and smallest duikers
of Africa; left: blue duiker—Ceph. monticola—male, southern Cameroon; right:
yellow-backed duiker, male, southern Sudan. 19. Left: Jentink duiker—Ceph.
jentinki—male, Liberia; right: yellow-backed duiker, male, southern Cameroon.
20. Dental comparison, top: Jentink duiker, male; bottom: yellow-backed
duiker, male. These two can be distinguished by differences in the shape of
the palate (see arrows). Note the deeper groove in palate of Jentink duiker.

open forest and use my long legs to outrun my two heroes. Fortunately the gorilla is content with his success and retreats. We continue stalking for a while and reach camp at nightfall.

My crew is buoyant, and everyone is proud as punch that we have reached this distant unknown area. I wait fifteen minutes for the purification drops to do their job disinfecting my freshly filled water bottle, then mix one quart of water with mineral and vitamin powder for a tasty drink that replenishes my body's depleted reserves. I always carry a little bottle of disinfecting drops in my pocket; five drops are enough for four pints.

I take off my cotton belt and hang it within reach. It weighs a ton because I carry four reduction shells and five big .460 cartridges on it. They are securely stored in four-inch-long cases made from bicycle-tire inner tubes. They fit exactly over the belt, and small holes are punched on one side in one-inch intervals in an upper and lower row to host the cartridges. The friction is so high that they cannot fall out. They sit so tightly that no noise is generated, but I can remove the appropriate cartridge with one pull. Additional pockets for my precious Damascus knife, knife sharpener, and sunglasses add weight.

After the ritual evening shower, I dress in my knee-length woolen socks to protect against mosquitoes. It is important not to *ever* walk barefooted since parasites like sand fleas and worms can easily enter unprotected skin and set up housekeeping. Tonight it's cooling off so rapidly that I dress in my featherweight parka and trouser liner. They insulate very well and I use them inside the poncho liner that acts as my sleeping bag. All this weighs very little and is stored in a drum to stay dry until I need it again.

I cut up some dried plums, apples, and apricots into a cup, fill it with water, and secure the lid to keep out ants while it soaks overnight. Early the next morning the camp boy brings me a cup of steaming hot rice. I pour my fruit mix over it, then add some sugar and my *poki* honey for an absolutely delicious breakfast. Unfortunately hordes of obnoxious black ants mar an otherwise relaxing morning spent enjoying the songs of birds and insects.

We continue along the swamp but can't find open areas until the very end. These swamps are virtually impenetrable. Of course elephant move across these nasty areas freely. There are plenty of fresh tracks, but all are small. Perhaps it's the wrong season for tuskers or perhaps they are on the march elsewhere searching for ripe fruits. Maybe it's just plain bad luck.

We whack on through the swamp with machetes to an open spot only to be eaten alive by tsetse flies and black horseflies, so we beat a hasty retreat into the forest. Gilbert loses his way in the vast swamp and its tributaries. I have to take GPS fixes twice to find our way back to base camp.

By 5 P.M. we reach camp under rolling peals of thunder. Tonight even the Pygmies build a shelter. They have a plastic tarp but prefer to build their traditional igloo-shaped huts using bent branches and large phrynium leaves. In the huts they have their fires going to warm them in the chilly night. As a bonus, the smoke drives away mosquitoes. They just stretch out on a bed of leaves without even a cloth to cover their bodies. At 3 A.M. heavy rain falls, lasting until morning. I am well protected under my tarp and doze contentedly.

It is our thirteenth day, and we have fifteen days left. We have two possibilities: either return in a loop toward the river crossing where our ferryman waits, or move in a big half-circle far away toward a swamp called Ngolongolong. I visited there last year (chapter 4), and sent another hunter there during this expedition. In the middle of the rain forest lives a small population of dwarf bushbuck, which are called Ngolongolong by the Pygmies. Buffalo always visit this swamp, and elephant bulls like it, too. We have to cover some twenty-five miles as the crow flies to reach it, and from there it is thirty-three miles back to the village.

There is no path or trail to the Ngolongolong Swamp, so we would have to navigate by GPS across unknown territory. Since it worked perfectly before, I decide to take a chance. I program the coordinates into the unit and set course for the swamp, but this segment of the expedition will be different. If major obstacles should arise, we will have no time to go back the way we came. We will have to forge ahead for five days directly toward the big river and somehow find a fisherman to help us cross it—not an easy task with twenty miles between fishing camps.

Due to rain, we do not leave until 10 A.M., and we do not advance far because after fifteen minutes the sharp eyes of my Baka detect a promising tree with a small fissure. The minute black stripe and heavy traffic of little stingerless bees promise tasty *dandu* honey. The operation takes time, but finally the tree is felled by two Baka working with their axes in turn while everyone else sits around watching and chatting happily. We are rewarded with a huge pot full of dark brown liquid honey. It's an auspicious beginning for the ambitious second part of our expedition. The Baka see this as another sign of the white man's powerful magic.

After an hour and a half we move on. We closely follow the direction of the compass, regardless of the difficulty cutting a path through dense undergrowth along creeks and muddy swamps. We are very relieved when we reach a ridge that goes in our chosen direction, and can easily follow the usual game trail. From time to time we faintly glimpse huge trees on the next ridgeline some miles away through the widespread treetops.

We call here and there and bring in several duiker, but I am reluctant to shoot a small one because we still have enough meat. This is a veritable paradise for duiker calling; they just gallop in.

My experts find yet another hive of "true" bees and, of course, they can't leave it. It is in a difficult location—about forty-five feet up a massive tree with a trunk that measures at least ten feet across—so they have to climb and cut it out there. For safety they cut some fine liana, which they knot around the trunk and the climber's waist as a safety belt. We don't need to cart a Baka with a broken leg around these boondocks.

Meanwhile, the others weave a basket of very fine liana vines and place a bundle of leaves and burning embers in it. Soon it is smoking well, and this is pulled up with a long liana and hung on the trunk at the opening to the beehive.

Salomon cuts the trunk open, puts his arm in up to the shoulder, and pulls out one honeycomb after another. About twelve altogether, and all twelve are empty! His arm swells to double its normal size, and he resembles a pincushion with stingers sticking out everywhere—such agony for only a handful of honey.

We continue our walk and encounter a truly monstrous tree. Its trunk protrudes in several directions for ten feet at the base and measures about thirty feet in diameter. A small opening and traces on the ground give away a scaly anteater's habitat. It must have moved in sometime during the previous night. The Baka stick their spears in the cave and reach far inward in several directions. All four big parts of the tree are hollow and subdivided.

Gilbert's son is armed with a knife and my lamp and maneuvers himself into the cave. I hope there is no snake. It would be horrible to find a python hissing at him! He investigates the larger chambers, which are big enough for him to turn around in, but they are empty. The anteater must have gone deeper because small tunnels lead far under the ground. It's a small, well-protected burrow and the Pygmies finally give up.

By 5 P.M. we have our fill of hiking and camp at a clear creek. Again heavy thunder threatens rain, so we prepare a well-protected camp but it only sprinkles. This area seems ideal for elephant hunting, but where are the big ones? Today we found the fresh tracks of one medium bull and two smaller ones.

Amazingly we managed three miles of straight-line distance on this "honey-day," which is good for dense jungle travel. The easy walk on the ridge made up for the time lost at the honey shops.

The night is warm, and everyone is eager to reach our new goal. We are off by 8 A.M. and with many a moan, take four hours to climb a high hill. Perspiration flows freely, and the GPS reveals that by noon we have gone only $2\frac{1}{2}$ miles. From the crest we have a nice view of a row of green hills through an opening in the canopy made by a fallen log.

When we descend, my second tracker detects excavations made twenty or more years ago to dig up wild yam roots. The plant is a fine liana that winds through the foliage and is not even as thick as a little finger. Its roots, which grow underground to a depth of three or more feet, tastes like potato and all my Baka swarm out to search for *temmeli*. Bosco digs passionately and is rewarded with over ten pounds of thick, juicy roots.

I get a nice surprise while calling duiker that afternoon. A grizzled veteran sneaks in, and I quickly realize that this is an outstanding animal with very prominent horns. When he pauses behind some foliage at forty yards, I position the red dot of the scope on his shoulder and fire. He runs some twenty yards and collapses.

This might be my oldest duiker ever. His muzzle has gone white, the skin on his head is partially hairless, and his teeth are worn down to the gum. This Peters duiker (*ngendi* in Baka) probably would not have survived another year. His thick horns are long for his species, measuring close to five inches. He should be No. 2 in Rowland Ward's *Records of Big Game*; I already have the No. 1 ranking!

The meat will be tough, and as the Baka cut up the 50-pound animal, thin, 4-inch-long filaria move in the muscles. These worms are present in all game and are transmitted during the day by small, active red flies. Humans also contract the worms and almost all the locals suffer from it. *Loa loa*, as it is called, first results in allergic reactions such as itching and swelling of joints, then progresses to elephantiasis—monstrous swelling of the legs due to obliterated vessels. I certainly won't eat any of this duiker, even though cooking will destroy the slimy little devils.

After our tough morning climbing high, steep hills, we have an easy walk through lowland open forest on wide elephant trails. This area looks very promising for elephant. Fresh tracks here and there repeatedly raise our pulse rates. Anticipation—what a high!

One track looks good; the three nails of the round front foot are very well defined. We let the porters rest while the trackers and I stalk. Tension rises as we find fresh droppings and wet urine. The droppings consist of big heaps of fiber balls. This means the bull is at ease and moving undisturbed while answering nature's call. If he were stressed out and anxious, he would let it go while walking and just leave a single ball here and there on the trail. Worst for the pursuer is when the excrement is full of liquid. This means the elephant is really scared and will hike at full speed. Then it's almost impossible to catch up because elephant usually move during most of the night as well as the day. To put things in perspective, the Gold Medal winner in the Olympic 100-yard dash would come out a poor second to a rapidly walking elephant!

This bull produces small, applelike droppings—a bad indication of his probable body and ivory size. We creep as silently as possible through the forest, avoiding contact with branches that scratch against clothing and immediately reveal the presence of humans to game. The Baka trackers in front of and behind me are stripped down to short pants and glide noiselessly like snakes along the trail while I clumsily work my way through the many obstacles of a rain forest.

A light rain sets in, which is ideal for stalking. The carpet of leaves on the forest floor gets soaked and no longer crunches. Sometimes we lose five minutes in places where our prey moved off on a tangent and we have to relocate its trail. The fact that we can close the distance every time he changes directions is a good sign.

Another hour passes. Tension rises and falls. Suddenly the tracker abruptly motions us to stop. We listen intently and hear the sound of bending and breaking treetops: Our bull is feeding close by!

We move ahead very slowly. My rifle is loaded with a solid, and the cocked safety lever is in the medium, easy-to-switch-off position. Suddenly, a huge gray back moves away through the green wall of leaves and we follow. There is absolutely no way to get ahead of him in this dense thicket to get a look at his tusks. Is he a worthy bull? He is bigger than his small front footprints indicates.

Our stress hormones are surging. My heart beats at its upper limit, and perspiration flows freely. Even after bagging twenty elephant, it still gives me an adrenaline high to stalk this mighty beast. For what seems an eternity, we slowly follow ten yards behind the huge bottom that smells like a circus arena.

The trail opens up at a fork and the elephant stops, not sure which way to go. He listens and tries to get wind with his long trunk. As he turns his head sideways we can judge the tusks. They protrude about forty inches from the gum. That will make the length a good five feet including the portion embedded in the jaw. They are of medium thickness, about seven inches in diameter, and nicely stained. The deep nailprints in the track of his front foot were an accurate indicia. He carries nice ivory for his relatively small frame.

This is definitely a good bull, but not the huge tusker of my dreams. Each tusk will weigh twenty-six to thirty pounds—fair for these times. Still, my three best bulls from this area had forty to fifty pounds a side. These are top weights for Cameroon, and the potential is there to find more such bulls. I have often come across very promising tracks.

The Baka desperately motion me to shoot and can't understand my hesitation. For them it's a magnificent bull, a *semée* of the quality they formerly worshipped and did not dare to kill. I am torn between desire and the notion of waiting for a bigger one. I have to decide quickly. So far we have had the faint breeze in our favor, but usually at noon wind direction starts shifting, and could do so now at any moment.

I almost bow to my tracker's wishes, but decide to wait for a better bull. I turn around to withdraw; he might charge if he realizes danger is so close. The Baka follow very reluctantly. They wish me to hell and deeply regret not having a gun. At this moment they might even attack the bull with spears like their ancestors. A deep thrust into the guts would eventually make him sick, thereby forcing me to kill him. This actually happened to an acquaintance in the Congo who initially had not wanted to shoot.

Back where the porters are gathered, I receive more reproachful glances and do not feel as popular as before. They have endured a lot to reach this bare backside of beyond. Some still carry heavy loads, except the porters of the rice bags who have only half of their original burdens.

By 4 P.M. we rest at a lovely place in an open forest with no undergrowth; a small, clear creek flows in a bend around our camp. I pick a spot thirty yards away from the crew and sleep very well.

Today will be tough. We have some hills ahead and it is difficult to judge how steep and high they are. This is the only disadvantage of the 1:100,000-scale topographic map. Drawn from aerial photos, it accurately shows the smallest creek because of the surrounding vegetation. But it is not good about showing height lines, so one never knows whether to expect a slightly rising slope or a steep, demanding climb from hell.

I take the GPS fix and position the transparent film with lines on the topo map. I pinpoint our position and choose the best route across a plateau toward the hills. We have only twelve more miles before we reach the Ngolongolong Swamp—the place where the elephant dance. I have a choice of two routes: One is to move left and wade up a creek, but the creek is deep and we will have to whack our way through dense, difficult vegetation. The other choice is to negotiate some steep hills, but once on top we will have a ridge to follow in a large arc, eventually descending on a short route toward the Ngolongolong Swamp. I opt for the latter, which will be faster and easier after the tough initial climb.

At first we march comfortably on a broad elephant trail. Hunters have used this trail, and some very old cuttings still remain. Twice we call duiker, which is easy to do during a march. We motion the porters to sit, then move fifty yards farther up the game trail and call. I prefer the standing position, because it allows more freedom to swing the gun and turn: The antelope can come from any direction. My camouflage works well, and several duikers come close.

But again, this is not my day. The first animal stands behind a large fallen log with just its back line visible, and I miss. My second chance is ruined by an arm-thick sapling in the line of fire that deflects the bullet as the duiker moves through dense undergrowth.

By noon we reach a large creek. It would be interesting to explore its origin. The map shows that the game-rich plateau we crossed earlier today continues for another fifteen miles, and I notice promising fresh elephant tracks leading in that direction.

After a refreshing pause we tackle the ascent, and it's tougher and steeper than expected. Baka are not used to steep hills, and they complain incessantly while suffering under their loads. Finally we reach the top and relax on a large game trail on the crest. I'm thankful they don't have a porter's union since the shop steward would undoubtedly be my already big-pain-in-the-rear Gilbert!

A horde of white-nosed monkeys pass by in the trees high over our heads. My companions draw them in like magic with an imitation of the call of the crowned eagle (*Stephanoaetus coronatus*), a high-pitched whistle repeated in short intervals. The monkeys descend from their lofty stronghold, crying excitedly. Soon a particularly large male sits just twenty yards above in some branches and watches us, his curiosity evidenced by his ecstatic yelling—more proof of a virgin area. Hunted simians wouldn't venture within a mile of us.

The Baka suffer today as we climb up and down hills, topped off by a huge, very steep hill at midafternoon. Even the eager camp boy sighs, and everyone is content to rest while the *patron* tries to take GPS positions. Gilbert again locates wild yam roots and digs out another ten pounds. My army definitely marches on its stomach!

It gets easier on top as we follow a level elephant path in open forest. It's duiker paradise again. Several times we see them feeding, but at the last split second the opportunity to aim properly is always lost. The only time I fire, it turns out to be a black stump behind which a bay duiker disappeared.

Several times we cross bull elephant tracks, but they are always a day old and none are really big. There is no water up here, so we keep walking, having already covered a good distance today. As it gets dark we hurry to find a decent campsite, or at least water. The side of the ridge falls away steeply and is densely covered by vegetation with no game trails leading down. It would be too difficult to descend, and there might be steep parts where we couldn't continue. One thing I do know: If it's too steep for the animals, it's too steep for us! We might have to rely on the water-producing liana.

Finally the ridge descends and we become hopeful. Dusk is coming as Gilbert suddenly hears a noise in front. Pigs? He and I stalk ahead. Short of a clear creek he motions me to wait while he sneaks ahead quickly and silently to check the water. At exactly this moment the porters descend the hill and yell for us with the monkey cry. They can't see our tracks in the twilight. Usually during stalking the tracker stops cutting. He just breaks twigs or bends small saplings aside, making it difficult for the others to follow.

Gilbert hurries back excitedly. A single huge elephant bull just crossed in front of him at the creek. He starts arguing with the porters about their noise, but that's useless at this time of day after one of our toughest marches. They can't be blamed for much while looking for a place to build camp at dusk.

We rush to the creek just thirty yards away. The bull's passage stirred up the yellow soil, and the water is still troubled. We try to follow in the forest, but it is impossible in the rising darkness, so we soon give up. But knowing Gilbert I will not believe it's a big bull unless I see the ivory myself. I hope the bull was not disturbed by the porters' noise and will linger nearby so we can get a crack at him in the morning.

Today, for the first time since our departure fourteen days ago, I have dry boots due to the long walk on the arid ridge. It's amazing how wear-resistant these Vietnam boots are, but that honor goes only to the original BDU version from the U.S. The Asian imitations do not last more than one safari in the rain forest.

My camp boy works like mad in the swiftly encroaching darkness to clear a spot and hang the mosquito net. We skip mounting the rain fly since the sky is clear, and there are no trees around to hang the rope. I regret not being able to take this boy back to Germany. There is a lot of work waiting in and around my house!

After a shower and a frugal dinner, I anxiously watch repeated sheets of lightning to the north, but the sky stays clear and I fall exhausted onto my cot. I am awakened by nearby thunder around 10:40 P.M. We start working rapidly. The camp boys cut two small trees and drive them into the ground to support the rope, then pull the tarp across. Thin strips of inner tube are tied at the ends. They provide a firm but flexible pull to keep the tarp taut, and their other ends are easily attached to thick grass and twigs. There's even enough time enough to dig a shallow trench around the tarp to drain the water.

It pours cats and dogs, and my small horde gathers under the tarp. I am fine in the middle on my cot under the mosquito net, and the Baka huddle close to warm themselves and me. I soon fall asleep, and the crew eventually returns to their fires.

Early the next morning, I can't wait to see the bull's tracks to find out whether I missed a close encounter with a big tusker, but as we cross the creek and look around, it's impossible to find the track. The beast went into the dry forest, where just a broken branch, twisted liana, and scratched root evidences its passing.

Last evening's torrential rain wiped out all other signs. If I had wounded an animal yesterday and stopped pursuing it due to nightfall, it would be gone forever. I contentedly slap my .460 Weatherby. Another reason to "carry enough gun" in the rain forest!

But there is another reason to worry. I have only twenty-three small loads left for the reduction shells, and there are still eleven days left to hunt. I must remember to fire only if no object intrudes in the line of fire.

We climb up a short way and continue our hike on the high ridge toward the large swamp. We were lucky to find the small creek yesterday that cut across our line of march. It remains the only one we find until late afternoon.

As we trot along the well-beaten trail, a huge gorilla suddenly breaks out of some dense undergrowth and charges while yelling wildly. Everyone is scared to death and madly running off in sixteen different directions!

I manage to grab my rifle from the tracker's shoulder just before he takes off. In a swift move, I eject the reduction shell, load a regular cartridge, and fire into the ground near the aggressor. The deafening noise and a small fountain of dust and shattered earth make him stop and retreat abruptly. Another narrow escape! I do not want to bear scars like some of my Baka or be mauled to death in the middle of nowhere. That beast could definitely tear a human from limb to limb.

The huge silverback male was probably kicked out of his band and is angry at anything and everything. A dominant male will not usually wander far from his band and generally allows smaller males to do the defensive charging while he stays well in the back. It takes a while before all the porters come back. Everyone laughs and recounts the details of his neighbor's fast escape.

We walk all day and remain on the ridge longer than planned. The original route would have led us straight down an extremely steep and slippery slope through very dense thickets. It will be better to follow a wide arc and enter the Ngolongolong Swamp from the side.

Several times we cross the tracks of medium bulls, but decide not to waste time following every one to check for size. We will deviate from our chosen path only for genuinely promising tracks, or if we detect an animal close by.

The locals prefer not to name the elephant and instead refer to it as "animal," "beast," etc. This practice can also be found in our own ancient history when people did not want to call a thing "devil" or "ghost." This kept them from accidentally conjuring up the evil thing, and I recognize this trait among many tribes. This is quite obvious when I inquire about the local game and visibly discomfit my hosts.

By 4:30 P.M. we find a game trail and descend from our high ridge. We reach another small creek on the slope with a nice open area in which to camp, but I have to wait another hour for my luggage to arrive. The Baka found honey in a huge tree again, requiring heavy cutting without much reward since the honeycombs were not well filled—or so they said!

When I am finally lying on my cot and starting to relax, I hear termites gnawing on my plastic tarp and parts of the mosquito net. I have to save the net by placing some phrynium leaves from my shower underneath. I crawl out and check with my flashlight to find a horrific scenario: A large front of fat, green caterpillars is advancing on my sweet little home. As I stomp around crushing them with my heavy boots, I suddenly realize that the quickest have already invaded my mosquito net. I don my leather gloves since their small hairs contain venom that causes burning and swelling, and pick them off.

These ugly little monsters leave wet, fatty stains on the mesh, and it is a desperate fight for over an hour as they march in new waves out of the bush. Talk about army ants! I just wanted to relax after a hard day's walk! Finally I triumph, but I am reluctant to jump into my cozy cot before making sure the little brutes are not snuggling in my bed. I don't dare return until 11 P.M. and sleep restlessly with nightmares of battling man-sized caterpillars.

I'm glad when day breaks and eager to leave, but it's Murphy's law today: During the night the skull of the bay duiker fell into the fire and was burned, so that trophy is gone for good.

By 8 A.M. we resume our march toward the Ngolongolong Swamp and about half an hour later we reach a river that originates from it. My GPS unit shows only three more miles north-northwest to actually reach the swamp. Normally that would be a good day's walk, but here the forest is more open and a well-beaten game trail leads along the river toward the swamp—apparently a magnet for wildlife.

Suddenly we are in a chicken farm. A bunch of guinea fowl are scattered around, so I stalk one. It sounds hilarious to hunt jungle chicken with a .460 Weatherby, but the reduction shells allow the loading of .38 shot shells that give good patterns up to fifteen yards—enough to bag two fat chickens. This assures a tasty dinner, provided the cook stews them for a few hours. Otherwise, they will be tougher than the soles of my worn-out boots!

At noon the typical cawing sound of heron alerts us: We have reached the Ngolongolong Swamp. Being extremely careful and keen to find valuable game (maybe even a huge elephant bull), we sneak through the foliage on large, trampled elephant trails, my rifle loaded with "big stuff" and at the ready. Ah—anticipation is so sweet, so much a part of hunting!

As we reach the edge of an opening, we stop while still in cover to scan the beautiful scenery revealed to us. Bright sun bathes a grassy, 300-by-600-yard meadow containing a four- to six-yard-wide clear, shallow creek running down the middle.

A scene similar to my three previous expeditions here greets my eyes: A herd of buffalo, varying in color from bright red to dark brown, is grazing peacefully in the meadow's midsection just 100 yards away. We watch the row of oxpeckers and some white herons sitting on their backs, picking at ticks. Among them is a huge bull with a widespread set of horns and a body frame some 30 percent larger than the others. However, he is safe from me since I don't want to slow down my worn-out crew with heavy loads of smoked meat, which they would love to carry and consume en route!

Many fresh tracks testify that a variety of other game, including good-sized elephant, have visited this Garden of Eden recently. I'll try my luck tonight, and will camp here while the crew proceeds to last year's campsite almost an hour away. I study the salt lick I created two years ago. The shallow mud hole has been greatly increased by many visiting animals, which have licked well into the eight-foot-high embankment encircling the site.

Now it's a small cave in which even I can stand upright. This makes me confident about encountering game toward the active evening hours, and I arrange my mosquito net with its tarp cover some thirty yards to the rear in the forest. Nearby, a large well-trampled elephant path leads toward the salt lick.

First I take a refreshing shower with the waterbag, then move back to the clearing. My tracker and camp boy sit with me behind a large tree, and we watch some bushbuck peacefully grazing. But Africans like to stalk—they can't just sit and wait. As the Baka tracker gets restless, he starts making noises and wants to join his brothers who are talking and relaxing at a cozy campfire. Africans chat endlessly, and even after a fortnight in close quarters, they can still find tales about which to babble.

The tracker and camp boy sneak out in a big loop across the forest toward the main camp, and I enjoy nature alone. Well, not truly alone, since at least an "air wing" of horseflies and tsetse are already happily gathering around, trying to find an entrance in my clothing. Their stings swell immediately with a nasty burning sensation, so I tighten the waist on my trousers, stick a net under my cap to cover my face and neck, unroll my sleeves, and thrust my hands in them like a muff. Now all access is barred, so go find another meal!

After about an hour the sound of small sticks breaking and birds' cries of alarm stir me. Some bushpigs move into the open and feed on the lush green grass. The ground around the small creek is treacherous. Once in a while a pig sinks up to its belly in black mud, but it apparently welcomes the accident, which kills ticks. It's fun watching the noisy, grunting, squealing litter. Among the eight pigs a larger, older one catches my attention. A jet-black forehead and a red muzzle indicate it is the alpha male. I can see the boar's tusks from seventy yards—a worthy trophy, but I wait for bigger quarry. After half an hour they get my wind and move off quickly. Now it's time for the more cautious game, and tension and anticipation rear up. But the scene stays quiet as no other game join the bushbuck that are feeding two hundred yards away.

The natives are right: Sitting and waiting is a poor tactic in Africa. Several days' perspiration in my clothing must be giving off a strong human scent to the surrounding area. I suppose I could have left off my sweat-stained apparel after my bath. Right! Run naked after a wounded animal and get eaten alive by voracious clouds of insects? No, thanks!

Despite my camouflage, I am constantly exposed by birds and traveling monkeys that realize the danger and alert the forest with warning cries well understood by other animals. My hopes of a big, lone elephant bull wandering into the open are in vain, although shortly before dusk the noise of a dry twig breaking indicates a bigger animal moving in the forest.

When it is completely dark I slowly creep back to my little camp, enjoy some snacks, and relax on my cot. It's a full moon tonight, and after 10 P.M. the yellow ball will be high enough to light up the swamp. Perhaps that will allow me to watch and eventually follow a worthy bull in the morning. After a nice nap, the bright moonlight awakens me.

Carefully I retrace my steps and return to my vantage point. My nerves are taut. What adventures will the night bring? When I reach the edge of the forest, a surge of adrenaline floods my system as three large, gray shapes wade through the swamp. The tusks are glistening, and one is bigger than the others, but a closer look reveals they are only Pygmy bulls. Still, it's fascinating to watch them for almost an hour. Fortunately, the slight night breeze follows the running water to the right so my odor is blown away from the bulls. One whiff of me and they would depart in panic.

After midnight I become fatigued and the stage remains empty. Apparently the wind is circling and the game is aware of a human intruder in their quiet refuge. So I return to my comfortable cot and sleep well until morning.

Another hour at my outpost reveals no game at all, and my Pygmies arrive with a carefully guarded pot. Good boys—they bring me warm breakfast rice. I enrich it with some sugar and dried fruit; then we break camp. This still-hunting was not rewarded by game, but that wonderful time is very much alive in my memory.

The following days are spent walking hard, with only occasional duiker hunts and some exciting stalks along fresh elephant tracks or sudden encounters with small jumbos providing welcome breaks. Three days later we reach another interesting swamp where I took a nice bull last season. I am curious about the remaining bones. They are widely scattered, but I pick up the second vertebra as a souvenir.

Tracks reveal that my German friend, Fritz, passed through on his hunting expedition about a week ago. Three days after he left for the next camp, a huge bull strolled through the swamp. Big footprints indicate a valuable bull. I've known about this one for some years now, and maybe we will meet him on our way out. If not, then during my next expedition—*insha' Allah* (if God wills).

Three days later I encounter my friend and his crew at the last swamp, and we talk for the rest of the day and evening. Too many exciting adventures to relate. These precious moments of companionship on a lonely jungle hunt are pure pleasure. This is a hunter I like—not trophy-crazy but a hard hunter who appreciates every minute detail of a foot safari with Pygmies.

Fritz has a very special present for me—the bullet I used to kill the big bull in the last swamp a year ago. He found it in the third vertebra. The full-metal-jacketed bullet traversed through the mighty elephant head and is still completely intact. Even the grooves of the .460 Weatherby Magnum barrel are visible. It is a worthy souvenir. He could not have given me a more appreciated present. Thank you, Fritz!

We have to wait a day because a porter, Samedi (Saturday in French), has a severe attack of malaria. Chloroquine cures him quickly, and I use the rest period to have my clothes washed and relax under the mosquito net, talking to Fritz.

While watching the crew dig out a special honeycomb, we spot guinea fowl and I stalk them by myself. It's fun to shoot one with the reduction shell of the mighty .460 Weatherby Magnum, and it's a welcome change of food for tonight.

After more days of walking we are back in civilization after weeks in one of the last lost places in the world. I will never forget this safari, even though the promise of El Dorado in the lost swamps did not prove true. We covered around 170 miles as the crow flies in three and a half weeks. I didn't kill an elephant or other large game, but the pure enjoyment of the trip transcends the kill. This is why we call our wonderful sport "hunting" and not "killing." Lord, I love it so!

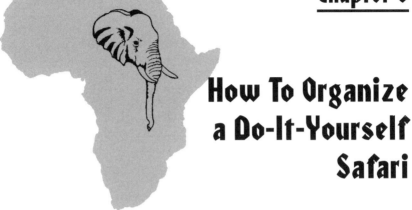

Chapter 6

How To Organize a Do-It-Yourself Safari

Do-it-yourself hunting is a fascinating challenge, but not many people dare to venture out in the bush alone. In southern Cameroon around sixty nonresidents try it each season. Of these, only half-a-dozen dyed-in-the-wool hunters still do it in the traditional style by hiring porters and trackers and venturing into the wilds for weeks on foot.

The major challenges are finding a viable, productive hunting area and recruiting a good, reliable crew of trackers and porters. The latter usually takes two to three safaris to get right, and requires knowledge of the local mentality, game territories and behavior, and fluent French.

Physical fitness, an open mind, and the fortitude to endure dirt, heat, bugs, and miles and miles of walking are absolutely necessary. There is no master-and-servant relationship between black locals and white hunters on a foot safari. It is a partnership, and we sit and eat together at the campfire morning and evening.

Such a traditional safari will be a lifetime memory—hopefully a very positive one. The trophies that decorate your home after such a hunt will always revive memories of that adventure.

The Cameroonian embassy provides two vital documents: your visa and your temporary gun import certificate. Preparations beyond that depend upon where you plan to hunt. For example, hunting in the game-rich savannas of northern Cameroon is relatively easy.

After you arrive in Garoua, a cab ride will take you to the hunting department of the Ministry of Environment, where the helpful clerks will establish a Big Game Hunting Permit for about CFA Fr 425,000 (the Communauté Financière Africaine or African Financial Community consists of several west African countries, including Cameroon, in a monetary union with a common currency—the CFA franc. The CFA franc is related to the French franc at CFA Fr 100 for French Fr 1; $1 U.S. equaled CFA Fr 515 in 1996).

One hunter-friendly regulation is that trophy fees are payable only after the kill, so there is no monetary loss when game animals on the permit are not taken.

In 1997 the major trophy fees for nonresidents were: elephant, giant eland, bongo, and lion—CFA Fr 1,000,000; buffalo and roan—CFA Fr 500,000; waterbuck—CFA Fr 250,000; sitatunga and hartebeest—CFA Fr 200,000; warthog, giant forest hog, bushpig, *kob de buffon*, bushbuck, yellow-backed duiker—CFA Fr 100,000; and the smaller duiker—CFA Fr 50,000.

It is best to reserve a hunting zone by fax or letter before leaving home. Unfortunately for the do-it-yourself hunter, of the twenty-four designated zones in the north, only zones one and four are free. A friend recently shot a giant eland (*Taurotragus derbianus gigas* or central African giant eland) in zone four. Zone twenty-three is leased to an employee of the Ministry of Environment, but one can hunt in it as well. The same goes for zones six and ten, which are reserved for the Lamido of Rey Bouba, who rarely uses them.

Then one has to organize transportation. Hired vehicles are expensive, but the price usually includes a local driver. Both may be found through a hotel's reception desk or at the gathering place of bush taxis.

Remember that Africa is a country of intensive bargaining where every white man is viewed as a millionaire and the prices are excessively high. Test the market by asking several people, and possibly contacting your church's missionaries. Some are very helpful; others are dummies.

Never hire someone on an "open" basis: "Do not worry, we will arrange the price later; it will be right." That leads to terrible complications because the price will be very high, and you will already be stuck somewhere in the bush.

It is far more difficult to arrive in the capital city Yaoundé, then head south into the rain forest. The hunting permit is still obtained from the Ministry of Environment, but here it may take up to several days longer. I once had to stay in Yaoundé for a whole week because the only two persons able to sign were far away from Cameroon.

Dealing with the authorities is always a major problem for do-it-yourself hunters. Since Cameroon adapted French bureaucracy, which is no easier than the German, paperwork and other formalities require a lot of precious time and impose a lot of unnecessary stress. This begins with the hunting permit, continues with trophy certificates, and ends with export and veterinary papers and shipping.

Fortunately, a small travel agency—Kamba—can now alleviate this hassle. They specialize in all the paperwork and related tasks. It must be made clear, however, that they are not professional hunters and do not organize or outfit the hunt. But the agents of Kamba, which means elephant in the Pygmy language, cater everything else. They meet the traveler at the airport, bring him safely through all the tricky formalities and luggage control, accompany him to a decent hotel of his choice—that alone saves quite a lot of money—and arrange transportation by rented car, pickup, or public transport to his hunting area.

Amazingly, this agency effectively arranges most visits for a relatively small amount of money. The white visitor doesn't have to bargain to reduce excessive "white tourist" prices. Fees are set lower at the outset. Sometimes the agency even provides English-speaking guides for those who can't speak French well enough to make all the arrangements.

The agency guides will accompany the hunter to the local authorities—three different administrations must be visited—and do all the paperwork in the hunting area. They will negotiate with a village chief to find porters and trackers, but the hunter has to choose his own personnel and do the hunting himself. They are tour guides or private secretaries, not hunting guides.

After the hunt the tour guides will bring the hunter safely back to the city and take care of paying trophy fees, paperwork such as export papers and veterinary certificates, shipping with registered forwarders, and even bring the hunter back to the airport.

Although I am an experienced hunter in Cameroon, the agency's help greatly reduces my stress and saves me considerable time, which I can use to hunt. As of February 1999, Kamba's fees are:

- Meeting a traveler at the airport, getting him through customs, handling all paperwork, and bringing him to a recommended hotel of his choice: $150.

- Assisting in town and the countryside: $50 a day plus expenses while traveling.

- Preparing a complete dossier and issuance of the hunting permit, which means the traveler gets his permit immediately at the airport: a flat 25 percent of the official fees.

- Preparing all export papers including vet and CITES papers (they really know their business here): $150.

The ivory export permit I used to beg, plead, and even apply pressure through the embassy for years to get is now ready in just two days! I strongly recommend the services of the Kamba agency, which is run quite efficiently by a team of experts.

The authority of the state is fading faster and faster as crime rates in the big cities rise drastically. In the past, Douala was the place to avoid, but since 1997 it is more dangerous in Yaoundé. Several employees of well-guarded embassies have been carjacked, and an ambassador was even one of the victims.

In the northern part of Cameroon, in a line from Banyo to Batouri, certain parts of the road are notorious for hold-ups. The bandits, mostly from neighboring countries, come out of the bush well armed with fully automatic AK-47s once a week or so, stopping cars and robbing the passengers. So far no harm to life or limb, but for how long?

Common wisdom has it that bush taxis—large vans with wooden benches crammed with as many as twenty-eight people (plus four in front)—are not suitable for westerners. They are not very reliable, have long delays, and are relatively unsafe and terribly uncomfortable. Nevertheless, I have traveled in them a lot since they are sometimes the most reliable (and usually only) means of transportation. Such a journey certainly provides an interesting and close look at African daily life. I value those memories, but if I can hire reasonable private transportation, I will do so.

So far there are no hunting zones demarcated in the south; nevertheless, a daily fee of French Fr 250 must be paid in the region of Mouloundou, which has abundant wildlife. The hunter must register in Yokadouma, headquarters for the southeastern region's tourism administration.

One goes to the village where the hunt will start and negotiates with the local chief. Tradition requires giving presents such as a knife, fishhooks, a cap, or other small items to this almost absolute ruler. Once you gain his co-operation, he will choose porters and trackers for you and put a favorable spell on your safari.

If the chief is not in a favorable mood, no one will hire on as a porter or tracker, making it impossible to hunt near that village. They will be afraid of accidents and scoring zero on game due to "bad magic." Offering more money will not help in this situation. The white hunter will not care about any spell, but that aspect is extremely important to the crew.

In central Cameroon where I used to hunt quite extensively, it was traditional to bring a five-gallon jar of red wine and a twenty-pound bag of salt to distribute among the villagers. On every safari a big celebration was organized by the chief the evening before we departed for the bush. It started with a ceremony in which the chief diluted some manioc flour in water, burned some herb over it, spit into it along with the village elders, and sprinkled this magic potion over the assembled guns and us. Then a wild party began where everybody got drunk, and it was quite difficult to pull all our people out of the various huts early the next morning. So many things must be arranged for a three-week safari into the bush!

The caravan sets out: fifteen heavily loaded porters with fifty-pound packs of food and gear, two trackers, and two white hunters venturing into an area of uninhabited bush measuring 100 by 150 miles. There are no track roads—not even footpaths—and it will be several days of tough walking with no outside assistance.

On a self-organized safari the hunter has to judge the size of the trophy himself. Trackers appraise an animal only according to body size—the more meat, the better. They don't give a hoot about trophy quality.

The tracker walks in front, followed by the hunter, who must maintain a healthy distance of at least six feet.

The tracker cuts the way with his machete, and if a snake appears, he can easily swing the blade too far behind him, striking a person following too closely. That would be quite a disaster.

It is important to create confidence in a crew of black Africans. A cornerstone of success is to remain calm and ponder solutions to the ever-present problems. Postponing judgment until the next day can't hurt. Also, it is important to show courage and provide daily meat for the pot. One must be very firm, but never unkind.

Once I had a Canadian hunter with me who wanted to shoot an elephant very badly, but he climbed a tree in front of some bushpigs with a rifle in his hand! Of course he never got an elephant, even though I put him on a good fresh track. He was afraid to follow it alone with his crew; he thought he needed my gun as "backup." How can such a person create confidence and expect to be guided toward elephant by his tracker? It's OK to get scared, but you don't show it to your crew. Poor guy—on top of it all he got a bad case of jaundice, a souvenir from an earlier trip to the CAR.

Motivation is another key to success. Sometimes Africans can be stimulated by very simple means. Promising more money can help, but other things are more important. Once, I made a three-week safari into a very remote area, traveling a sixty-mile footpath. After our extremely enjoyable hunt we had to trek back out again, and the crew was heavily loaded with trophies and smoked meat.

A German friend really wanted to take advantage of the few remaining days before his flight home and hunt yellow-backed duiker, which were easier to find close to the waiting vehicle. I wanted to get out quickly to explore some other areas in Cameroon's far north. Both of us were strong walkers; our long legs allowed long strides, and we moved at considerable speed. Amazingly, half of our young and eager porters responded to the unspoken challenge and followed us closely—even though they carried a load of at least sixty pounds each!

During most long-distance marches we would stop at noon or early afternoon, make camp and relax, and eventually do an evening stalk if there was game around. But now we wanted to come out as quickly as possible. The problem was the weaker porters who wanted to stop and rest.

I promised everyone an extra day of pay and that afternoon pulled out the big magic: thick, green, shiny pills (plain aspirin). These were the secret of the tall white boss—the reason he was able to walk so long and so fast.

The porters' eyes got big and everyone rushed to get one of the magic pills. It was more than suggestive medicine because it really did help ease their sore muscles. By evening we had covered the first thirty miles. With our feet and legs aching, we just set up the shower, washed away sweat and dust, rested, and stretched out on cots under the mosquito net.

The next day was a 180-degree turnaround. Everyone was tired and slow to start. I rushed our porters, made jokes, and ensured that we set out as early as possible to take advantage of the chilly morning hours and cover as many of the remaining thirty miles as possible.

By noon the crew's morale was shot, and nearly everyone wanted to camp. My friend and I were also tired, but we wanted to continue, so I promised two precious bottles of beer and a German schnapps for each porter who kept up and arrived with us. Again I distributed the magic pills, and with renewed spirits our crew started out again.

We reached our destination by evening, but it was an exhausted, dragging crew that stomped in among the few huts. All but two porters made it; the laggards arrived by noon the next day. Our success was due to the magic pills, which inspired enough confidence to cover a tremendous distance in just two days.

I immediately went to purchase beer. That cheered everyone up, and sparked jokes and laughter. I had brought little bottles of highly concentrated German schnapps in my truck—about 55 percent alcohol. It gave a nice burning sensation, and for years afterward, all the members of this crew kept asking me for more of this delicious potion! This was the only safari crew to ever manage this kind of distance in a mere two days.

Equipment

Belt: Do not put a lot of very heavy items on your belt; it will be too bulky and weigh you down. Take only the essentials such as a short, pointed knife, preferably a stainless steel model by Damascus-U.S.A. Damascus steel will stay razor-sharp for a long time and is easy to resharpen, a necessity on a long hunt. Never, ever let your crew touch it. Turn your back for an instant and someone will try to touch up the edge with a rock!

Carry at least seven easily accessible spare cartridges for the big bore. I make shell holders out of four-inch-long pieces of bicycle inner tube, as described earlier. A .460 Weatherby does not need many cartridges even for a big elephant bull, so I load two in the magazine—one solid and one softnose—followed by a reduction shell in the chamber for the daily duiker and small game. In my belt are three extra half-jacketed rounds (for shoulder shots), four full-jacketed bullets, and three spare reduction shells.

Add the invaluable Leatherman or similar multitool (Gerber, Buck, et al.) and a small sharpening device. That's all the experienced jungle hunter needs besides a small pocket camera to take snapshots along the trail.

Rucksack: All other gear for daily use should be in a small pack carried by a porter who remains close by: GPS unit, electronic diary or notepad to store all the small details of a hunt, a snack, and a small container with a lid to hold nuts or other food for lunch. Don't forget a lightweight one-quart drinking bottle, such as a simple PET bottle that you can give away afterward, and the all-important water-purification drops.

Add a single lens reflex camera with a lightweight body and a variable 28-200mm telephoto lens, soap, snakebite kit (Sawyer pump instead of antivenin that requires refrigeration), repellent spray of 100 percent DEET, folding ultrathin mat for a nap, and a roll of tape to keep debris out of the muzzle brake or bore. During the rainy season add a thin thirty-foot rope and a thin polyethylene tarp to create a shelter in case of sudden rainfall. The rope is fastened in an instant and the tarp pulled over it as a tent. Downpours can be massive, and in central and northern Cameroon the tarp needs to be thicker since hail is frequent.

Luggage: The very best and safest way to transport gear is to use small plastic drums (Unitec Inc.) that can be purchased new or used in most big cities. These drums are easily locked, and keep goods safe from water and other damage.

Rifle: Hunters constantly ask to accompany me, and sometimes I agree. But if they want to hunt elephant, I insist they carry a .460 Weatherby or equivalent caliber. Most hunters protest vigorously and assure me that their deadly .416 or .458 Winchester Magnum (or even .375 H&H Magnum) has killed other large game easily and will surely do for elephant. My reply is a resounding "No!" This is not open for discussion. I tell these experts to either get a .460 or equivalent caliber or forget about going with me. I always follow Ruark's advice: "Use enough gun." Otherwise I might end up having to send a companion home to mama in a box.

I do not take any other hunters with me in my party. Instead, I send each hunter friend out on his own with his own Pygmy crew, each in a different direction. A safari lasts for three or four weeks, and it is vital to be able to defend your crew and properly kill an elephant under all possible circumstances. In the dense maze of the rain forest one can often only guess at the angle and which part of the game is exposed. The hunter usually gets only one chance at a big bull and this opportunity must be maximized, even if the situation is far from ideal.

There is a vast difference between hunting elephant in savanna or light, dry bush and hunting in dense jungle, so a caliber with deep penetration and maximum stopping power is needed. I do not want a wounded elephant running around, and, more importantly, I do not want injured hunters or porters lying around. If a hunter wants to forgo jumbo and hunt the elusive forest buffalo, he can use a .375 H&H Magnum.

With my reduction shells, a less noisy second gun is not required. Even a shotgun produces a significantly loud report that is easily recognized by elephant as dangerous and might scare that valuable animal away. The reduction shells give out a dull crack like the breaking of a large branch. They can now be purchased in .375, .458, and .460 from Damascus-U.S.A. The inserted .38 caliber cartridges are easily handloaded in regular .38 cases. Also .45 caliber bullets are readily available.

For several seasons I have carried a unique Bullpup rifle in .460 Weatherby Magnum that was specially developed for me by Mountain Rifle Inc. (*Note:* Due to the untimely death of its owner, Mountain Rifle is no longer in business.) The prototype was improved in several ways after a couple of safaris, so I now consider this the ideal rifle for a dense forest: an overall length of thirty-seven inches and weight of just eight pounds two ounces with a HoloSight red point. The thumbhole stock design provides a very steady grip, and the laser sight makes it possibile to shoot from the hip. Some readers might be amazed by the rather low weight of this mighty caliber, but I found an extremely efficient muzzle brake made by Mountain Rifle that helps keep weight down.

Recoil reduction: My initial experiments involved several tests comparing the effect of modern muzzle brakes on recoil and noise level. I mounted a French Bullpup rifle in .375 H&H Magnum on a stable three-foot sled with a hard plastic end. The sled was standing on a long glass plate that minimized friction as the sled slid backward as a result of recoil.

Recoil and its reduction were measured by the distance the sled traveled backward. Recoil reduction is easy to determine. Percentage of recoil reduction is shown by the percentage of rearward travel with a muzzle brake compared to 100 percent of recoil.

Loudness was measured at two-kilohertz frequency from six feet behind the rifle with a precision Model 2236 instrument by Brüel & Kjaer. It was found to be in the range of 60 to 140 decibels (dB).

Different ammunition gave off different levels of noise and recoil according to powder charge and bullet weight. Each time, a shot was fired from the same gun with and without a muzzle brake. All muzzle brakes had the same threading and were easy to screw on. The hair trigger was pulled from a distance with a wire. The results were:

No. 1: Best was the muzzle brake from Mountain Rifle Inc. Two large holes on both sides resulted in only 37 percent of the original recoil, a reduction of 63 percent! The noise level increased slightly from 127 dB to 128.4 dB.

No. 2: Second best was a German prototype consisting of two aluminum tubes screwed together with many equally spaced $1/10$-inch holes. It resulted in only 39 percent of the original recoil, a reduction of 61 percent. The loudness increased very little, from 127 to 128.5 dB.

No. 3: Third best was another American muzzle brake from Sam Johnson (Answer Products, 1519 Westbury Drive,

Davison, MI 48423, U.S.A.). It showed 57 percent of the original recoil, a reduction of 43 percent. However, loudness increased significantly from 126 to 131 dB.

No. 4: Fourth best was a muzzle brake from France. Supradax, weighing five ounces, reduced recoil by 43 percent. The loudness increased from 126 to 133 dB.

No. 5: Fifth was a muzzle brake by Colorado Hi-Tech Muzzle Brakes (3102 Beacon Street, Colorado Springs, CO 80907, U.S.A.). It reduced original recoil by 42 percent, and the noise level increased from 126 to 128.7 dB.

No. 6: Another German prototype muzzle brake (three cylinders of thin steel plate equally pierced with 0.2-inch holes) reduced recoil by 38 percent. The loudness increased from 127 to 128.5 dB.

There is a caveat to my tests to the extent that the friction in the sled is rarely linear or consistent. The problem is basically twofold:

First, friction changes depending upon impact. If a force of ten pounds drives the sled one foot, a twenty-pound load would not necessarily drive it two feet because the force is not linear. It increases incrementally, so small increases in pressure will result in large gains in distance.

The second problem is contact. Depending on the gun and the pressure properties of the load, the sled will torque or rise, lessening contact and resulting in less friction to stop its travel. Consequently, loads that cause the most muzzle rise seem to produce the most recoil since there are periods when the sled is not in contact with the table below.

You had better believe noise level is a major concern. I've observed elephant and other valuable game hear a relatively distant shot and immediately haul their butts out of the area as fast as they could!

Photographic Equipment

Take plenty of color slide and ASA 200 print film, a lightweight single-lens reflex camera, and a good quality weatherproof pocket camera. Shoot twice as many pictures as you want, so you will be sure to get some good ones. A 28-200mm telephoto lens is lightweight and extends photographic possibilities immensely.

A tripod is not necessary. I always carry an extendible ski pole as my "third leg" to creep through tangled roots and cross mangrove swamps and slippery fallen logs. It helps to keep one's balance and prevent falls, as well as reduce back pain from strenuous bending under low tree branches. If you remove the top and insert a one-ounce screw-on, table-top tripod, the pole doubles as a camera tripod.

Health

Most African countries are home to the worst malaria-inducing parasite, *Plasmodium falciparum*. It causes *falciparum* malaria and is more or less resistant to the usually prescribed preventive medicine.

Doctors usually recommend taking Lariam while visiting these areas. In about 30 percent of all cases, however, Lariam produces serious side effects. For this reason, some commercial airlines such as Lufthansa do not allow their flying personnel to take it.

I was in Cameroon with a friend from New Zealand who suffered severe depression and an irregular heartbeat after two preventive doses of Lariam. I advise my fellow travelers and patients to take a combination of half a pill of 250-mg Chloroquine, plus two pills of Paludrine daily for up to four weeks after leaving an area where malaria is prevalent, and to carry a standby medication like Lariam or Halfan in case of an attack.

It is important to prevent mosquito bites, so always carry a mosquito net with you and put it up even in hotels; U.S. Army mosquito netting is very good. Also take repellents and always tuck long trousers into high boots during the late afternoon and evening since mosquitoes usually attack the lower legs. It is also wise to wear gloves at night, even under the mosquito net. While tossing and turning during sleep, one's hands often meet the net and the crafty little devils sting right through the mesh!

Eighty-five percent of white residents in Africa do not follow a malaria-prevention regimen. Instead, they "hammer" the occasional attacks with three pills of Halfan. Halfan can be purchased prescription-free in almost all African countries (Cameroon, $10; Zambia, $15).

I strongly recommend shots against the following diseases: yellow fever, polio, tetanus/diphtheria, hepatitis A and B, and in northern Cameroon, meningitis.

After returning home, it is wise to have stool and blood screens for parasites including filaria (worms) and Lyme disease if bitten by ticks. Better safe than sorry!

Political Structures

The old feudal structures are integrated into modern administrations in Cameroon. Recent legislative changes in 1995 confirm local traditions up to the province levels. Each village is ruled by a local chief, who is now elected by the population, but in almost all cases the chief comes from the same family. The county commissioner must confirm the election. The state does not pay the chief, but the villagers have to work in his fields to recompense him for his duties.

One of the chief's duties is to fix and collect the annual head tax. It varies according to age, family, and individual wealth and is usually between $20 and $40. Those who cannot pay or refuse to pay are brought to the district jail for forced labor. This motivates almost everyone to pay quickly and get a tax receipt. At the numerous and often bothersome roadblocks, police always check both identity card *and* tax receipt. Without both one has to vacate his transport and remain with the police to straighten things out. You thought European and U.S. tax authorities were rough? Count your blessings!

Always respect the chief and try to have friendly relations with him. His influence on the villagers is extremely high, and a hunter cannot succeed without his support.

Unfortunately, corruption is a common problem in most developing countries. In Cameroon, state employees are poorly and irregularly paid, so graft is rampant—a fact of life.

One chief in my old hunting area had many problems with the authorities due to buffalo poaching and injury to one of his hunters, but another poaching of two elephant by the chief's eldest son solved the problem. One pair of tusks went to the owner of the rifle and one pair went to the officer judging the case: The chief was released from prison.

Unfortunately, one must always be suspicious and can rarely trust local people. Sometimes I think stealing is the national sport. Even my longtime tracker, with whom I shared a very close relationship through many hunting adventures, would have no scruples about seizing an opportunity. The never-ending stories at the evening campfires all involve what was stolen, when, from whom, and by whom.

To provide a view of black Africa's daily realities, I'll tell two stories from my former porter and tracker, Jean Bosco:

Story one: After killing an elephant with "just" twenty pounds of ivory, Jean Bosco met another black hunter with a rare treasury of forty rounds of .404 ammunition. Jean exchanged his ivory for the cartridges plus $50. The second hunter had no money to pay the balance, so one tusk was deposited with Rene, Jean Bosco's friend and father-in-law.

Later the buyer still had no money and persuaded Jean's father-in-law to trade the tusk for ten cartridges of .458 Winchester Magnum. The second hunter gave the cartridges to his brother Pierre, who should have gone to the village and handed them over to Jean's father-in-law. But Pierre, a notorious ivory poacher, happily took the precious .458 cartridges, borrowed a rifle and even more ammo from the local chief, and poached heavily.

Pierre did not share the tusks he obtained with the chief as arranged, but kept all except two very small tusks for himself. "The big bulls were bad magic. They all managed to escape with the bullets in the body," was his excuse. So, except for Pierre, everyone got cheated, and I am sure that somewhere down the line someone eventually got to him.

Cartridges are extremely valuable and highly coveted so a traveler should not relinquish them. An unusual   caliber is a very good defense against the heavy pressure that will be exerted, even by authorities, to get your extra rounds. After switching to the extremely powerful .460 Weatherby Magnum, I rarely encountered demands for cartridges. There are not many rifles of that caliber in Cameroon.

Story two: Jean Bosco planted seven acres of cocoa trees in his home village, half of them the so-called German cocoa—high-growing trees lasting up to seventy years. They are very resistant to disease and were imported during German colonial times. Their disadvantage is that they do not produce cocoa beans for the first seven years.

The other half of his field was planted with rapidly growing hybrids—bushy trees that produce cocoa after only four years. Their disadvantage is that they are sensitive to diseases, so the plantation must be sprayed twice a year with insecticides and the undergrowth of plants and other trees hewn out.

In January and again in May, Jean sent $400 to his sister to pay for the work and expected a nice clean place upon returning to his village in October. What he found instead was a rapidly growing secondary forest and his valuable cocoa trees almost strangled. His sister betrayed him, paying some $80 to local workers and using the rest for her own purposes.

To get an idea of the mentality of the indigenous people, I recommend that one read about African history, native customs, and tribes. A very cheap and useful resource is public libraries, a sound way to prepare for a do-it-yourself safari!

Cameroonian tribes are completely different from one another, and most do not share any common language. In the north the common language is Hausa, a major tongue of the dominant Fulani (also Fulbe or Peul) tribes. In the west, near the Nigerian border, they use Pidgin—a distorted English—and in central Cameroon they speak Bamum (also Bamoun or Mum), the language of a formerly strong kingdom with a capital at Foumban that ruled several tribes. The tribal languages vary in the extreme, much like Swedish and Spanish, so it is useless to learn more than a few words of the local language.

Anthropology, the science of human races, distinguishes between the tall Hamitic Fulani in northern Cameroon and the much more Caucasian-looking Bororo. The latter have high foreheads, slender lips, sharply outlined, pointed noses, and cream-of-coffee skin tones. The male Bororo put quite a bit of makeup on their skin and look rather feminine. They traditionally live as cattlemen and are a common sight in the daily life of Cameroon. In many places they are seen beside the roads herding their Zebu cattle from the north down toward Yaoundé and even Douala to sell them there. Scientists believe they are the last remains of the original Caucasian population in northern Africa before the Negroid tribes moved in.

The situation in southern Cameroon is similar with Pygmies and Bantus, as the tribes of larger black people are called. Not much scientific information about Cameroonian Pygmies is available, and the small volume of material that does exist is written almost entirely in French.

At one time, Pygmies (from a Greek word meaning half an arm's length or distance from elbow to knuckles), who called themselves Baka, were approximately fifty-six inches tall. They hunted only with spears, never used crossbow or snares, and did not fish. They settled only temporarily in leaf huts in the rain forest, and were strictly segregated from the Bantus. Now this has changed completely. Baka settle along the track roads, fish, hunt with snares and crossbow, work banana and cocoa fields for Bantus, and are a good five inches taller, probably due to better nourishment.

Still, characteristics such as the sharp-featured faces, yellowish skin, and sharply filed or cut-out front teeth distinguish Pygmies from Bantus. In elder Baka, mutilated teeth are common in about eighty percent of the population. Among the young, tooth mutilations diminish, but the majority still endure it.

The diversity of Cameroon's people, landscape, and animals makes it one of the most fascinating countries to hunt. It is not an easy country in which to hunt, and few attempt it. But if successful—getting in and out alive—the experience ranks as one of the most gratifying for any modern-day Nimrod. After twenty years hunting on my own in Cameroon, and after thirty safaris, I still love going back.

Overview of the Cameroon

Kamerun as German Colony

Most friends are surprised to hear Cameroon described as big-game hunting country. Not many know where to find it on a map. The name is more likely to stir German hunters, since *Kamerun* was one of the few German colonies. One of the most popular German writers of hunting stories was Professor Ernst A. Zwilling, mentioned in the foreword, who wrote several books on Cameroon that sold into the hundreds of thousands. It put the name *Kamerun* on the tip of every German tongue and ignited the imagination of Deutsch hunters such as yours truly.

This fascinating country is situated close to the equator where West Africa becomes Central Africa. The name Cameroon originated as a distortion of the Portuguese word *camarões*. The Wouri River estuary was named Rio dos *Camarões* (River of Prawns) by Portuguese explorers in the fifteenth and sixteenth centuries because they bred in incredible numbers in the fish-rich delta near Douala. *Camarões* designated the river's neighboring mountains, and "Cameroons" referred to the mountains until the late nineteenth century.

Back then, Cameroon was known only as a dreadful coast full of mangrove swamps, impenetrable jungles, mosquitoes, and hostile black tribes. No country was interested in taking on this hostile region as its colony.

When the German Empire decided to follow other great powers and colonize, Cameroon was one of the few remaining spots "up for grabs." Chancellor Bismarck vigorously objected to colonization since he preferred to stay on good terms with Great Britain, but public opinion and the emperor prevailed.

In 1881 the renowned merchants Woermann of Hamburg founded a trading post in Douala, so it was logical for the scientific explorer Gustav Nachtigal to hoist the Empire's colors there on July 14, 1884. Nachtigal was named German consul general at Tunis and ordered by the German government to establish *Kamerun* as a colony. A British consul sailing for the same purpose arrived just five days later!

As contacts with the coastal tribes were established, their resistance to allowing white people to enter the interior was slowly worn down. The black chiefs profited from buying European goods and reselling them at enormous profit, so they tried everything imaginable to prevent white people from crossing the dense coastal forest. The new colony consisted of a checkerboard pattern of large and small tribal areas in the south, and a Muslim Fulani (also Fulbe or Peul) kingdom in the north. Other regions were ruled by independent sultans.

Once the jungle belt was penetrated, German law and order were slowly established despite strong resistance from the Muslim kingdoms in the interior. It was not until 1891 that the famous Lieutenant C. von Morgen was able to traverse from the south to Lake Chad in the far north.

In 1893–94 he demarcated the borders of the English colony of Nigeria and the French colony of Ubangi Shari.

Measuring around 316,000 square miles, the colony was larger than the entire German Empire. In 1899 a census counted just 425 white persons, and in 1908 only 1,128 more. The German government invested heavily, building roads and railways, helping create large banana, coffee, tobacco, cotton, and cacao plantations.

The tribes of western Cameroon were more cultured than those in surrounding areas. Most renowned was Sultan Njoya of the famous Bamum (also Bamoun or Mum) tribe, who created a special written alphabet in his language and recognized the advantages for his peopleunder German sovereignty. Njoya readily flew the German colors and was even allowed to have his own army.

After World War I, *Kamerun* was divided. The majority of the region was put under French mandate and a small western strip was placed under British control before the country reunited and achieved independence as the United Republic of Cameroon (*République du Cameroun*) in 1963. French and English are the official languages, but it is rare to find anyone speaking English, French being the tongue of the majority.

In 1996, Cameroon consisted of 183,568 square miles and a population of 13,609,000. During colonial times the population was around 2.5 million, with 35 percent concentrated in the cities and the fertile grasslands of western Cameroon. Today the big urban centers of Douala on the coast (with over a million inhabitants) and Yaoundé 300 miles inland (750,000 inhabitants) continue to attract new residents from the countryside. The rest of the country is very sparsely inhabited. Settlements in the far south are situated close to dirt-track roads, while beyond the meager network of roads stretch hundreds of miles of forest inhabited only by a variety of wildlife.

Climate and Zoology

Cameroon stretches long from north to south, and encompasses completely different climatic zones, so the vegetation and wildlife vary greatly. In the south, bordering Congo and Gabon, the land is covered with primary rain forest. The rain forests gradually change to gallery forests surrounding open savannas in central Cameroon, then to humid and dry savannas in the far north.

Primary rain forest, featuring large trees shading smaller trees and a few bushes, is much more open than secondary rain forest, where heavy and dense undergrowth blocks the way. The densest vegetation is found in the gallery forests—small, extremely thick woods along watercourses.

The Adamawa or Adamaoua region, which is mostly a highland, creates a sharp geographical break between central and northern Cameroon. It is named after the Muslim conqueror Modibbo Adama, who founded a powerful Fulani kingdom that extended into Northern Cameroon in the last century.

Close to the Nigerian border, mountains nearly 10,000 feet high protect the remnants of the heathen Kirdi tribes. As recently as thirty years ago they were still being sold as slaves. The Muslim Fulani took them on their pilgrimage to Mecca; they were officially called servants but were sold and remained there as slaves to their new owners. What a disgusting way to pay for a religious pilgrimage!

Cameroon's wildlife is extremely interesting to serious hunters: One can find the shy bongo, the mighty Lord Derby eland, the wary and nocturnal sitatunga, and the forest elephant with its gleaming yellow ivory. Pigs appear in three varieties: the highly sought giant forest hog, the common and colorful Cameroonian variety of bushpig, and the warthog in the north.

Buffalo occur in two forms. In the north it's the Nile buffalo, also called the northeastern or equinoxial buffalo and in the south it's the red or dwarf forest buffalo. In the northern form the horns have a wider sideways spread, whereas in the southern form the horns curl upward. Northward, the color grows steadily darker, becoming pitch-black in the savanna, while the southern dwarf buffalo ranges from yellow to red.

Common but extremely rare to bag is the small, nocturnal water chevrotain. The most common of the many slender duiker subspecies such as the Peters duiker, blue duiker, and bay duiker are easy to hunt. Some regions hold the Gabon or white-bellied duiker (*Cephalophus leucogaster*) and the second smallest hoofed mammal in Africa, the Bates pygmy antelope (*Neotragus batesi*) that lives in cacao and coffee fields close to human settlements.

Wildlife and Local Customs

Unfortunately, the local population has absolutely no sense of conservation. Everyone is out for himself, trying to get as much game meat as possible to eat and sell. Snares are the main "hunting" method; they are made of fine steel cables and set out in incredible numbers. Animals that walk on well-traveled trails become very scarce within a day's walk of any settlement.

In a remote area that is very good for bongo, I once counted about 150 newly positioned snares in one valley. They are not set as quick-killing head cables, but as foot snares that catch a forefoot and lift the animal into the air, resulting in a slow, painful death. I could cheerfully punch out anyone using such inhumane contraptions on any sort of game.

During the dry season local people leave their villages and live far out in the bush for weeks, checking their cables every two or three days. They vacate camp and return to the villages, but the cables remain indefinitely. Animals snared after the hunters leave usually die and rot, so wildlife is rapidly diminishing. The concept of conservation does not exist in any form: The people just don't care!

The existence of large areas far beyond the settlements with no access track allows reservoirs of wildlife to proliferate. During the rainy season surplus animals migrate from the hinterlands into empty areas closer to roads, and are eventually subjected to wide-open poaching.

Fortunately, modern rifles and shotguns are still rare. However, the few there are "work," as the locals say, all day and especially at night. At night it is relatively easy to quietly stalk within close range of antelope and buffalo and kill them at short distances by "jacklighting," fixing flashlights on the hapless beasts for an easy kill.

The venison is boned out and cut into ten- to twenty-pound pieces of about an arm's length. Each piece is pierced lengthwise by a fresh, green branch and put over a quickly built wood fire. This blazing hot fire turns the fresh, juicy venison into hard, black-charred chunks that keep well and can be preserved for months with repeated smoking.

The pieces are cut differently for the bigger animals. Elephant meat is cut into larger pieces than buffalo. Still, a buffalo will provide around twelve chunks and an elephant proportionately greater quantities. With elephant there is additional profit in the large amount of intestines with inch-thick walls; they are highly prized.

Prices for smoked venison vary according to distance. The more remote and difficult the transport to meat-hungry city dwellers, the higher the price. The price also varies according to the type of game, but not necessarily taste and tenderness!

The highest prices are paid for the bigger animals because black Africans believe that meat from powerful animals will give them power. The most highly prized are elephant, giant snake, gorilla, and buffalo in that approximate order. Unfortunately, the rewards of this cruel poaching are not invested in better living but usually in booze and dope.

It is illegal to transport and sell game meat obtained by poaching, and roadblocks are installed to control this trade. But criminals are ingenious, and federal game agents, seldom decently paid, are more than willing to close their eyes for some pocket money or a piece of meat. For years smoked meat was safely smuggled from central Cameroon into Douala in the bellies of empty diesel tanker trucks—to heck with a little gasoline smell.

The rain forest hosts chimpanzee and gorilla as well as the shy and very desirable spiral-horned antelopes such as bongo and sitatunga. You can also find three different types of wild boar, various species of duikers, Nile and dwarf forest buffalo, and a few varieties of elephant.

The tree-rich savannas of the north are home to sparse and isolated populations of the colossal Lord Derby eland as well as great numbers of waterbuck, western hartebeest (*Alcelaphus buselaphus major*), *kob de buffon* (western or Buffon kob), and roan antelope (*Hippotragus equinus*).

One of the most beautiful antelope is the graceful harnessed bushbuck, much more colorful than its southern cousins—Cape bushbuck (*Tragelaphus scriptus sylvaticus*), Limpopo bushbuck (*Tragelaphus scriptus roualeyni*), and Chobe bushbuck (*Tragelaphus scriptus ornatus*). A striking feature of this slender animal is its overall bright chestnut color with white stripes.

Even lion (*Panthera leo*) can occasionally be found in middle Cameroon. When I hunted the Pangar River area in 1988, there was still a pocket of lion that preyed heavily upon the herds of tame Zebu cattle driven by the Bororo tribes in week-long trips from the north down to the big cities. These nomads had even put a price of around one thousand dollars on one particularly active cat.

Of course, the king of all animals is the always-impressive elephant (*Loxodonta africana*). In the north, bush or savanna elephant seldom carry tusks with more than twenty-five pounds of white and usually very fissured ivory. Almost all elephant hunting is done around the Waza, Bouba Ndjidah, or Faro National Parks. The legal minimum weight is eleven pounds per tusk.

In the south roam the smaller, round-eared forest elephant (*cyclotis*) and a very small variety called the Pygmy elephant (*pumilio*). It is undecided whether the latter, which live in the same areas as the larger forest elephant, are a different subspecies or just a smaller version. Both carry beautiful yellowish, straight ivory, sometimes called rose ivory because of the bright pink hue that appears when one puts a light inside the hollow base of the tusk.

Hunting season starts in December and ends in May. The rainy season ends in December and begins again around mid-March in the south and May in the north. Hunting in central Cameroon is not possible before the tall elephant grass is burned down around mid-January.

In almost all areas hunters have to stalk. Driving is possible only on a few logging roads in the south and on relatively good track roads around the national parks in the north.

Hunting in Cameroon is a dicey proposition; you can't say, "I want a certain animal." One has to bag what one comes across, and it can be a very different animal from the desired quarry.

Most big-game hunters classify game according to the degree of difficulty, in about the following order:

1) Sitatunga
2) Giant eland
3) Bongo
4) Giant forest hog
5) Forest elephant
6) Yellow-backed duiker
7) Dwarf buffalo

This ranking by difficulty varies according to the terrain. I once found an isolated swamp with a few sitatunga. Each time I went there, at least four were grazing in full daylight.

Cameroon offers several interesting species of smaller animals, such as African golden cat (*Felis aurata*), Congo clawless otter (*Aonyx (Paraonyx) congica Lönnberg*), and several others that are mostly nocturnal. Any encounter with them is accidental, and collecting one as a trophy is especially rewarding.